$175.00

ICONS OF BUSINESS

Recent titles in
Greenwood Icons

Icons of Horror and the Supernatural [Two Volumes]: An Encyclopedia of
Our Worst Nightmares
Edited by S.T. Joshi

ICONS OF BUSINESS

An Encyclopedia of Mavericks, Movers, and Shakers

VOLUME 2

By Kateri Drexler

Greenwood Icons

GREENWOOD PRESS
Westport, Connecticut • London

Library of Congress Cataloging-in-Publication Data

Drexler, Kateri M.
    Icons of business : an encyclopedia of mavericks, movers, and shakers / Kateri Drexler.
        p. cm.
    Includes bibliographical references and index.
    ISBN 0-313-33862-0 (set : alk. paper)—ISBN 0-313-33863-9 (vol 1 : alk. paper)—
    ISBN 0-313-33864-7 (vol 2 : alk. paper)
        1. Businesspeople—United States—Biography.   2. Businesspeople—United States—
Directories.   3. United States—Biography.   4. Business enterprises—
United States.   5. Corporations—United States.   I. Title.
    HC102.5.A2D74 2007
    338.092'273—dc22   2006031209

British Library Cataloguing in Publication Data is available.

Library of Congress Catalog Card Number: 2006031209
ISBN: 0–313–33862–0 (set)
        0–313–33863–9 (vol. 1)
        0–313–33864–7 (vol. 2)

First published in 2007

Greenwood Press, 88 Post Road West, Westport, CT 06881
An imprint of Greenwood Publishing Group, Inc.
www.greenwood.com

Printed in the United States of America

The paper used in this book complies with the
Permanent Paper Standard issued by the National
Information Standards Organization (Z39.48–1984).

10 9 8 7 6 5 4 3 2 1

Contents

List of Photos

Preface

Business icons, moguls, tycoons—the people who create and master industries, bringing them to their fullest fruition—are usually many different things to different people. To some they are exemplars and saints who show us that democratic capitalism creates innovation and economic well-being. To others, they are villains and demonstrate all that is wrong in a system that tolerates and even seemingly encourages economic disparity between the top and bottom rungs of the socioeconomic ladder.

The actions of these chief executive officers (CEOs) are at times mythologized as business school students and middle managers voraciously read accounts of their leadership strategies and yearn to emulate their success. Is it surprising, then, that people like Bill Gates (Microsoft), Jack Welch (General Electric), Richard Branson (Virgin Group), and Herb Kelleher (Southwest Airlines) became folk heroes whose superstar status was rivaled only by famous popular culture icons?

The "CEO as miracle worker" phenomenon most likely began when Lee Iacocca led Chrysler through what was thought to be an impossible situation. When Chrysler not only survived but became a serious rival to the other top auto manufacturers, it was Iacocca who got most of the credit. Then along came CEOs such as Gates and Michael Dell, who continued to log fantastic growth rates long after their companies became behemoths.

Can this be credited to the special skills these CEOs hold, or might it be a mixture of many factors, including the strength of the economy? While there may be nothing like a bear market to tame an executive ego, when the sobering macroeconomic realities hit, we still expect CEOs to rise above the minor obstacle of a flailing economy. Most executives are also usually compensated as though they can do that.

The line between visionary leader who overcomes a stale economy and other barely insurmountable obstacles and the executive who becomes a loose cannon may be quite thin, though. In recent years, we have seen CEOs and top executives held to a higher standard than ever before. Some say it is about time—that we ignored for too long excesses and criminal activity that significantly hurt not only company stakeholders but also overall investor confidence in the market. Others believe that the urge to blame is more basic: Americans enjoy playing a role in building someone up, and then once that person rises out of our reach, they enjoy tearing him down. With the conviction or indictments of top corporate executives Ken Lay, Jeffrey Skilling, Martha Stewart, Bernie Ebbers, Ralph Nacchio, and others, the justice department is succeeding in its efforts to hold executives accountable. More than seven hundred people have been charged since the Corporate Fraud Task Force was formed in 2002 in the wake of a series of corporate accounting scandals.

What are we to make of leaders of industries, then? Are they knights endowed with special qualities who can lead the way and navigate us through the threats and opportunities that businesses face in a global economy? Or have we made them into superheroes only to condemn them when we see their mortal side?

Most successful businesspeople seem to be quite complex, and they have both fans and detractors. The exact combination of luck, determination, creativity, and other skills they use is hard to discern given the complexity of their personalities and their business endeavors. Books on leadership, management, and strategic thinking line library shelves. Psychologists and academics have published forests of articles on the attitudes and behaviors that distinguish top executives from the only moderately successful. As we try to probe the lives of successful businesspeople in order to understand them, we search for clues. Are there particular ingredients we can add to our own lives to make us more succesful? Are the same leadership lessons from multibillion-dollar companies transferable to smaller businesses? Would the skills and personalities that these business titans used have allowed them to be successful in other careers as well?

Martha Stewart achieved some success as a stockbroker; Kelleher was a successful attorney; Jack Welch, a respected chemist; Howard Schultz, a fast-rising executive. However, others floundered until they found their niche. One management analyst, Michael Lewis, once wrote, "In no other epoch in history would Gates have risen to prominence, much less become the world's richest man. In ancient Greece, he'd have been a clever slave; in the British empire, a scrupulous bookkeeper."

Could it all be just a matter of genetics, as Warren Buffet believes? Buffett says that successful businesspeople are "wired in such a way that when they see business questions or problems or activities they tend to get the picture very quickly.... They don't get tangled up in prejudices or biases they may have. They just tend to get the right answers. It's sort of like 'Why was Ted Williams a great hitter?' There's just some coordination that goes on that made him a little bit better at meeting the ball than other people. And that's what happens with business. It certainly isn't a function of IQ to any huge degree. It's just some wiring that takes place. It's not a function of education in my view. It's about seventy-five percent DNA."

If we can assume that leaders have skills that are responsible for their success, might these skills be transferable to other people? How important is personality in the equation?

Welch was seen by many as a human dynamo, who through sheer force of personality and brilliance of vision transformed General Electric into an engine of perpetual high performance. Likewise, the freewheeling, straight-talking Kelleher, Ted Turner, and Branson have used their charisma and passion to drive everyone around them, but Phil Knight, Gates, Buffett, and George Soros have taken a quieter, more introverted approach.

While many, such as Welch, Iacocca, and Carlos Gutierrez believe in creating a clearly articulated vision with measurable results, others such as Andrew Grove, Turner, Soros, and Donald Trump trust more in reacting to environmental opportunities and threats as they come. The Internet had been around years before Welch embraced it and saved millions of dollars. Grove turned Intel in a completely different direction, seemingly on a dime, as a result of a quickly shifting competitive marketplace. His decision to get out of the memory chip business—the business upon which the company was founded—shocked even Intel insiders.

Some managers believe in implementing specific and strict management or quality programs, such as Six Sigma and Total Quality Management, while others such as Kelleher believe that employees who work freely work better than if they spent time analyzing certain aspects of their jobs.

A few leaders, such as Oprah Winfrey, rely mainly on gut instinct, or intuition, to make critical business decisions. Winfrey has said, "The only time I've made a bad business decision is when I didn't follow my instinct. My favorite phrase is: 'Let me pray on it.' Sometimes I literally do pray, but sometimes I just wait to see if I wake up and feel the same way in the morning. For me, doubt normally means don't. Doubt means do nothing until you know what to do. And I'm really, really, really attuned to that."

Some of the business icons in these volumes, such as Grove, Gates, Schultz, and Jeff Bezos, made their mark through innovation—creating a product, service, or market that didn't exist before. Others, such as Sam Walton and Winfrey, have said they never had the great idea but were good at building upon those of others. Walton claimed that the key to his success was extreme devotion to copying the methods of other successful discounters.

While several CEOs have had very high IQs and translated those into business products, others, such as Branson, Anita Roddick, and Stewart seem to have created empires out of common sense and ideas anyone could have come up with.

Although corporate cultures and structures vary greatly among the different companies who have achieved megasuccess, most of those companies' leaders pay a lot of attention to the people they hire. Welch even went so far as to cull his people down, year after year, firing the bottom ten percent. However, Knight and Bill Bowerman thought that they could work with the people they had, training their current employees to the necessary level. Some leaders brought in high-level staff from the outside, while others such as Kelleher and Welch believed in promoting from within. Regardless of their personal style of management, most CEOs surround themselves with people whose complementary personalities seem to act as checks on their own. Kelleher, for instance, had Colleen Barrett, whose systematic attention to detail was the perfect foil for his idea-driven approach. Winfrey had Jeff Jacobs, whom she called a financial bulldog, to make up for her lack of expertise in that area.

In some corporate cultures, such as Southwest Airlines, the Virgin Group, and Harpo, Inc., the work environment is fun and enjoyable, while others' environments are much more serious. Some CEOs encourage their employees to take time off to spend with their families, while others encourage just the opposite. Some companies, like Southwest and Kellogg, have a lot of middle managers, while others have very few. Some leaders have seen mainly success, while others have experienced significant failures and yet pulled themselves up again without a loss of enthusiasm.

Perhaps the answers lay not so much in what these CEOs do or how they act but in inherent personal qualities. Indeed, if we look to their early lives, we can sometimes see evidence of future success. Buffett, for instance, had the equivalent of over $42,000 saved by high school after starting to invest at age 11. While in college, Donald Trump read federal foreclosure listings for fun and bought his first housing project before he graduated. Winfrey could read at age two, and although she was just five years old when she started school, she insisted on beginning in first grade instead of kindergarten. The following year she skipped another grade. There may even be some evidence to show that some people may be born with some of the qualities we associate with success—notably, ambition. But, then again, others such as Welch, Carly Fiorina, Roddick, and Ben Cohen surprised even their closest friends when they developed business skills later in life. Could their success be a result of these CEOs' family situations? Most of our icons grew up in a middle-class socioeconomic environment, but some, including Donald Trump, grew up in higher-class households, while others such as Iacocca, Bezos, and Branson had poorer roots. Schultz spent most of his childhood in the projects. And while some of our icons had supportive family environments, others, including Winfrey, struggled with theirs.

What we find by analyzing the profiles included in this set is that the personalities and leadership styles of these business icons are as varied as the organizations they manage. The skills and traits that served them well at some points may have served them poorly at others. Success, however, seems to be a magnifying glass, bringing some traits more clearly into focus while at the same time distorting their importance.

It is a natural tendency to want to emulate other's techniques and strategies. Once a management philosophy is shown to work, in fact, others rush in to follow, as they did when Jack Welch showed that the Six Sigma leadership strategy he implemented turned GE into a finely tuned, more profitable company. Thousands of companies have since implemented it. Warren Buffet has even created a term, "the institutional imperative," for this tendency of corporate management to imitate the behavior of other managers. The leaders profiled here have mainly developed their own differing management philosophies, which seem to be developed not from studying other companies but from their own value systems.

Can we see the same level of success in the future as we have in the past? As Sam Walton said, "Of course it could happen again. Somewhere out there right now there's someone—probably hundreds of thousands of someones—with good enough ideas to go it all the way. It will be done again, over and over, providing that someone wants it badly enough to do what it takes to get there."

CRITERIA

To determine the people to showcase in this set of business icons, we considered contemporary leaders whose companies were market leaders in a number of different industries or industry niches. The leaders profiled here represent a wide range of industries. Some are CEOs of long-established businesses, and some are entrepreneurs who started with very little. All have achieved measurable and significant success by responding first or most effectively to new market opportunities or competitive pressures. The business executives presented are still currently being asked for advice and strategy, though some have retired or moved into consulting positions. Their leadership qualities and skills continue to endure and are still analyzed by others hoping to apply them to current situations.

DESCRIPTION

The information in the profiles included in *Icons of Business* was put together using a variety of sources, including research texts, management books, biographies, autobiographies, interviews, and company Web sites. The profiles contain a section on the subjects' early years, giving an overview and illustrating significant events. From there we move into their career paths, explaining the roads they took that led to their eventual successes. Their personal lives are explained in a small section covering marriages, births, deaths of loved ones, and other crises and situations that may have had an effect on their eventual successes. Any major philanthropic endeavors they undertook are highlighted here. A major section on their leadership lessons is presented, and these include at times not only what our business icons have self-reported but also other tactics obviously used that may have been evident only in retrospect. Because wealth often leads to power, a section on how they wield that power in the political sphere is included. To balance our portrayals, we have included a section of criticism of each of our subjects, the length of which varies by the person being discussed. While some have had an enormous number of critics, others have seemed to escape with little public criticism. Possible future impact is also included, with discussions based on statements made by our subjects or inferred from their strategic decisions. Each profile also includes a timeline, quotes by and about the subject, and company information.

Herb Kelleher

Herb Kelleher is the founder and chairman of the board of Southwest Airlines. Before stepping down as CEO in 2001, Kelleher had managed to take the startup airline serving three cities in Texas to the most profitable in the industry, making a profit every year for thirty-two years—an unsurpassed record in the highly turbulent, frequently unprofitable airline industry. Most of its competitors have struggled to achieve more than a couple of years of consecutive profitability. In 2004 the company earned $442 million—more than all the other U.S. airlines combined. It now flies about 5.5 million people each month, and in May 2004 for the first time Southwest boarded more domestic customers than any other airline.

While Kelleher was CEO and president of Southwest Airlines, he also produced the highest return to shareholders of all companies listed in the Standard & Poor's 500. Southwest, with its low fares, is also credited with expanding the market of airline travelers. When the airline first started operations, the main type of passenger on all domestic flights was the businessman, and the fares were steep. Only about 15 percent of American adults had ever flown on a commercial airline flight. [Today, that is around 85 percent.] Southwest played a crucial role in this increase.

In 1998, *Fortune* called Southwest the most successful airline in history. It also landed in the top ten of *Fortune*'s Most Admired Companies in each of the past six years—a distinction shared only by Berkshire Hathaway, General Electric, and Microsoft. Southwest has also achieved high levels of employee satisfaction. It was included in *Fortune*'s list of the 100 Best Companies to Work for in America three years in a row, and has consistently enjoyed lower turnover rates than other U.S. airlines. Kelleher has been named by several publications as CEO of the Year.

The company made it possible for the middle class and working class to fly. It is the only airline to earn a profit every year for the past three decades. The airline has overcome many obstacles, including the $12.8-billion loss the industry took between 1990 and 1994 and the downturn in airline economics because of September 11, 2001.

In 1993, the U.S. Department of Transportation labeled Southwest the dominant airline in the United States because of the effect it was having on the rest of the industry. It coined a new term—*the Southwest effect*—that described the change in fares and passenger volumes that is observed when Southwest enters a market. According to the report, when Southwest announces service on a new route, other airlines serving that route almost immediately reduce their fares, and sometimes increase their frequencies of service. As a result, they reported, the net effect of Southwest's entrance into a new market had been to reduce fares by an average of 65 percent and to increase passenger traffic at least 30 percent in every new market it entered, with a 500 percent increase in one market.

The airline industry is still emerging from very tough times. Largely because of September 11 and its aftermath, the rest of the airline industry laid off thousands of people and lost more than twenty-two billion dollars. However, even during these times, Southwest didn't lay off a single employee and remained profitable every quarter. Many managers and employees took a pay cut during this time in exchange for stock options. [Southwest at the time was financially better off than any of the other airlines.]

"If you treat your employees well, they'll treat the customers well and if they treat the customers well, the customers will come back and that's what makes your shareholders happy."

Herb Kelleher

Kelleher has been the driving force behind Southwest's remarkable success and the innovative ways in which that success has been achieved. Southwest's business model is to provide reliable, low-cost travel by using its resources efficiently. It enters markets in which traditional airlines are based but Southwest offers much lower fares. Southwest flies point to point, versus the hub-and-spoke model used by most other airlines. It flies only Boeing 737s, serves no meals, charges no fees to change same-fare tickets, has no assigned seats, and has no electronic entertainment on its planes.

More often than not, analysts credit the company's success to Kelleher's eccentric, charismatic leadership more than Southwest's business model. Kelleher has provided Southwest Airlines employees with a sense of mission that connects to their own values, ideals, and aspirations while also generating a culture that is famous for being fun and irreverent. [The walls of the company headquarters are plastered with more than ten thousand photos that include employees' pets; Kelleher dressed like Elvis, the Easter Bunny, or in drag; flight attendants in miniskirts; and Southwest planes gnawing on competitors' aircraft.] Kelleher is legendary among the employees, known as a smoking, whiskey-drinking, Harley-riding, wisecracking, and self-effacing man. He encouraged the flight attendants on Southwest flights to amuse the passengers by singing the flight instructions, hiding in overhead storage compartments, joking, bantering with the passengers, or holding trivia contests.

"Respect people for who they are, not for what their titles are."
Herb Kelleher

The airline is now flying more than seventy million passengers a year to sixty cities across the United States, using over 430 jets. Kelleher is still intimately involved in the company, handling critical government affairs, scheduling, aircraft purchasing, and general strategic planning.

The United States Airline Deregulation Act of 1978

The United States Airline Deregulation Act of 1978 was a dramatic event in the history of economic policy. It was the first thorough dismantling of a comprehensive system of government control since 1935. It was also part of a broader movement that, with varying degrees of thoroughness, transformed such industries as trucking, railroads, buses, cable television, stock exchange brokerage, oil and gas, telecommunications, financial markets, and even local electric and gas utilities.

Most observers agree that airline deregulation has been a success. The overwhelming majority of travelers have enjoyed the benefits that its proponents expected.

Deregulation also has given rise to a number of problems, including congestion and a limited reemergence of monopoly power and, with it, the exploitation of a minority of customers. It would be a mistake, however, to regard these developments merely as failures of deregulation: in important measure they are manifestations of its success.

The most important consequences of deregulation have been in the areas of fares, productivity, and safety:

Fares. Between 1976 and 1990 average yields per passenger mile—the average of the fares that passengers actually paid—declined 30 percent in real, inflation-adjusted terms. Average yields were declining in the decades before deregulation as well, thanks largely to the introduction of jets and jumbo jets. The best estimates, however, are that deregulated fares have been 10 to 18 percent lower, on average, than they would have been under the previous regulatory formulas. The savings to travelers have been in the range of five to ten billion dollars per year.

Productivity. The other major accomplishment of deregulation has been the improvement in airline productivity. Deregulation fostered this improvement by removing the previous detailed restrictions on airline prices and on where they can fly. Decontrol of prices allowed airlines to fill their planes by offering large numbers of heavily discounted fares for seats that would otherwise go unused. Decontrol of routes permitted them to plan their operations as they saw fit. And deregulation has compelled improvements in efficiency through the intense pressures of the price competition it unleashed. Carriers have put more seats on their planes—the average went up from 136.9 in 1977 to 153.1 in 1988—and succeeded in filling a greater percentage of those seats—from an average of 52.6 percent in the ten years before 1978 to 61.0 percent in the twelve years after. By wiping out all these restrictions and freeing carriers to enter any market, deregulation produced an estimated 25 percent increase in the average number of airlines per route despite the recent mergers.

The instances of sharply increased price discrimination that deregulation has made possible are both a competitive and monopolistic phenomenon. They reflect intense competition for the travelers most likely to be attracted by price differences among competitors. They also have promoted economic efficiency in very important ways. The deeply discounted fares to discretionary air travelers have helped fill planes and, by doing so, helped make possible more frequent scheduling, which is particularly valuable to the full-fare travelers.

Safety

Air travel is unequivocally safer now than it was before deregulation. Accident rates during the twelve-year period studied were 20 to 45 percent below their average levels in the six- or twelve-year period before deregulation. Moreover, by taking intercity travelers out of cars, the low airfares made possible by deregulation have saved many more lives than the total number lost annually in air crashes.

THE EARLY YEARS

Herbert D. Kelleher, known to all as Herb, was born on March 12, 1931. He was raised in Haddon Heights, New Jersey, mostly by his mother, who raised him alone after Kelleher's father passed away when Kelleher was only twelve. Harry Kelleher, Herb's father, had been general manager at a Campbell's soup factory. As a young boy, Kelleher would work at the Campbell's factory during his summer breaks and sometimes after school. He started as a soup chef and worked his way up to warehouse foreman, and, later, to part-time analyst.

Kelleher, the youngest of the four children, was raised in a family with three boys and one girl. One of Kelleher's brothers, Richard, died in January of 1942 during combat in World War II. Kelleher remembers his family feeling very duty bound, and after Richard died, his other brother, Harry, went into the Navy despite a heart murmur. Harry Kelleher passed away in 1973, and his sister Ruth moved to New York to work as an expediter for RCA, leaving Kelleher alone with his mother.

Ruth Moore Kelleher spent countless hours talking to her son about a wide range of topics, including ethics, business, and politics. She taught him to be respectful of others and nonjudgmental. In their conversations, some of which lasted until three or four o'clock in the morning, Ruth told him not to judge a book by its cover and especially not to judge people by the titles they carry. This lesson was reinforced when a very dignified gentleman in their neighborhood, the president of a savings and loan, was convicted of embezzlement. Ruth taught Kelleher that every person and every job is worth just as much as any other person and any other job.

During Kelleher's years at Haddon Heights High School he stayed very busy. He was an all-around athlete, playing football and basketball and running track. He lettered in basketball, was the captain of the football team, and was also was the president of the Junior class. While attending high school, he worked for $2.50 an hour at the *Philadelphia Bulletin*.

In 1971, a person could fly with Southwest from Dallas to Houston for twenty dollars. Other airlines were charging almost three times that.

After completing high school, he went on to acquire a bachelor's degree, majoring in English and minoring in philosophy, from Wesleyan University. He was an Olin Scholar and graduated cum laude. Although he had initially pursued higher education because of an interest in journalism, a trustee had persuaded him to go to law school, and he eventually received his law degree from New York University in 1956. He earned a place on the university's law review and graduated as a Root-Tilden Scholar.

Frank Borman

A hero of the American space odyssey, Frank Borman led the first team of American astronauts to circle the moon, extending man's horizons into space. He is internationally known as commander of the 1968 Apollo 8 Mission.

Frank Borman retired from the Air Force in 1970 but is well remembered as a part of this nation's history, a pioneer in the exploration of space and a veteran of both the Gemini 7 Space Orbital Rendezvous with Gemini 6 in 1965 and the first manned lunar orbital mission, Apollo 8, in 1968.

Borman became a special advisor to Eastern Airlines in early 1969 and in December 1970 was named senior vice president of the Operations Group.

He was promoted to executive vice president of General Operations and was elected to Eastern's board of directors in July 1974. In May 1975 he was elected president and chief operating officer. He was named CEO in December 1975 and became chairman of the board in December 1976.

During his tenure as CEO of Eastern, the airline industry went through the enormous change caused by deregulation. As Southwest was growing, Eastern was faced with hardship. During this period Borman originated several unique programs including profit sharing and wages tied to company profitability. These programs produced the four most profitable years in the company's history, but Borman could not deal effectively with the unions, and the programs were abandoned. The resulting losses led to the sale of the airline to Texas Air Corporation, and Borman retired from Eastern Airlines in June 1986.

CAREER PATH

After graduating from law school, Kelleher earned a great job working as a clerk for the New Jersey Supreme Court. By 1959, he had joined the firm of Lum, Biunno, and Tompkins out of Newark, New Jersey. Kelleher practiced at the firm for two years before he decided to move to San Antonio, Texas, with the intention of starting a firm of his own. Upon arrival, however, Kelleher went to work for Matthews, Nowlin, Macfarlane, & Barrett as a partner. The firm specialized in helping people start new businesses. In this environment, Kelleher was able to analyze why some start-up companies made it and some did not.

In 1962, Kelleher served as Governor John B. Connally's Bexar County campaign manager. The contacts he made during the campaign became many of Southwest's first shareholders.

In 1967 Kelleher met with a client, Rollin King, who had an air charter company, Wild Goose Flying Service, which flew between San Antonio and small South Texas cities, such as Del Rio and Laredo. The air transportation service at this time was much different from what it is today. The government largely regulated the air service and there were monopolies among many carriers. There also were not many point-to-point flights. Oftentimes, passengers would have layovers before catching another flight to get to where they were going.

King proposed expanding his air service to the three largest cities in Texas, offering low fares, convenient schedules, and a no-frills approach that was completely contrary to the standards of the established airlines. He wanted Kelleher as a partner and famously described his plan on a cocktail napkin. Service between Dallas, Houston, and San Antonio was being provided by Braniff Airways and Trans-Texas Airways (later Texas International Airlines), but tickets were usually sold only as part of a leg of longer, interstate flights. Kelleher thought King was crazy, but after doing some homework, decided that he was in. King convinced his banker, John Parker, of the Alamo National Bank in San Antonio, to conduct a feasibility study for an airline that would serve the market at a time when the three cities involved were among the fastest growing in the nation. An independent marketing consulting group, hired with $150,000 donated by seven of their San Antonio friends, helped to convince King and Kelleher of the project's viability.

In 1967, a new airline, Air California, had made an initial public offering before it had actually started flying. This provided the model for King and Kelleher, who used Air California's investment bankers and two of its founders to raise money for Air Southwest.

Southwest was incorporated as Air Southwest on March 15, 1967, with Kelleher, King, John Peace (University of Texas board of regents chairman,) John Murchison (brother of Clinton Murchison, Jr., of the Dallas Cowboys,) Charles Kuhn (Dresser Industries executive), and Robert S. Strauss (Democratic Party leader and future ambassador to Russia) as its first board of directors. Wilber Morrison of Pan American Airlines later joined Southwest's board. In November 1967 Kelleher filed an application with the Texas Aeronautics Commission to serve Dallas, Houston, and San Antonio. The application was a state matter because Southwest wasn't proposing to fly out of state; it didn't fall under the regulatory guidelines of the Civil Aeronautics Board. On February 20, 1968, the commission voted unanimously to grant Air Southwest a certificate of public convenience and necessity that would allow it to begin service. The following day, however, Braniff, Trans-Texas, and Continental Airlines obtained a restraining order from the Travis County District Court that temporarily prohibited the agency from issuing the certificate. Thus began a four-year legal battle.

Kelleher led Southwest's legal fight but lost the first round in Austin State District Court, which found that the three cities Air Southwest proposed to serve already had sufficient air service. Kelleher appealed to the Third Court of Civil Appeals, which, seven months later, upheld the lower court's decision. The investors were ready to admit defeat, but King and Kelleher were not. Offering to hold off on charging legal fees until the company had some money and agreeing to pay all court costs and expenses out of his own pocket, Kelleher filed an appeal with the Texas Supreme Court; to everyone's surprise, by unanimous vote the Supreme Court overturned the lower court's ruling. In all, Kelleher was involved in thirty-one separate administrative or judicial proceedings. He made three trips to the U.S. Supreme Court, which ultimately upheld Southwest's right to fly in Texas. December 7, 1970, the date of the Supreme Court decision, is considered by many to be the beginning of deregulation in the airline industry.

In 1971, Air Southwest became Southwest Airlines. In January, King and Kelleher hired Marion Lamar Muse, the former president of Detroit-based Universal Airlines, to run Southwest, which had $148 in the bank and past-due bills for more than $133,000. Faced with starting an airline virtually from scratch after much of its original investment had already been used to pay expenses, Muse called on his industry contacts to raise capital. Muse himself gave fifty thousand dollars, and his friend Wesley West wrote a check for $750,000 to help restart the company.

In just 120 days the company hired and trained pilots, flight attendants, mechanics, and other personnel; completed negotiations for space at three airports; hired Bloom Advertising to design an initial campaign; and completed the purchase of three Boeing 737–200 aircraft. King, Kelleher, and Muse were able to purchase the planes at 90 percent financing, a move previously unheard of in the industry. But plans to raise additional money through an initial public offering just before service began were interrupted by yet another battle. Braniff and Texas International complained to the Civil Aeronautics Board (CAB) that Southwest's operation might violate its intrastate exclusivity. Kelleher moved swiftly to argue the Southwest case. He flew without a change of clothes from San Antonio to Washington, where he pleaded before the CAB for several days in the same rumpled suit.

Back in Dallas, only two days before Southwest's scheduled inaugural flight, Kelleher received word that the CAB had thrown out the objections of Braniff and Texas International. But he also learned that the two carriers had won a restraining order barring Southwest from beginning service. The order was issued by the same Austin judge who had issued the original injunction against the TAC decision. Kelleher immediately flew to Austin, where the Texas Supreme Court held an emergency session to hear the case, voided the injunction, and forbade the judge from involving himself with Southwest again.

On June 18, 1971, a Southwest Airlines plane flown by Capt. Emilio Salazar began service out of Love Field. Southwest was employing fewer than seventy people and had four planes; the new airline was barely making it with minimum operating capital by the end of the year. Southwest was only five months old when Muse had the idea of offering a ten-fare on the last flight of the week from Houston to Dallas. The plane was needed back in Dallas anyway for weekend servicing, and the crew had been ferrying it back empty every week for five months. Within two weeks, the flight was carrying a full load. Muse then slashed fares on the last flight of each day in each direction.

By the next fall, Muse had raised regular fares from twenty dollars to twenty-six dollars and the weekend and night fares to thirteen dollars. The two-tier fare system, one of the most important innovations in airline marketing history, was born. The larger airlines, however, were not finished with their fight against Southwest. Braniff lowered its Dallas-Houston fare to just thirteen dollars. In an action that became characteristic of the airline, Muse responded with newspaper advertisements claiming that "Nobody's going to shoot Southwest Airlines out of the sky for a lousy $13," offering customers their choice of either a thirteen-dollar-fare or a full-fare ticket plus a fifth of premium liquor. The bottles of liquor did not cost thirteen dollars, but a businessman could put the twenty-six dollar fare on his expense report and take the liquor home free. With 80 percent of its customer base choosing to pay full fare, Southwest won this 1972 fare war and became the largest distributor in Texas of Chivas, Crown Royal, and Smirnoff.

To enhance the company's image further, Muse began a marketing campaign that clad female flight attendants in hot pants and emphasized the slogan, "We're spreading love all over Texas," a pun on the company's home base at Love Field. In 1977, Southwest listed its stock on the New York Stock Exchange under the trading symbol LUV. In 1972, Dallas-Fort Worth Airport (DFW) and the cities of Dallas and Fort Worth sued Southwest in an attempt to force the carrier to move form Love to DFW. Love Field is considerably closer to downtown Dallas than DFW, and after a two-year battle, Southwest won the privilege to remain at Love Field as long as the field was a commercial airport.

In April 1974 the Dallas City Council attempted to close Love Field to commercial traffic but did not succeed. In 1978, in an attempt to curb Southwest's growth, the major airlines at DFW sought support from Congress to bar flights from Love Field to anywhere outside of Texas. Finally, in 1979 a compromise known as the Wright Amendment (named after majority leader Jim Wright, a Democrat from Fort Worth) was ratified. This measure limited service from Love Field to Texas and the four surrounding states, Arkansas, Louisiana, Oklahoma, and New Mexico. Congressional representatives from districts not served by Southwest introduced legislation to repeal the act in hopes of bringing nonstop Southwest service and low fares to states that did not border Texas.

> *"We've never tried to be like other airlines. From the very beginning we told our people, 'Question it. Challenge it'."*
> Herb Kelleher

King resigned as an officer of the company in 1976 but remained on the board of directors and flew the line for two years as a captain. When Muse left the company in March 1978, Kelleher was asked to run the airline on an interim basis until a new president and CEO could be hired. In August 1978, Howard Putnam, a United Airlines executive, was hired as president and CEO. Putnam subsequently left in September 1981 to take over the ailing Braniff Airways. At that time, Kelleher left his San Antonio law firm for good and began running Southwest full time. He was named permanent chairman, president, and CEO on February 23, 1982.

With the Airline Deregulation Act of 1978, which permitted competition on routes across the country that were previously virtual monopolies, Southwest again expanded. By the end of 1981 it had added service to Amarillo, New Orleans, Albuquerque, Oklahoma City, Tulsa, and thirteen other cities. In early 1982, it added service to San Diego, Kansas City, Las Vegas, and Phoenix—its first service to cities outside of Texas and the surrounding states. Of course, in compliance with the terms of the Wright Amendment, direct service to these cities was not available from Dallas's Love Field.

When Southwest entered the San Francisco–Southern California markets in the late 1980s, US Air had a 58 percent market share in those routes. By the mid-1990s, Southwest had driven U.S. Airways completely out of them. Southwest took over the San Jose–Los Angeles market in 1991 just as American Airlines was pulling out of its unprofitable San Jose hub. With the inauguration of service to Baltimore Washington International in 1993, Southwest served both coasts for the first time. The acquisition of Salt Lake City–based Morris Air at the end of 1993 facilitated Southwest's expansion into new cities in the West and Northwest. By the end of 1994, Southwest had a presence on each coast and a solid presence in the Midwest via Chicago.

> *"The rule at Southwest is, if somebody has an idea, you read it quickly and you respond instantaneously. You may say no, but you give a lot of reasons why you're saying no, or you may say we're going to experiment with it in the field, see if it works."*
>
> Herb Kelleher

It was during the early 1990s that Southwest first hit the national radar screen. The 1990–1994 downturn in the industry in the wake of the Gulf War contributed to the decline of other airline businesses. While they were pulling back and reducing their presence in many markets, Southwest continued its growth.

Southwest Airlines has also been innovative and a leader in its time. The airline was the first to introduce senior discounts, Fun Fares, Fun Packs, same-day airfreight delivery service, and ticketless travel, along with other programs. Southwest introduced ticketless travel on January 31, 1995. This enabled Southwest to save money by having less paperwork for the company and travel agents, quicker processing, and shorter lines.

Southwest Airlines "services twice the number of passengers per employee than any other airline."

PERSONAL LIFE

Kelleher met his future wife, Joan Negley, on a blind date when he was in college. A Texas native, Joan was attending Connecticut College in New

London when Kelleher's team played the Coast Guard Academy there. They went to dinner on a double date with one of Kelleher's friends, but when the bill came, neither of the men had any money, so their dates had to pay. He called Joan "J. P." after that, for J. P. Morgan.

Despite Kelleher's financial faux pas on their first date, he and Negley were married in 1955. After graduating from law school, Keller worked for the New Jersey Supreme Court, which had essentially the same schedule as Joan's college. They spent a couple of weeks in Texas at Christmas and Easter and a month during the summer before finally deciding to move there.

A few years ago, while still Southwest's CEO, Kelleher battled prostate cancer. He dealt with it in what some said was typical Kelleher fashion. He enjoyed meeting the people at the University of Texas M. D. Anderson Cancer Center, where he received daily doses of radiation. He would go right back to his office after each treatment. Kelleher tried to stay light-hearted and humorous and did not give up his smoking and drinking habits. In an interview with Mark Morrison for *Business Week Online*, Kelleher recounted his attitude toward treatment. He would tease the nurses, "I'd like to ask you why, if this is so good for me, all of you run out of the room before you turn the machine on. Don't you want to share the benefits?" Someone asked him if he was scared while in the waiting room before one of his treatments, and he replied, "Yeah, I'm scared. You know what I'm afraid of? I'm afraid I'm going to die of boredom, waiting to get in there." About his battle with cancer, he said, "It wasn't really much of a battle. I just kind of kicked its ass—with the help of the University of Texas of course. You either get it, or it gets you."

> *"I'm most proud I think of the fact that Southwest Airlines has never had an involuntary furlough. We could have made more profits during recession, but that's a very short term approach to things as far as I'm concerned."*
>
> Herb Kelleher

Southwest is a major supporter of the Ronald McDonald Houses, which provide a home away from home for families of critically ill children who are undergoing treatment at nearby medical facilities. The Southwest annual "Home for the Holidays" program, which received the President's Award for Private Sector Initiatives for 1986 and 1987, has enabled thousands of poor senior citizens to visit friends and relatives during the Christmas season at no charge. Southwest also assists victims of floods and other disasters.

LEADERSHIP LESSONS

Southwest has succeeded in large part because of the unique corporate culture, the concentration on lowering costs, and high levels of coordination among all the employees. One of the reasons for Kelleher's success may also be longevity. Kelleher was a main part of the leadership structure when the airline began and remains so in his role as chairman of the board today. No other air carrier has had the same continuity of leadership as Southwest. Kelleher himself has often said that he has no identifiable leadership style other than just being himself and encouraging others to do the same. His guiding tenet has been that he would rather have a company bound by love than by fear.

The mission of Southwest Airlines is written as "dedication to the highest quality Customer Service delivered with a sense of warmth, friendliness, individual pride, and Company Spirit." Kelleher has said that he values employees above all other stakeholders because he believes that if they are treated right, they will treat the customers right, which in return creates wealth for the shareholders. Kelleher does not adhere to specific quality programs such as Six Sigma and total quality management because he believes that freedom is better for his employees than trying to analyze certain aspects of the job.

Focus on Relationships

Southwest has a very different corporate culture from that of other major U.S. airlines, but this culture has evolved over time. Kelleher created a work environment based on relationships. He ensured that the employees had shared goals, shared knowledge, and mutual respect. His personal actions also exemplified to employees the importance of relationships. They always felt as if they could call him directly with any problem or concern at any time of the day. He would listen to anyone, regardless of his or her position or the nature of the problem. He did not have an office with a window because he did not want to set himself or his position apart. This management philosophy has been called "servant leadership" by some management analysts.

Lead with Credibility and Caring

Kelleher and his management team excelled at gaining the trust of managers in the field and frontline employees. They built trust over time by being up-front and consistent in their message.

Kelleher has often referred to Southwest employees as his extended family. He believes employees should come to work to be themselves and feel comfortable because this makes them more dedicated. They will be more effective and productive and work together better if they are happy about being there. To help create this extended family, Kelleher made sure that when a major event took place in an employee's life, Southwest acknowledged it. When someone has a baby, is ill for an extended period of time, or has a death in the family, for instance, they receive a communication from the general office. To help in times of personal catastrophe, Southwest also has a Catastrophic Fund. Their human resource department was named the People Department instead so that no one would consider the employees resources to be used.

"We're in the customer service business and we happen to operate an airline."
Herb Kelleher

Foster Communication

Southwest is known not only for its friendliness toward customers, but also for its friendliness internally. Early on, Kelleher incorporated cross-training among the different careers at Southwest. The employees are able to learn the responsibilities and pressures of each job. That enabled Southwest's employees to be respectful and helpful toward one another.

Kelleher communicated with his employees via videotapes, newsletters, weekly updates, and visits to the field. The communications informed the employees of what was happening inside the company and industry. The Message to the Field is an annual meeting for all the employees, at which people are recognized and the culture is reinforced. Kelleher believes that all milestones, major and minor, should be celebrated. Celebrating successes and accomplishments allows the people of Southwest to feel appreciated and acknowledged for their hard work, and it reenergizes them. Although many companies celebrate, Southwest tries to celebrate much more. The celebrations are also a chance for the employees of Southwest to get to know one another and build relationships with people outside of their daily job.

Kelleher created the "Southwest Shuffle," which entailed several hundred employees singing, or rather rapping, about how much fun they have on the job. This was shared throughout the company. It has also been customary to film every minor and major event. Kelleher arrived wearing a straitjacket to deliver the 1996 Message to the Field, "Still Nuts after All These Years."

Establish Shared Goals

Before Southwest arrived on the scene, the airline industry had a tradition of deep divisions: pilots, flight attendants, gate agents, ticketing agents, ramp agents, baggage transfer agents, cabin cleaners, caterers, fuelers, freight agents, operations agents, and mechanics, had distinct functionary boundaries and status. They lacked shared goals, shared knowledge, and respect for the roles played by the others.

If a delay occurred at the gate in getting the plane off the ground, it often deteriorated because of finger-pointing and blame avoidance among the employee divisions. Southwest countered this tendency in the early 1990s by instituting a "team delay," which allowed less precise reporting of the cause of delays, with the goal of diffusing blame and encouraging problem solving. In addition to the team delay, Southwest has about ten other delay categories, far fewer than at other major airlines, and they use a less precise performance measurement. This allows the company to look at the problem as situational rather than assigning blame to an individual or group. Punitive measures are only taken when a delay is caused by personnel.

Early in the airline's existence, the question of laying off employees came up. Kelleher was so against that idea that he instead decided to sell one of their four planes and operate with only three. The mandate to not lay off any employees still exists at Southwest and could play a big part in the establishment of shared goals.

Develop Coordination for Quick Turnaround

Southwest's outstanding performance has been achieved in part through high levels of coordination among its frontline employee groups, particularly in the flight departure process. This process is one of the core processes of an airline's operations. Repeated hundreds of times daily in dozens of locations, the success or failure of this process can make or break an airline's reputation for reliability. In the flight departure process, representatives of twelve distinct functions, who often do not communicate well with each other, perform a complex set of tasks between the arrival of the plane and its next departure. The flight departure process is further complicated by rapid changes in weather, connections, and gate availability, such that information is often inaccurate, unavailable, or obsolete. Well-coordinated organizations have a competitive advantage through their ability to achieve higher quality at lower cost by achieving faster cycle times and by providing a more coherent interface to customers. The flight departure process requires a high degree of coordination under time constraints for its successful completion.

Over time, Southwest became able to unload passengers, refuel, clean the cabin, reload new passengers, and take off within fifteen minutes, cut drastically down from the fifty-five minutes it originally took.

The coordination observed at Southwest is powered by relationships among employees and goes beyond the more familiar concept of teamwork. It comes from not only how they act but also how they see themselves in relationship to one another.

One of the most important objectives of the hiring process, in fact, is to find people who are very team oriented, even when hiring pilots or mechanics. Employees are selected with the participation of station management and the People Department using a time-consuming process. Southwest spends more money to recruit and train than any of the other airlines. The training of new employees serves to build coordination as well. Each employee learns about the jobs of each other functional group that interfaces with the job for which he or she is training.

Walk the Line

Southwest has a program called "Walk the Line," which enables people to try someone else's job for the day. Over 75 percent of Southwest's thirty thousand employees have taken part in this unique program. It is training not only in a particular job but also in how everything works, such as how the pilot and first officer communicate. By conducting the "Walk the Line" program, Southwest enables employees to learn about the other job functions in order to see the larger picture. Kelleher admits it is an administrative "nightmare," but insists that it something worth continuing. The program also creates more job security, which has allowed Southwest to have a smaller labor force and more productive employees than its competitors.

Share the Profits

Southwest was the first airline to provide a profit-sharing plan, which has proved to be very profitable for many employees. The start of the program was in 1974; employees owned 13 percent of the company. When budgets got tight or such tragedies as September 11, 2001, occurred, and Kelleher would have to cut costs, he offered employees stock options for taking a lower wage. Kelleher doesn't believe the profits are the only reason his employees take stock options, however. He has said that he thinks people are willing to take that risk because they want to feel fulfilled in the workplace, and Southwest offers that.

Train through Frontline Leadership

Ironically, although Southwest Airlines is known as a flat, team-based company, it has more supervisors per frontline employee than any other airline in the industry. This directly contradicts many contemporary management thinkers, who have argued that more supervisors equate to more bureaucracy.

For Southwest, however, leadership at the front line plays a critical role in organizational success. Rather than undermining coordination among frontline employees, supervisors play a valuable role in strengthening coordination through day-to-day coaching and counseling. At Southwest, each supervisor is responsible for ten to twelve frontline workers. Southwest supervisors are "player coaches," having managerial authority but also performing the work of frontline workers. Supervisors take part in frontline work on a regular basis, even highly physical work such as baggage handling. Supervisors' working side by side with frontline employees is conducive to building shared goals and developing the credibility and knowledge needed for effective coaching.

Keep Jobs Flexible

Traditional organizational practices often demand that individuals disconnect themselves from nonwork aspects of their identity. Relationships at Southwest typically extend beyond the work itself, spilling over into friendships and taking on some characteristics of family ties. There seem to be powerful benefits to blurring the boundaries between work and nonwork aspects of life for Southwest and its employees.

Southwest has been recognized for its innovations in achieving scheduling flexibility for frontline employees through shift trading. In effect, this approach to achieving scheduling flexibility requires employees to use their workplace relationships to negotiate flexibility with each other, further integrating workplace relationships with family ties. Southwest's shift-trading approach to achieving flexibility also reduces the administrative burden associated with flexibility and instead places it in the hands of employees to negotiate with one another.

Southwest recognizes this scheduling flexibility as a major benefit for both the organization and its employees, enabling employees to meet their family commitments without neglecting their work commitments. As a result, Southwest has foregone workplace innovations that might have helped performance in principle but that would have reduced employees' ability to schedule their work around family obligations. For example, some airlines have attempted to schedule the same employees to work together on particular flights over the course of an extended period, hoping to build more permanent teams. But Southwest decided against such scheduling practices, not wanting to reduce the scheduling flexibility enjoyed by Southwest employees. In effect, Southwest did not want to sacrifice the family relationships of its employees.

Have a Strong Leadership Team

There is a highly functioning, well-integrated top management team in place at Southwest. The team's long management meetings reflect Southwest's approach to decision making. Managers from different business areas are knowledgeable about issues beyond the expertise suggested by their titles, and they build on each other's thoughts. Long meetings can be an enormous expenditure of valuable time, but they may be worthwhile. The time invested in developing shared goals, shared knowledge, and mutual respect among senior managers may actually save time in the long run by resolving functional disputes early on.

Most management positions at Southwest are filled through internal promotion and through lateral moves across departmental lines. Kelleher chose long-time colleague Jim Parker to succeed him as CEO and long-time colleague Colleen Barrett to succeed him as president and chief operating officer. In selecting Barrett, Kelleher also left Southwest with the legacy of having the first top female executive in the U.S. airline industry. Barrett, a fifty-nine-year-old Vermont-born grandmother, has been with the company since its beginning; she started as Kelleher's legal secretary.

Make Unions Partners

Because of its reputation for teamwork, most people assume that Southwest Airlines has no unions or very few unionized employees relative to the rest of the airline industry. However, Southwest has the highest percentage of unionized employees of any airline in the United States. It prides itself on outstanding relationships with its unions, including the traditional unions such as the International Brotherhood of Teamsters, the International Association of Machinists, and the Transport Workers Union. Kelleher's approach was to welcome the unions and to work with them to better the employees' lives. One union asked to see the company's books, and Kelleher agreed. He wanted everything to be open between them. Since his departure, however, Southwest has had increasing problems getting issues resolved with the unions. Kelleher has been called in since retiring to work on conflict resolution with the unions.

Build Relationships with Suppliers

Kelleher believes in developing relationships that last over time, and this is true with suppliers, as well. He didn't continually look for better prices, service, or perks, and he wasn't afraid of giving a supplier a perceived advantage by being their sole source. Boeing is the only supplier of planes for Southwest. The airline has been the launch customer, as well, for three Boeing models, but Boeing has not tried to take advantage of the fact that they're a

---

In 2004, Southwest operated 2,800 daily flights to sixty airports in fifty-nine cities across the United States.

---

sole supplier of Southwest Airlines. Kelleher has worked hard to build relationships with the company.

General Electric has been the sole supplier of the aircraft engines, as well. Kelleher was apprehensive because he didn't really know the company at first, but he spent a lot of time with its employees and discovered that in the engine division, they were same kind of people as at Boeing: If they give you their word, they keep it.

Identify the Niche Market

Southwest Airlines was founded to serve a unique market within the airline industry. Herb Kelleher and Rollin King, Southwest's founders, wanted to provide frequent, low-cost, short-haul service in busy markets of fewer than five hundred miles. They considered automobiles and bus service their major competition. Southwest's flights were typically nonstop from originating airport to destination. This point-to-point service differed from the hub-and-spoke strategy employed by other airlines. Their competitors would bring in passengers to a central distribution point (the hub) and provide service outward to other destinations (the spokes). In this arrangement, passengers traveling from small markets could be consolidated together in hubs to create the economies of scale needed for efficient service.

The hub-and-spoke strategy gives airlines more pricing power. A hub generates up to 20 percent more revenue per plane than a comparable

---

Southwest has won the Triple Crown (best on-time record, best baggage handling, and fewest customer complaints in the industry) over thirty times. It has won five Annual Triple Crowns.

---

point-to-point flight. Southwest, as a point-to-point carrier, had neither hubs nor pricing power. To serve this market niche, it was imperative that Southwest have a quick-turnaround strategy at the gate to keep its costs lower.

With its ticket pricing, Southwest created a market of air travelers that did not previously exist. The company opened up air travel to the masses, when it had previously been primarily used by wealthy businessmen. Southwest continues to do this in the markets it enters. A Department of Transportation report noted Southwest dominance in the hundred largest U.S. city-pair markets. Southwest had created those large markets because of its low fares; the markets themselves were not large when Southwest entered them.

Reduce Costs

The short-haul flights that Southwest uses are inherently costlier per mile flown than long-haul flights are, making Southwest's tremendous profitability record quite impressive. The company has had to reduce costs and maximize efficiency in all other areas.

Kelleher was very cost conscious. He wanted to reduce all of Southwest's costs except wages, benefits, and profit sharing. Kelleher oversaw all of the cost reductions, even supervising such expenses as snacks and drinks on the plane. Using mainly the same type of planes allowed a significant cost savings: mechanics and pilots only have to be trained on one type of aircraft, reducing the cost of maintenance and training. Kelleher would intently watch the cost per seat per mile; fractions of a cent in savings could add up to millions of dollars. He thrived on operating below the industry average. Southwest's unit cost ran 30 percent below most of its competitors under Kelleher's tenure.

Kelleher communicated the cost savings and ultimate impact on the bottom line to the employees. He once sent a memo to his employees informing them that the company was about to have an unprofitable quarter. In that memo, he asked each employee to save five dollars a day. It didn't matter if they were flying the airplanes, serving the coffee, or changing the tires, he said. He signed the memo, "LUV, Herb." Southwest cut 5.6 percent from its operating expenses that quarter, a huge amount that enabled the company to make a profit.

Prepare for the Bad Times

Preparing for bad times was always on Kelleher's mind. He assumed that in the airline industry, bad times were always around the corner. His strategy was to have a lot of capital, without which he couldn't fight a war of attrition.

As the strongest airline in the industry financially, Southwest is prepared if somebody wants to charge the same fares. In its position, they can last years in a fare war in order to be successful.

When September 11 occurred, Southwest Airlines had the strongest balance sheet in the American airline industry. It had proportionally the greatest liquidity and was able to maintain profitability while other airlines were applying for government help on a massive scale.

Refrain from Extensive Planning

The ability to respond with rapidity to change is enormously important, especially in an industry where the principal capital assets are traveling at over five hundred miles an hour. If one airline pulls out of a market, another can be serving that market within hours. Within this type of framework, it is difficult to have long-term plans. Kelleher has pointed at his head and said, "We have a business plan: it's up here." He avoided long-term planning in the detailed sense.

His planning, for instance, consisted of defining what Southwest was, what the company thought it should be, how it should function, and what kind of debt-equity ratio it should have. He focused on values, believing that having simple, clearly expressed values enables a company to move much faster because instead of studying things extensively it can make instantaneous decisions. Quickness is important in the airline industry, and beyond defining who the company was and its values, Kelleher did not do much planning at Southwest.

POLITICAL INFLUENCE

Southwest started making political contributions through its employee PAC in 1998, the same year it opened a Washington lobbying office and hired Tom Chapman as its lobbyist. Southwest pursued a strategy of political lobbying after a bruising political battle in which the larger airlines tried to shift a significant portion of the industry's federal tax burden to the short-haul carriers. Since then, the airline has contributed fifty thousand dollars to current Texas delegation members. Their main political action committee, the Freedom Fund, gave five thousand dollars to George W. Bush in his two presidential elections while giving nothing to his opponents. They gave Tom DeLay nine thousand dollars over the last five years. Kelleher and his wife, Joan, have given almost two hundred thousand dollars to the Republican National Committee (RNC) since the 2000 election cycle and have given $126,500 to the RNC's National State Elections Committee.

Kelleher's near-exclusive contributions to Republicans in the past several years may reflect the GOP's majority on Capitol Hill and control of the White

House. In earlier years, Mr. Kelleher gave to both Democrats and Republicans. Kelleher currently serves as an advisory council member to the U.S. Department of Homeland Security.

Southwest acknowledged using long-term strategies to create relationships with lawmakers who will help when important issues arise. When Southwest was preparing to go to Congress to fight the Wright amendment, which forced Southwest's operations at Love Field to refrain from serving any state that did not border Texas, they targeted campaign contributions to supportive members.

The airline contributed $2,500 to Senator John Ensign, a Republican from Nevada who introduced legislation to repeal the Wright amendment, and gave five thousand dollars to Senator Jon Kyl, a Republication from Arizona who subsequently signed on to become a cosponsor of Ensign's bill. Southwest also contributed a thousand dollars each to Republican representatives Jeb Hensarling of Dallas and Sam Johnson of Plano, who jointly sponsored a bill in the House to repeal the Wright amendment.

CRITICS

It is difficult to find critics of Kelleher. Even the unions like him and will make concessions for him because of his legendary status. Kelleher once had many critics and powerful enemies opposed to his involvement in the airline industry, who did everything they could to stop him, including legal and political action that lasted four years before their first flight. After Southwest was allowed to fly, the critics and political maneuvering continued. In 1972, Southwest was sued to oust it from Love Field, which would have severely impacted its business model. This resulted in five more years of litigation, including two more trips by Kelleher to the U.S. Supreme Court. In 1978, the Airline Deregulation Act became law, and the CAB authorized Southwest to provide interstate air service from Love Field. Then, however, Jim Wright, the majority leader of the House of Representatives, amended a House bill to ban all interstate air service from Love Field. The Senate refused to concur. Finally, the Conference Committee agreed on a compromise: nonstop interstate service could be provided out of Love Field to only the four states contiguous to Texas. Moreover, Southwest could not provide one-stop, through ticketing or market passenger service beyond those states. In 1994, a big effort was made to keep Southwest out of the two major computerized reservations systems used at the time—Continental's System One and United's APOLLO.

None of these actions had an effect on Southwest's ultimate profitablility, however. Kelleher's main critics currently are those opposed to his political contributions. During the contentious 2004 presidential election, Southwest would not allow a woman wearing a T-shirt with the pictures of President

George W. Bush and Vice President Dick Cheney and an expletive to board her flight. Critics became vocal against Southwest's and Kelleher's contributions at that time.

POSSIBLE FUTURE IMPACT

After Kelleher's departure, Southwest faced expected difficulty. The unions were not as amiable to work with, and Helleher's successor had a difficult time following him. After a grim tenure, Jim Parker quit as CEO and was replaced with longtime CFO Gary Parker. The big question now is whether Southwest can achieve the same level of success without Kelleher.

Kelleher was pressed back into service in the stalemated, embittered flight-attendant negotiations. He got the deal done finally, but expensively: a 31 percent raise over the contract's six years. It's settlements like that—and a 2002 pilots' contract raising pay a minimum of 20 percent over the past two years—in addition to soaring fuel costs, that have raised Southwest's costs. Its cost per average seat-mile of eight cents is creeping closer to that of the larger carriers. There is also additional competition for them today with JetBlue, AirTran, and United's Ted.

Southwest is the United States's only major short-haul, low-fare, high-frequency, point-to-point carrier.

Some analysts believe that Southwest is facing the same issues and challenges that other carriers have experienced and there is a risk that as a generational change occurs and the oldest Southwest employees retire, the company's low-cost culture will change. Keeping costs under control and keeping its culture alive are huge challenges for Southwest.

Southwest allowed itself to become the subject of a reality TV show on cable channel A&E called *Airline*. ("We all have our baggage" is the tagline.) The cameras follow Southwest employees as they deal with all manner of crisis.

Kelleher has started the Center for Entrepreneurship at the University of Texas at Austin because he wants to help Texas continue to be a friendly place for entrepreneurs. The Kelleher center will add to existing programs at the Red McCombs School of Business while creating a forum for successful entrepreneurs, business people, students, and faculty.

TIMELINE

1931	March 12, Born in Camden, New Jersey.
1953	Graduated from Wesleyan University.
1955	Married Joan Negley.

1956	Graduated from law School from New York University.
	Began working with the Supreme court as a clerk and stays until 1959.
1959	Started work as an associate with Lum, Biunno, and Tompkins.
1961	Started work as a partner with Matthews, Nowlin, Macfarlane & Barrett.
1966	Began work as legal counsel for Air Southwest Company.
	Filed an application on November 27th for the start up airline to fly between Dallas, Houston and San Antonio.
1968	February 20th, The application was approved.
1969	Became senior partner with Oppenheimer, Rosenberg, Kelleher & Wheatley and worked there until 1981.
1971	Became legal counsel for Southwest Airlines. (previously Air Southwest) until 1981.
	January, Lamar Muse became CEO.
	June 18, Southwest made maiden voyage with service between Dallas, Houston, and San Antonio.
1972	All Houston service was moved to Houston's Hobby Airport.
1973	Southwest had its first profitable year. Southwest applied to expand service to the Rio Grande Valley.
1974	Southwest boarded its one-millionth passenger. The terminal at Houston's Hobby Airport was remodeled by spending four hundred thousand dollars to add two new boarding gates and departure lounges.
1975	Southwest was granted permission to fly to the Rio Grande Valley.
1976	Southwest service expanded to Austin, Corpus Christi, El Paso, Lubbock, and Midland/Odessa. Southwest also added its sixth Boeing 737.
	"LUV" was added to the stock exchange as Southwest went public. Southwest also carried its five-millionth passenger.
	Filled in as CEO, president, and chairman of the board for Southwest president Lamar Muse. Later in the year, Howard Putnam became CEO and president and Kelleher remained chairman of the board.
	United States Airline Deregulation Act of 1978 was passed.
	Southwest expanded service outside of Texas to New Orleans. Self-ticketing machines are also introduced in ten cities.
1977	Southwest Airlines added the twenty-second Boeing 737 to its fleet. The 737 was christened *Rollin W. King* in honor of the company's cofounder.
1978	September, Became permanent president and CEO along with his previous duty of chairman of the board. Southwest celebrated a decade of service.

1979	Southwest added flight service to San Francisco, Los Angeles, San Diego, Las Vegas, and Phoenix.
1980	Southwest hit a mark of 9,500,000 passengers flown.
1981	For the fourth consecutive year, Southwest was ranked number one among airlines in customer satisfaction.
1982	Service to St. Louis and Chicago's Midway Airport were added.
1983	'Fun Fares' was introduced and Southwest celebrated fifteen years of low fares.
1984	Weekend Fun Packs, which include round-trip tickets and hotel stays, were introduced. Southwest took over TransStar Airlines.
1985	Southwest won its first Triple Crown: best on-time record, best baggage handling, and fewest customer complaints. Southwest also worked with Texas and California to promote Sea World; a 737 was painted with a whale design and named *Shamu One*.
1986	Service to and from Oakland International Airport began.
1987	Southwest hit its one-billion-dollar mark.
1988	Twenty years of service.
1990	Southwest began service on the East Coast. The second annual Triple Crown was won.
1991	Southwest won its third consecutive Triple Crown. Southwest took over Morris Air.
1992	Ticketless travel was made available everywhere, and Southwest won its fourth consecutive Triple Crown.
1993	Southwest.com debuted. Twenty-five years of service was celebrated and the fifth consecutive Triple Crown was won. Service to Florida was also added.
1994	Service to Southwest's fiftieth city, Jacksonville, Florida, was introduced.
1995	Southwest becomes the fifth-largest U.S. air carrier.
2000	"SWABIZ" was introduced online to assist business travelers.
2001	Southwest marked its thirtieth year of service. June, Kelleher stepped down as CEO and president.
2003	A&E Television Network filmed a behind-the-scenes look at commercial air travel.
2004	Southwest announced its thirty-first consecutive year of profitability. The sixtieth airport, Philadelphia, is added to service.

RESOURCES

Bird, J. B. Herb Kelleher: An Entrepreneur for All Seasons. *McCombs School Magazine*, May 12, 2003 (http://www.mccombs.utexas.edu/news/magazine/03s/kelleher.asp).

Dodge, Robert, and Gillman, Todd J. Looking for Mileage from Their Donations: American, Southwest Target Federal Giving as Wright Debate Simmers. *Dallas Morning News,* August 27, 2005.

Drake, Susan M. *Light Their Fire: Using Internal Marketing to Ignite Employee Performance and Wow Your Customers.* Chicago, IL: Dearborn Trade, 2005, pp. 25, 56–59, 152, 159–160, 168.

Frieberg, Kevin, and Jackie Freiberg. *Nuts! Southwest Airlines' Crazy Recipe for Business and Personal Success.* Austin, Texas: Bard Books. 1996.

Gittell, Jody Hoffer. *Southwest Airlines Way: The Power of Relationships for Superior Performance.* New York: McGraw-Hill, 2002.

Gunther, Marc. *Faith and Fortune: The Quiet Revolution to Reform American Business.* New York: Crown Business, 2004, pp. 17, 61–74, 78, 93, 181.

Hiam, Alexander. *Motivational Management.* New York, NY: AMACOM, 2002, pp. 1, 28, 34, 212.

Hunter, James C. *World's Most Powerful Leadership Principle: How to Become a Servant Leader.* New York: Crown Publishing Group, 2004, pp. 47, 84–89.

Johnson, Steven Kyle. Southwest Airlines: A Case Study in Strategic Planning. MBA report, University of Texas at Austin, 1987.

Kelleher, Herb. A Culture of Commitment. *Leader to Leader* 4 (Spring 1997): 20–24.

Krames, Jeffrey A. *What the Best CEOs Know: 7 Exceptional Leaders and Their Lessons for Transforming Any Business.* New York: McGraw-Hill Companies, 2003, pp. 11, 21, 31, 173–174, 177–192.

Kuile, Roger C. Airline Deregulation Act. MBA report, University of Texas at Austin, 1985.

Morrison, Mark. Herb Kelleher on the Record, Part 1. *Business Week Online,* December 12, 2003.

Putnam, Howard D. *Winds of Turbulence.* New York: Harper Business, 1991.

Serwer, Andy, and Kate Bonamici. The Hottest Thing in the Sky. *Fortune,* March 8, 2004, pp. 86–106.

Shapiro, Linda. Southwest Airlines: A Case Study in Airline Deregulation. MBA report, University of Texas at Austin, 1985.

Useem, Jerry. America's Most Admired Companies. *Fortune,* March 7, 2005, pp. 66–70.

COMPANY INFORMATION

P.O. Box 36611
2702 Love Field Drive
Dallas, TX 75235
www.southwest.com
New York Stock Exchange symbol: LUV

AP Photo/Jack Smith.

Phil Knight

Phil Knight and his running coach at the University of Oregon, Bill Bowerman, created the Nike company, the footwear and clothing empire, in Beaverton, Oregon, in 1962 with an investment of only five hundred dollars each and an intense love of running. It became the world's leading athletic shoe and sports apparel maker, a multibillion-dollar company endorsed by superstars like Michael Jordan and recognized around the world for its Swoosh logo. Nike posted revenues of $13.7 billion in 2005 and now owns about 40 percent of the U.S. athletic footwear market and 34 percent of the worldwide market. It has been the clear industry leader and has made Phil Knight the twenty-second richest American, valued at $7.4 billion. Knight is revered by many as an entrepreneurial legend and marketing genius for his success in turning the once humble sneaker into a must-have fashion item. Although he resigned as CEO in 2004, Knight has remained as chairman of the board. His awards include: Most Powerful Man in Sports, *Sporting News,* 1992; Pioneer Award, University of Oregon, 1982; and one of America's top managers, *Business Weekly,* 1997.

The seeds of the Nike company were planted when Knight, a business student and runner at the University of Oregon, began wearing the footwear inventions his coach, Bill Bowerman, designed. The University of Oregon campus had long been home to a successful track program, and Bill Bowerman had been the head coach there since 1948. Bowerman liked to tinker with new track shoe designs for his players, attempting to improve their speed and decrease their injuries.

The partnership between Knight and Bowerman began in 1962, not long after Knight decided to take some time off after completing his MBA at Stanford University to travel the world. While he was in Japan, he contacted Onitsuka Tiger Company and convinced its managers that there were great marketing opportunities in the United States. When asked what company he represented, Knight made up a name, Blue Ribbon Sports, and ordered shoes that were delivered to his parents' garage. He and Bowerman each contributed five hundred dollars to pay for the product.

The idea behind Blue Ribbon Sports was to import high-tech, low-priced athletic shoes from Japan and sell them in the United States to compete with the German-made shoes that then dominated the market. Bowerman worked constantly on ways to improve the shoes, and Knight sold the products and managed the financial end of the business. By 1964, they had sold eighteen hundred pairs, mostly peddled out of the trunk of Knight's car at track meets. Four years later, a Bowerman-modified design, the Cortez, became Tiger's best selling shoe. Between 1962 and 1971, revenues in the business grew from eight thousand dollars to $1.96 million, and the number of employees grew from the two founders to forty-five. In 1972, after a falling-out, Blue Ribbon Sports ended its partnership with Onitsuka Tiger and agreed that it would no longer sell Tiger brand shoes. Knight and Bowerman decided to manufacture 330 pairs of their own latex-and-leather design. Its distinguishing feature was a unique lightweight sole that was made with a waffle iron that belonged to Bowerman's wife. The two sold out their entire supply at $3.30 a pair and gave birth to their own corporation. The Nike brand shoes were worn at that year's Olympics by four of the top seven finishers in the marathon.

It would take only a few years before their Nikes, featuring the now-famous Swoosh symbol, made them the dominant athletic-shoe company in the nation. Their company was the brash and exciting challenger on the scene. The timing and image were perfect, riding the growing interest among baby-boomers in physical fitness and jogging. Surprisingly, there were just a handful of sneaker styles for all activities before Nike entered the game in the early 1970s. From 1917, when Keds, the first popularly marketed sneaker, was introduced, until 1970, sports footwear underwent little change. Aside from Bowerman's innovative designs, Knight's savvy alliances with sports celebrities and cost-effective promotional programs, they were also quite fortunate to be starting out during the country's biggest fitness boom. They did their part to contribute to this boom, as well. Their first employee, runner Steve Prefontaine, marketed running as a serious sport, and Bowerman himself helped make jogging a national pastime by writing a book and studying how running's popularity had occurred in Australia.

Through the use of continued innovative designs and business strategies, by 1980 Nike controlled half of the market for running shoes in the United States. That year, with 2,700 employees and a successful track record, Knight and Bowerman took the company public. When they did, they renamed the company Nike, after the winged Greek goddess of victory. By 1987, the company had 487 separate footwear styles. By recruiting some of the world's best-known and well-liked professional athletes to represent the company and because of Knight's ingenuity and marketing savvy, there are now sneakers for basketball, running, bowling, tennis, aerobics, and so on—many at prices of a hundred dollars or more per pair. People have been convinced, in part by Nike, that they need the best sports shoe in order to perform their best.

The company continued building its brand through a steady focus on high-performance athletes. Athletes were responding. By the end of 1982, every world record in men's track, from the 800 meters to the marathon, had been set by athletes wearing Nike's high-performance shoes. In 1990, Nike had grown to 5,300 employees and two billion dollars in revenue. Between 1993 and 1997, the company scored record growth, tripling in size. By 2001, the company had grown to more than twenty-two thousand employees operating on six continents and almost ten billion dollars in revenue. Today Nike remains the driving force in its industry. It still offers some five hundred generally well-regarded shoe models, and even more types of apparel. It operates giant Niketown superstores and has opened a few Jordan-themed specialty outlets, and it continues selling billions of dollars in product each year in more than a hundred countries. Through its network of suppliers, shippers, retailers, and service providers, Nike provides employment for close to one million people worldwide.

The firm drew passionate criticism for exploiting foreign and child workers. Early on, Knight had decided that the company would contract all of its manufacturing, and most of the factories it used were and are still in developing countries. Nike became the symbol for globalization and the problems that occur because of it. This controversy threatened to tarnish Knight's and the brand's reputation in the late 1990s, but strong management and a willingness to face ethical issues and respond to public pressure by adapting some manufacturing processes has seen Nike emerge in a better shape than some other multinational companies with similar issues.

Knight has encouraged innovation, the company's main focus, through the use of an unusual management style. Nike has never been a top-down organization, and Knight credits Nike's "distributive leadership" with the company's successes. He encouraged people to be bold and to make their ideas happen, and this still happens today. Rarely at Nike are there management mandates to do something. It is firmly understood that real innovation doesn't come from

Fact: The word *Nike* is the name of the Greek goddess of victory.

upper management. The company is fast paced and creative. As a result, there is little patience for a long-term perspective. It is a culture that admires high-performance heroes who defy the odds. Though Nike has become a "big company," at heart many employees, particularly those who have been with Nike for some time, still view it as an agile, even rebellious company. Nike's organizational culture is about sports, fitness, performance, risk, excellence, and winning. It is a competitive culture that attracts sports-oriented, competitive people who pride themselves in being performers. At Nike the athlete is king, and making cool products for athletes is the ultimate achievement.

THE EARLY YEARS

Philip H. Knight was born in Portland, Oregon, on February 24, 1938. He grew up in the upper-middle-class Portland suburb of Eastmoreland. His mother, Lola, was a homebody, thought to be a recluse later in life. His father, William (Bill), had been a state representative at the age of twenty-six. He could wield political power to his advantage and likely taught his son a little of politics, which he would later use on a much larger scale in his career. Bill left politics for labor law and eventually found his way into a particular niche representing newspaper publishers. Then in 1953, a plane crash killed the young publisher of the *Oregon Journal*, and, though a strange choice, Bill was handpicked by the publisher's widow to take over. Bill was a staunch Republican, and the newspaper was quite liberal. Knight was fifteen at the time and was a good student. He was on the honor roll in high school and was well liked, though very quiet. He took sports seriously, and though he couldn't play football or baseball well, he excelled in track and was one of the city's best performers. He also wrote for the sports section in the high school paper.

Knight was never easy to get to know; he was remembered as "the shy guy with the grin." In his youth, for reasons his friends can't remember, he was nicknamed Buck. Classmates pigeonholed him as an accountant, and he indeed became a CPA, but Knight wasn't that careful with details. He overlooked maintenance on his car and often misread road maps. But he laughed at his mistakes, and friends thought he just assumed that wherever life took him, he'd be okay. He didn't have great ambitions, at least none that he let others know about.

Fact: Nike paid thirty-five dollars for the Swoosh logo.

When the class of 1955 graduated from high school, the yearbook editor assigned one of Bartlett's quotations for each graduating senior. Knight's caption read, "A more pleasant, willing lad I ne'er did meet." Knight went on to the University of Oregon, where his father had gone before him. He joined the Phi Gamma Delta fraternity and was known as a straight arrow who rarely drank too much. He was elected as president of his fraternity.

He spent a lot of time running and joined the track team under Coach Bill Bowerman, who, in addition to training his athletes, would experiment with their equipment to try to reduce their times and injuries. As part of that experimentation, he constructed prototype track shoes with lightweight leather and later nylon uppers. Bowerman believed that he could create measurable difference in times by decreasing the weight of a shoe by an ounce. Knight was eager to try out his coach's creations.

Knight studied accounting at the University of Oregon and received his BS in 1959. Knight did a stint in the Army reserve before going on to Stanford School of Business, where he studied accounting. He received his CPA, but to friends he didn't seem outstanding in any respect. It surprised them greatly that he achieved the level of success that he did. Although he was not an honor student in college or at Stanford, he did fairly well. In one business class, he had to come up with an idea for a business. He brainstormed the concept of manufacturing shoes in Japan and selling them in the USA. The thrust of his argument in the paper was that cheaper labor coupled with efficient manufacturing processes could threaten the dominance of German companies such as Adidas and Puma in the track shoe market.

CAREER PATH

After graduating from Stanford in 1962, Knight took a trip to Japan to meet with the top executives from Onitsuka Tiger, a shoe company. Knight's goal was to convince the executives to distribute shoes to the United States for him to sell. The company agreed, and Knight placed the order.

While Knight was creating the concept of his future business, he practiced as a certified account with Price Waterhouse and Coopers & Lybrand. He left this job in 1967 to focus on his company, but when he found he couldn't make enough money selling the shoes, Knight had to take a job at Portland State University teaching accounting.

Initially, Knight took on the finance and marketing functions, leaving Bowerman to create shoe designs. Knight's first retail outlet was the back of his car, from which he would sell track shoes at high school track meets. In 1965, Jeff Johnson, who had been working for Adidas, joined the duo as the company's first full-time employee and taking the sales function from Phil, started selling shoes out of a van at the track meets. The company at the time had revenues of only twenty thousand dollars. Knight knew Johnson because they had once competed against each other.

The second employee picked up by Knight and Bowerman was runner Steve Prefontaine. Prefontaine was the first athlete to wear the Blue Ribbon

Sports shoe, today known as Nike. Prefontaine's efforts in making running a popular sport helped create a larger market for track shoes. He was killed in a car crash in 1975. Another early employee (and Knight's former student) was Penny Parks, who helped keep the company's books.

By 1966 the first of the Blue Ribbon Sports outlet stores was opened in Santa Monica, California, by Jeff Johnson. Johnson created ads and stationery on his own and rarely communicated with Knight. Blue Ribbon Sports began doing so well that Knight could resign from Portland University and continue focusing on growing the business.

Knight almost named Nike "Dimension Six." His coworker Jeff Johnson came up with the name Nike from a dream.

In 1967, Knight and Bowerman incorporated Blue Ribbon Sports, and in 1971, Blue Ribbon Sports and Onitsuka Tiger had had a falling-out that resulted in litigation. They decided to go their separate ways in 1972, leaving Blue Ribbon Sports, Inc., on its own. Knight and Bowerman decided to forge ahead and continue to create designs, have them manufactured, and sell them. Their first shoe was not a running shoe: it was a football shoe. The decision to manufacture and market a football shoe was their way of striking out on their own while still bound by noncompete arrangements with Onitsuka. Since Onitsuka did not have a football shoe, Knight felt that he could successfully argue, if necessary, that they were not competing with Onitsuka at all. Unfortunately, that first shoe did not perform as Knight had hoped. Built in Mexico, the shoe was not tested to perform in cold, snowy conditions on the football field and ended up disintegrating. The company quickly gained a reputation as a cheap shoe. Over time, however, they would overcome this disastrous beginning and become known for quality and creative designs.

Knight and Bowerman then decided to have 330 pairs of their own latex-and-leather design manufactured. Bowerman had been experimenting with his wife's waffle iron and incorporated the results into his shoe design. The company first needed a name for their shoes. Knight thought of the name Dimension 6, but Jeff Johnson came up with something better. Nike, the name of the Greek goddess of victory, came to Johnson in a dream one night. With this, they had a name, but they still needed a logo. Knight was under pressure to create one because he had shoeboxes in Mexico that were waiting to be printed. He needed a logo. Knight turned to Carolyn Davidson, a graphic design major who worked on several designs, including a "fat check-mark," known today as the "swoosh." Knight chose her rendering of the Swoosh, telling her, "I don't love it, but it will grow on me." Knight paid Davidson's thirty-five-dollar invoice for the design promptly. Davidson continued to design for the changing company until her one-person design shop was too small to handle the company's needs. In 1983, after Nike had seen overwhelming success, Knight arranged a meeting with Davidson and gave her a gold Swoosh ring embedded with a diamond. She also received a certificate from Knight and an envelope containing Nike stock—how much stock remains a secret between Knight and Davidson. "The stock has split three times since I received it, so I can definitely say that I have been well compensated for my design," she says.

The Nike brand shoes were worn at the 1972 Olympics by four of the top seven finishers in the marathon. In 1981, Blue Ribbon Sports, Inc., merged into Nike, Inc.

PERSONAL LIFE

In 1967, Knight began dating Penny Parks, who was one of his students and worked as an accountant for Blue Ribbon Sports; she was nineteen and he was thirty. Six months later, they got married, and they quickly had their first son, Matthew. They eventually added another son, Travis, and a daughter, Christina, to their family.

Knight's older son, Matthew, died on May 23, 2004, at the age of 34. The victim of a scuba malfunction, Matthew Knight, died while in El Salvador working on a charity effort to build orphanages. Matthew had held a couple of positions at Nike, but opted not to pursue a career at the company. He and his wife, Angie, lived in Sherwood, Oregon, with their children, Logan and Dylan.

Knight and his wife were devastated. In a note to his staff, Knight told them that instead of sending him condolences, they should make a point of spending more time with their own families. "I wasn't a good enough manager, really, is what it comes down to," said Knight. "You have to manage your time [as a parent], and it's a pretty tough balance. It's a hard balance, and when the kid's not there anymore, you can't make up for it." At the time Knight was working on choosing a successor at Nike, and those working on the CEO search noticed an immediate change.

Though Knight is known for being reserved and quiet, he is also known for wearing his emotions on his sleeve—some employees have said that over the years they've seen Knight cry "countless times" when inspired by an athlete or employee. He is a very private person and has done few interviews. There have been no authorized books published about him. Interestingly, few employees, including executives, have ever been in Knight's office. The only thing that anyone seems to know about it is that Knight fashioned it in a Japanese style. So Japanese, in fact, that inside the office of the man who controls the most powerful shoe company in the world, no shoes are allowed-not even Nikes.

A very active man who enjoys watching sports just as much as he enjoys running, Knight is an avid sports fanatic who takes pleasures in live sporting events. Since retiring as CEO, he now spends much of his time attending sporting events.

The Knights contribute to their community, and over several years contributed hundreds of millions of dollars to the University of Oregon. They no

---

Fact: During Knight's college years, he recorded a time of 4:10 for the mile run.

---

longer do this, but they run the Phil & Penny Knight Scholarship and contribute to the community in other ways, whether supporting the Oregon Zoo or sponsoring the Aloha Knights, an amateur baseball team named after them. Knight's listed contribution to charities is one of the lowest percentages of total worth of any CEO. In 2004, Knight showed that he gave away only 1 percent of his net worth. A Nike spokesman commented on this saying, in essence, that Knight and his wife are intensely private people who rarely divulge their philanthropy.

Knight's combined salary and bonuses for 2006 were nearly $3.7 million.

LEADERSHIP LESSONS

Knight's management style has been mainly hands-off. He provided little or no direction to subordinates, leaving them to figure things out and create and implement new ideas on their own. Mark Parker, who has been at the company since 1979 and is copresident of Nike, thinks that is part of Knight's genius. He gives his people freedom to breathe. Knight is a man of very few words, usually. He uses a good deal of nonverbal communication, and his executives learn it. When he is asked a question, he may not answer or the answer may come in the form of a nod.

There were few corporate directives when Knight was in charge, and a system of "distributive leadership" was used throughout the company. Employees, including executives, were often moved around to different positions, reported to more than one person, and operated in a very atypical management setting. This approach worked well, especially in the early years of Nike's development, because the employees were motivated, inspired, and creative. As the company grew, however, they found they needed additional structure, although Nike still has an informal and fast-paced, creative culture.

Manage through Distributed Leadership

Nike uses a distributed, noncentralized, collaborative leadership model that celebrates the success of the team and creates an environment where leadership is situational. At Nike, leadership has not come only from its top executives. Instead, the firm distributes the responsibilities of leadership to virtually every employee at the firm, allowing the company to remain grounded in its entrepreneurial roots despite its evolution into a global corporate giant.

Knight liked to shuffle the employees and executives around. That habit created what Nike called its "matrix." In this type of management model, people answer to more than one boss. For example, a basketball-shoe marketer reports not just to the head of basketball but also to the heads of U.S. marketing and overall footwear—and, more informally, to anyone else who wants to add their opinion. Because Knight moved executives around, someone who was a boss one day could find himself a subordinate to his former charges the next. Rotating titles meant there might be half a dozen people in the company who had served in any one position, giving them license to critique the performance of the newcomer. In this situation, employees learn quickly that the only way to get things done is to come up with good ideas and build alliances.

This management style didn't mean that Knight would not make decisions without consulting others. Quite the contrary. It was characteristic of him to make big decisions without holding a vote.

In the wrong hands this management style could easily lead to chaos. Twenty-five thousand employees moving jobs, not knowing whether they will be the boss or the subordinate, answering to multiple managers, and not knowing what the boss will do next seems a sure recipe for disaster. But it wasn't at Nike, and that is largely because Knight inspired the employees to strive for something higher—to satisfy not just themselves but fans, coaches, and teammates.

Inspire

Companies that evolve quickly—sometimes too quickly—from start-up to megacorporation face the challenge of keeping the entrepreneurial spirit alive within the organization. Although Nike's rise has been fast and furious—from nothing to fourteen billion dollars over four decades, the company has managed to keep employees inspired, which contributed to the success of Knight's atypical management style.

To most of its employees, Nike is more a state of mind than it is a place to work. Knight truly has a passion for his company and athletics and still runs daily. Many of the company's employees are also athletes who truly believe that athletics represents the spirit and greatness of human beings. The triumph of a Michael Jordan, a Tiger Woods, a Mia Hamm, or a Lance Armstrong inspires many people, and Nike employees are especially attuned to that. Yet it is not just their victories that inspire. Every athlete knows that for every triumph, there are countless times when performance falls short. What also inspires Nike employees is the sheer determination that drives countless hours of tedious practice.

Stories about Bill Bowerman and past athletic stars are told to relate the company's heritage of innovation, commitment to helping athletes improve, and reliance on teamwork. In passing on these anecdotes, Nike helps its newest employees understand where the company has been and how it got to where it is today. The storyteller program has it roots in the 1970s, when newly hired employees attended a one-hour corporate history lesson; today, that history lesson takes two days to tell and is referred to as an orientation program.

Develop Talent

When Nike began it was structured as had been Bill Bowerman's work with a team of average track and field athletes. His approach was to develop the talent at hand through motivating, inspiring, challenging, and teaching. Bowerman created star athletes, including renowned long-distance runner Steve Prefontaine. This talent-development method has its parallel in Nike's corporate environment. The company looked for pockets of excellence where it could find them, and where it couldn't it tried to create them. The first Nike employees were not selected on the basis of excellence. Most of them were friends of friends, but once they were hired, they were transformed from average people to outstanding performers who helped shape the company. Nike cultivated a culture of rebellion and celebrated those who could do what some said couldn't be done.

Change the Composition of an Ineffective Team

Knight made tough decisions to change the composition of ineffective teams at Nike. He often restructured teams and the organizational chart, as was typical of his distributive leadership model. But he also made large, sweeping changes at the company when necessary.

Knight made some mistakes in his hands-off approach to management. When he took a couple of hiatuses from running the company, leaving others in charge unchecked, Nike ended up facing its toughest challenges, which Knight would have to correct when he took the reins again. The first time Knight left was for an extended trip to China. "I'm splitting from this turkey farm," he told longtime employee Bob Woodell in the spring of 1983 before taking an extended trip through China and putting Woodell in charge. Within months, the jogging craze ebbed and the aerobics craze began. Nike pooh-poohed the trend and kept focused on running and basketball.

Upstart Reebok snagged the new market, and Nike's U.S. revenues dropped 6 percent in two years to $730 million in 1985. Knight realized he had the wrong management in place. In the fall of 1984 he returned and took over from Woodell.

Tom Clarke, a longtime product developer who had been president since 1994, found himself running the company when Knight left again—this time for unknown reasons. Soon thereafter Nike hit the rocks once again. It failed to spot the slowing of demand for hundred-dollar-plus sneakers among U.S. consumers, got caught in the Asian economic meltdown, and reacted slowly as college kids switched from sporting Nikes to accusing the company of running sweatshops. Revenues, which had more than doubled to $9.2 billion between 1994 and 1997, stagnated, slipping to $9 billion in 2000.

By 1999, Knight was back; in May 2000, he sent Clarke off to head up new business ventures and retook the role of president himself. He revived the company by doing what he did best: finding and motivating talented people, then letting them do their thing, but keeping an eye out on the overall direction the company was taking.

When Nike missed the opportunity to enter the women's aerobic shoe market and let Reebok take control, Knight was distraught. He completely restructured the company and the way it did business. At that time Nike employed about two thousand people, and six hundred of them were laid off. More conservative executives were put in place to formalize the office. Over the next few years most of Knight's earliest employees who survived the layoffs, including Woodell, left, many feeling they had been frozen out.

By 1988, Knight noted in his letter to shareholders, "all of the vice presidents listed on the 1981 annual report have left." He set out to rebuild the company with a new team.

Bring in Outside Help

Knight revamped management and brought in key outsiders, stars like Mindy Grossman from Ralph Lauren to run apparel, Don Blair from Pepsi to be the CFO, and Mary Kate Buckley from Disney to head up new ventures.

Blair has been instrumental in restoring financial credibility and stability to the company, making earnings less volatile and fad driven. Since he joined Nike, its financials have improved. From 1999 to 2004, revenues increased from $8.7 billion to $12.2 billion, profitability rose from $451 million to $945 million, and share price increased from $60.9 to $71.1.

When it was time to choose a new CEO, Knight again went outside the company, choosing William Perez, fifty-seven, formerly chief of S. C. Johnson & Son, Inc.

Outsource Production

Nike is viewed as one of the corporate pioneers in terms of its production. Instead of trying to compete with its then-larger competitors, from the outset Nike designed its shoes in-house and outsourced virtually all of the manufacturing of its products to countries in Southeast Asia. Nike has never manufactured any of the shoes it sells. Virtually all are manufactured by independent contract manufacturers, many of whom produce for other globally recognized brands as well. Through outsourcing, the company significantly reduced its operating costs to the point where few other companies could surpass its profitability.

Approximately 650,000 people work in Nike-contracted factories worldwide. Today, the contract factory supply chain for Nike brand products includes over eight hundred factories. Most of the workers today are in Vietnam, Thailand, Pakistan, and Indonesia, although Nike has changed production facilities several times. In 1992 Nike had no companies or shoes made in Vietnam. Today, Nike shoes make up 5 percent of all the exports coming out of Vietnam, according to Knight. Nike also has manufacturing agreements with independent factories in Argentina, Brazil, India, Italy, Mexico, and South Africa to manufacture footwear for sale primarily within those countries.

Create the Market

Nike's view of itself has served as the basis for an effective marketing strategy: creating product need by promoting athletics as a movement. Early in Nike's life, it set out to create the demand for athletics, especially running. In 1962, Bowerman met exercise physiologist and coach Arthur Lydiard during a tour of New Zealand with the University of Oregon's world record four-mile relay team. Lydiard convinced Bowerman that the potential benefits of running extended beyond the track into everyday life. Upon his return to the United States, Bowerman started lecturing and writing about fitness. His 1967 book, "Jogging," became an instant bestseller and inspired America's jogging craze.

Soon after, Knight hired Steve Prefontaine, an Olympic runner, to help make running a more popular sport and create a larger market for track shoes. Nike ads frequently marketed the benefits of sports, rarely mentioning the brand. One of the television ads Nike ran in the mid-1980s was focused on the value of athletics to girls and women. In the ad, one girl after another makes a plea (presumably to her parents) that she be allowed to get involved in athletics. "If you let me play sports, I will like myself more....I'll be 60% less likely to get breast cancer....I'll suffer less depression....I'll be more likely to leave a man who beats me....I'll be less likely to get pregnant before I want to."

To create the movement toward their brands, Nike also promoted their products to high school and college athletics by donating equipment. Just as Microsoft gives away its Internet Explorer free as part of new computer purchases or Apple donates computers for schools to use to establish a preference for the product, Nike has long given away sports gear to high school and college teams. Nike marketers have long recognized the value of having top high school and college athletes and coaches sporting the firm's clothing and footwear. In some cases, having the Nike Swoosh appear on a college athlete may be just as advantageous as seeing the same equipment on a professional. Nike-sponsored American high school and college teams often sign contracts outlining strict terms of sponsorship.

Fact: Knight climbed Mount Fuji.

Providing products to athletes and signing endorsement deals were large parts of Nike's promotional efforts, but sponsoring road races and creating track clubs were equally important. One of the biggest successes was the Athletics West running club, based in Eugene, Oregon, in 1977. The club's purpose was to subsidize training and sponsor races for a group of athletes without overtly pushing the Nike name. Athletes were provided Nike gear that would be seen during races and competitions. Leaving references to Nike out of the club's name was one of the smartest moves the firm made. By distancing the Nike name from the club, the company avoided turning the group into an obvious commercial enterprise. Nike officials referred to this strategy as "whispering loudly"—allowing the consumers to figure things out for themselves.

Because athletes are not permitted to accept gifts or money of any sort in order to qualify for the Olympics, Nike circumvents this by donating to the U.S. Olympic teams via the schools, coaches, and teams associated with the athletes. And in return Nike earns significant media coverage and the potential allegiance of the athletes who receive the shoes and outfits.

Sell Where the Money Is

Since the early days when Knight and Johnson sold their shoes out of the backs of their cars at track meets, Nike has focused on going to where the customer is. Their main outlets are retail stores and the Internet.

Secure Retail Commitments. Nike products are sold in the United States through approximately twenty-eight thousand retail accounts. Outside the United States, Nike sells its products in 120 countries through twenty-three thousand retail accounts as well as via distributors, licensees, subsidiaries, and branch offices. In addition, the company has opened twelve Niketowns (megastores devoted to Nike products) in the United States.

During Nike's fast-growth period in the mid-1970s, the company hit a cash crunch and was having difficulty managing deliveries of its products. Retailers threatened to drop the Nike product line if deliveries were not made on time. But without a realistic estimate of product demand, Nike would have had to overproduce in order to ensure that its customers' needs were met, and the company simply couldn't afford to take such a risk. So Nike developed an advance-commitment program that would help the company forecast sales more accurately, while securing an upfront purchase commitment. Nike approached its largest customers and proposed its future program. Customers received a 5 to 7 percent discount for any order that they placed several months in advance of delivery, and they also got a guarantee that they would receive at least 90 percent of that order on time.

The Internet. Less than two hundred million dollars' worth of sports shoes and apparel is sold online today (out of seventy-seven billion dollars sold in the United States overall), but within the next five years the online figure could grow to four billion dollars. Although it has taken some time for Nike to establish a presence on the Web, the company is now ready. *Advertising Age* hailed Nike's site, saying, "Nike is an example of how to put together an integrated marketing campaign with the TV and Internet playing to their own—and each other's—strengths.... [It's] a good example to others who want to get the most out of their Net marketing bucks."

The most recent slate of Nike commercials encourages TV viewers to log onto the Nike Web site to choose a desired ending to its commercials. At the site, viewers can see several video clips with alternative endings.

Respond Quickly to Trends

Nike responds quickly to trends and shifts in consumer preferences by adjusting the mix of existing product offerings; developing new products, styles and categories; and influencing sports and fitness preferences through aggressive marketing. If the company cannot address continuing market changes extremely rapidly, Nike loses a lot of the market, as happened with women's aerobic shoes. Through its distributive leadership and encouraging everyone in the company to come up with ideas, Nike generally spots trends and movements and adjusts accordingly.

Innovate Continually

"Nike consistently comes out with products that people want to buy," said Bob Sweet, an analyst at Horizon Investment Services, which is based in Hammond, Indiana. This focus started with Bill Bowerman, who was constantly looking for ways to help his athletes improve through footwear design. The desire that led him to mix synthetic rubber and pour it into the back of a waffle iron drives the researchers at Nike today. Innovation is Nike's way of life and has pushed the development of new footwear and sports apparel technology. Knight continued to push technical innovation in Nike products with the launch in 1985 of the Air Jordan, which became Nike's best-selling shoe.

The company hosts twice-yearly design inspiration events—such as bringing in the manufacturer of a foreign car with a unique design for the team to contemplate. Some interesting, sleek, innovative aspect of that car might find its way into the shoe design.

While Nike has always invested heavily in research and development (R&D), its newest product, the Alpha line, is the result of a tripled R&D budget since 1995.

Sustainability

The evolution of corporate sustainability in Nike has been driven by internal employee concern and by external stakeholder pressure. In the late

1980s, Knight asked a group of people in Nike to suggest some scenarios for Nike's future. Some of the participants at that meeting mentioned that Nike needed an environmental program. They were concerned particularly with the environmental impact of manufacturing.

A steering committee was formed and eventually concluded that Nike needed an environmental department. In 1993, the Nike Environmental Action Team (NEAT) was formed. The focus for NEAT, headed by Sarah Severn, is to enter a new era of commerce where human and business needs stop depleting living systems. By 1996, NEAT had begun to focus on supplier education, pollution prevention, and the greening of materials used in the manufacture of their products. Footwear Sustainability initiatives began to emerge that focused on product life cycles and Nike developed specific initiatives to follow to achieve its goal.

Focus on Quality

The focus on product quality started with Bowerman, who continually pursued excellence. At Nike, "He was very conscious of quality," Knight told *The [Portland] Oregonian*, "and those are things that echo here to this day."

To make sure his guidelines for quality were followed, Bowerman would go over and over them at board meetings. Although Bowerman was often quite critical at these meetings, over time, Knight came to believe that Bowerman was Nike's most valuable asset. He stood up for what he believed in, and he believed the company had to keep improving to stay ahead.

Invest in Marketing

In addition to spending heavily on celebrity endorsements and donating products to amateur athletes, Nike has always been smart about its investment in marketing and promotional activities. Where the average U. S. corporation spends 4 percent of its gross sales on marketing, Nike spends multiples of that.

Brand It. Nike's driving marketing principle has been brand positioning. The company reflects the brand, and the brand represents innovation, inspiration, creativity, and energy. The company takes to heart its slogans of "Do the Right Thing," "Just Do It," and "There Is No Finish Line." Though Knight was not a big believer in advertising, he realized that there must be a large amount of money spent to brand Nike's products. Although the company now has the largest marketing budget of its industry, it was not always the

Fact: Steve Prefontaine was the first track athlete to wear the Nike shoe. Prefontaine also helped with the startup of Nike.

case. At first, Nike relied much more on promotions than on paid advertising to reach out to customers—mainly because that was all the company could afford.

Align Yourself with Image Leaders.   Nike's strategy of paying sports celebrities to wear its shoes was brilliant, and it seems to have been a major reason that the company has grown so much so quickly. Knight believed that if he could get a few "cool guys" to use his products, then his business would be a success. From the beginning, the company signed endorsement deals with leading athletes in a variety of sports, especially in tennis, basketball, and running. Having strong performers wearing its shoes helped to position Nike as a company of fellow athletes who understood the challenges faced by their customers. Nike also gave the best athletes an incentive to wear its shoes: a percentage of shoe sales. The revolutionary Nike Pro Club was a group of elite basketball players handpicked by the company, who were guaranteed a share of royalties on sales of basketball shoes. The first year of the program, each of ten players had a two-year, two-thousand-dollar minimum contract. And at the end of the year when basketball-shoe sales had quadrupled, they each received more than eight thousand dollars—much more than the minimum that had been set.

Tennis star John McEnroe became the first pro athlete to sign an endorsement deal with Nike. Although Nike invested heavily in endorsement deals with athletes, it wasn't until Michael Jordan came along in 1985 that the company hit the jackpot. Once Jordan became a Nike pitchman, the company supported its multimillion-dollar investment—its largest ever in one athlete—with a huge television advertising campaign directed by Spike Lee. Nike commercials led the way in linking basketball, fashion, and celebrity personalities, and the result was a huge surge in demand for its basketball footwear. With Jordan, Nike took the new tack of introducing a line of Michael Jordan shoes and apparel, complete with its own logo. Air Jordan shoes brought in a hundred million dollars in sales the first year. The company has since developed other successful lines for additional athletes. Following Michael Jordan as Nike endorser was football and baseball star Bo Jackson, who helped increase demand for Nike's cross-training shoe. The "Bo knows" series of commercials sparked yet another jump in demand for the company's shoes. Years later, golf phenomenon Tiger Woods was signed on as the newest Nike celebrity, getting ninety million dollars for a multiyear contract.

Nike has also ridden on the back of its sponsored athlete Lance Armstrong, who made a miraculous recovery from advanced cancer and went on to win a record number of Tour de France bicycle races. Nike codeveloped with Armstrong the popular yellow wristbands that sport the word "Livestrong." Sold for a dollar each, the wristbands have produced approximately twenty million dollars to date for cancer research. The bands have no Nike branding, but it's common knowledge that Nike is behind them.

Manage Globalization

Nike became the face of globalization because it was one of the pioneers in outsourcing. The contract manufacturers Nike uses are located primarily in developing countries, which means that Nike's business is deeply entrenched in some of the most difficult business, social, and environmental issues of the twenty-first century. Many of the countries Nike operates in compete aggressively for this business, which provides much needed wage-based employment in situations where unskilled labor is abundant and alternatives are limited. In a statement to the National Press Club in May 1998, Knight said that "the Nike product had become synonymous with slave wages, forced overtime, and arbitrary abuse," and pledged to change things. Nike was one of the first companies that needed to develop expertise in areas that went far beyond those conventionally associated with business.

Although Nike has some degree of control over what happens in the eight hundred factories it uses, because it doesn't own them the degree of influence Nike can exert varies. It is highly challenging in this situation to figure out how to actually "do the right thing," as required by one of Nike's recently adopted maxims. Simply withdrawing their business will not change the practices and conditions that exist in the factories. In fact, the loss of Nike's business would likely only exacerbate the difficult conditions faced by the workers. Nike has been trying to find a balance between using its business model and helping the countries in which it operates. Nike is in the midst of trying to regulate health and safety aspects of the facilities and trying to understand the cultural issues, including women's empowerment and education outside of the workplace, and really making the job a foundation for helping young women to improve their situations. To address its critics, Nike has become much more transparent. The company now lists its production facilities and mandates on its Web site. In 1998, Nike strategically hired Maria Eitel as vice president for Corporate Responsibility, signaling that the issues around corporate responsibility were considered important at the senior executive level.

The second issue in globalization is the worldwide market Nike now has access to. At first, the company had to learn how to market globally. It decentralized in the places in which it wanted to sell and followed strategies similar to those it had used in the United States (creating the market and providing product to teams and schools.) Nike was soon a world force, but Knight admitted that the company's globalization efforts had proceeded too fast and spread its resources too thin. He launched a massive restructuring program that included nineteen hunded layoffs and a significant reduction in the number of products carrying the Nike logo.

The Nike Sport Research Lab

The Nike Sport Research Lab (NSRL) comprises nearly 13,000 square feet in the Mia Hamm building at Nike World Headquarters. Over thirty staff members collaborate with designers to develop and test state-of-the-art sports footwear, apparel, and equipment. The research falls into three primary areas: biomechanics, physiology, and sensory/perception, taking into account four primary factors that influence usage and performance: geography, gender, age, and skill level. The NSRL is a showpiece of Nike's innovation. For more information, see http://www.nike.com/nikebiz/nikebiz.jhtml?page=6&item=research.

POLITICAL INFLUENCE

Knight's father was a staunch republican, but Knight personally has financially supported both parties fairly equally, donating $52,200 to Republican candidates and $57,100 to Democratic candidates in 2004. The Nike company has made a larger percentage of financial contributions to Republicans since 1999: 38 percent of the total donations went to Republican candidates, totalling $42,252, and 26 percent went to Democrats, totalling $31,252.

Nike has been very active in influencing government policies in the countries in which it operates, including the United States. Nike has government affairs offices in Washington, DC, Beaverton, Brussels, Beijing, Singapore, and elsewhere because it recognizes that government action, particularly on trade matters, can significantly influence the success its global business. It has strong, ongoing efforts to build relationships on a bipartisan basis with a broad coalition of parliamentarians, senators, representatives, mayors, ministers, ambassadors, and other national figures. Outside the United States it is Nike's policy not to make campaign contributions. In addition to its own political outreach, it belongs to multiple associations that play active roles in policy making and therefore wields its influence indirectly.

An example of the type of involvement Nike has is the environmental issue that arose when other outdoor apparel companies urged the U.S. administration not to abandon the rule prohibiting roads from being built in currently protected forests. One side said the issue was about protecting pristine wilderness lands, and the other said it was about protecting jobs and wisely using scarce natural resources. Because the Roadless Rule could have an impact on the quality of wilderness areas in the lower forty-eight states, it was possible that it could enable more Nike ACG (All Conditions Gear) customers to use their gear in those places. Supporting the Roadless Rule would enhance their relationships with outdoor retailers in the American West—a group that was important to the growing ACG business and with whom Nike wanted to develop closer relationships.

CRITICS

To its activist critics, Nike came to symbolize the many failings and deficiencies of an inequitable global market system. In the late 1990s it became the target of criticism claiming the factories in which its products were produced oppressed workers, made workers put in extensive overtime, did not pay minimum wage, and employed children. At first, Knight assumed this was a public relations problem and because Nike didn't own the factories and had no legal responsibility, the company would weather the criticism. That was not the case, and Knight recognized the damage it was doing when he addressed the critics in 1998, saying, "The Nike product has become synonymous with slave wages, forced overtime, and arbitrary abuse." He vowed to do something about it and has taken concrete steps even his harshest critics say have worked to substantially improve the situation. Because of this, the company was not hurt nearly as much as it could have been. It dealt expertly with negative reports, and in responding immediately to the commissioned report on its labor practices, the company took control of information dissemination. It placed full-page ads in seven major newspapers, urging consumers to visit its Web site and call an 800 number to receive more information on the company's plan to address the deficiencies cited in the report. The critics forced the company to deal with a social problem, and it could be argued that by doing so Nike has set the standard for other companies who use developing countries' labor sources. Eventually, Knight adopted the premise that the company should be concerned for moral reasons in and of themselves and added the "Do the Right Thing" slogan to his company.

> *"The trouble in America is not that we are making too many mistakes, but that we are making too few."*
> Phil Knight

At the same time Knight was leading the charge to change the way Nike's contracted factories operated, he was hit again by critics. In April 2005, Knight rescinded a thirty-million-dollar pledge to the University of Oregon because the university joined the Workers Rights Consortium, a student group that monitored working conditions in third-world countries and had sharply criticized Nike. Knight had given over eighty million dollars to the school and was the main contributor for a remodeling and extension of the library, which was named after him. For the same reason, Nike also withdrew millions of dollars in financial support from Brown University and the University of Michigan.

Another frequent criticism of Knight and Nike is their use of endorsements for athletes. By using the Nike logo on players' uniforms and saturating the market, critics say that Nike has overcommercialized athletes and their sports. These critics also say that Nike has created a culture that overidolizes athletes.

POSSIBLE FUTURE IMPACT

Since Knight has passed on his CEO title to Perez, he has still remained a part of Nike's everyday life. Knight seems to take a larger interest in the design and creativity of Nike's products now. Knight has been quoted saying, "At this stage in my life, the creative process is of great interest to me." He is currently chairman of the board and will likely also continue to be involved in Nike business decisions. He helped the new Perez recently acquire the sports apparel maker Starter, the Bauer hockey gear maker, and the high-fashion shoe brand, Cole Haan.

Knight is also now following his son Travis into animation. In 2003, Knight bought Will Vinton Studios, a Portland, Oregon, animation producer best known as the creator of the dancing "California Raisins" TV commercial. Travis had long been an employee there.

> *"At this stage in my life, the creative process is of great interest to me."*
>
> Phil Knight

At first glance, Knight's entry into animation may seem like a retirement splurge or a billionaire's favor to his son. While these justifications may be true in part, Knight's good business sense may also be the reason. According to the Wall Street Journal, of nineteen computer-animated films made since 1995, fifteen topped a hundred million dollars in U.S. ticket sales.

TIMELINE

1938	February 24, Philip H. Knight born in Portland, Oregon.
1957	Knight met Bowerman when Knight joined the track team.
1959	Knight earned a bachelor's degree in business administration with a concentration in accounting from the University of Oregon.
	Knight began active duty in the U.S. Army Transportation Corps; he stayed in for a year and on the reserves for seven.
1962	Knight earned an MBA at Stanford Graduate School of Business. Knight wrote a paper for business class regarding shoes that could be manufactured in Japan for lower costs and beat out competition from Germany.
	Knight acted on his idea and took a trip to Japan. Knight talked Onitsuka Tiger executives into distributing shoes for Blue Ribbon Sports, a company name he made up on the spot.
1963	December, Two hundred shoes from Onitsuka (Asic) Tiger arrive. Knight worked as a CPA at Price Waterhouse Coopers & Lybrand until 1967.
1964	With former coach, Bill Bowerman, invested approximately five hundred dollars to start up Blue Ribbon Sports. Blue Ribbon cleared $3,240 its first year.

1965   Jeff Johnson joined the Blue Ribbon Sports team as a salesman and sold shoes out of a van to high school students.

1966   The company's first retail outlet opened in Santa Monica, California, when Johnson rented space next to a beauty parlor.

1967   Blue Ribbon was incorporated into Blue Ribbon Sports, Inc.
Bowerman initiated the development of the Marathon running shoe, which had a lightweight nylon upper.
A sales office opened in Wellesley, Massachusetts, behind a mortuary, to handle east-coast distribution.
Became an assistant professor of business administration at Portland State University.

1968   Married Penny Parks and began to have their first of three children. Knight is thirty and Parks is nineteen.
The Cortez running shoe was made in Japan to Bowerman's specifications; it was one of Tiger's best sellers.
Johnson and Bowerman created the Boston running shoe, which had a full-length cushioned midsole.

1969   Resigns from Portland State University and devoted himself full time to Blue Ribbon Sports.
Blue Ribbon Sports employed twenty and had several retail outlets. Revenues approached three hundred thousand dollars.

1970   Bowerman created the "waffle sole" by pouring rubber into his wife's waffle iron.

1972   Business relations broke between Blue Ribbon Sports and Onitsuka Tiger.
Swoosh design was created by Carolyn Davidson for a fee of thirty-five dollars.
Johnson dreamed up the company's new brand name, Nike, the Greek goddess of victory.
A soccer/football shoe was the first Nike model to hit the retail market.
A Nike T-shirt to promote the shoe became the first apparel item.
Blue Ribbon Sports launched the Nike brand at the U.S. Olympic Trials.
The Moon Shoe debuted with the Waffle outsole.
Canada becomes Blue Ribbon Sports's first foreign market.
Revenues reached $1.96 million.

1973   Steve Prefontaine became the first major track athlete to wear Nikes and helped convert several people to the brand including Olympian Jon Anderson, who won the Boston Marathon, and Ilie Nastase, who was ranked the top tennis professional in the world.
Revenues reached $3.2 million.

1974   Blue Ribbon Sports opened its first American manufacturing facility in Exeter, New Hampshire.
            Revenues reached $4.8 million.
1975   Steve Prefontaine died in a car crash.
1976   The Olympic Trials were held in Eugene, Oregon, and Nike shoes were seen in abundance.
            Revenues reached $14.1 million.
1977   Blue Ribbon sports started Athletics West.
            Manufacturing factories were set up in Taiwan and Korea.
            Nike shoes were sold in Asia for the first time.
            Revenues reached $28.7 million.
1978   Revenues reached $71 million.
            Blue Ribbon Sports changes its corporate name to Nike, Inc.
1979   Nike was the number-one running shoe and controlled 50 percent of the athletic shoe market.
            Nike's "air" shoes, created by M. Frank Rudy, were patented.
            World Headquarters were opened at 3900 Southwest Murray Boulevard in Beaverton, Oregon.
            Revenues reached $149 million.
1980   Nike went public with two million shares of common stock and passed Adidas in sales.
1981   Blue Ribbon Sports, Inc., and Nike officially merged. The company is now known as Nike, Inc.
            Nike International Ltd. is formed to serve a growing foreign market that reaches into more than forty countries.
1982   The first Nike commercial was seen during the New York Marathon.
1984   Nike signed Michael Jordan to endorse the company. Jordan was twenty-one years old.
            Nike signed Charles Barkley and John Stockton.
1985   Air Jordan court shoes were introduced, along with apparel.
            John McEnroe went on a promotional "Tour through America."
1986   Nike's revenues exceeded the billion-dollar mark.
            The "Just Do It" campaign was introduced.
1987   Reebok passed Nike in sales by entering into the women's aerobic shoes market.
1988   "Just Do It" hit the advertising line.
1989   Nike returned to number one spot in footwear companies and stayed there.
            Bo Jackson was introduced as endorsing Nike.
            Nike relocated to the new World Campus in Beaverton.
1990   The first of twelve U.S. Niketowns was introduced in Portland, Oregon.

A hundred million dollars is spent on advertising, which includes more "Bo Knows" campaigns and new "Family Reunion" commercials.

Revenues reached $2.2 billion.

1991   International revenue topped $860 million.

Revenues reached $3 billion.

1992   Nike and the Athletic Congress agreed that every medalist on the USA track-and-field team will wear Nike apparel in the Olympics and other major events.

Niketown Chicago opened with 60,000 square feet of space.

International revenue tops $1 billion, an increase of 32 percent; it makes up 33 percent of Nike's total revenue; Agassi wins Wimbledon, defying 50–1 odds along the way; Lynn Jennings wins an Olympic Gold medal and 3rd consecutive World CC Championship.

Revenues reached $3.4 billion.

1993   Charles Barkley starred in another groundbreaking ad and created a stir by saying "I am not a role model."

Revenues reached $3.9 billion.

Nike assumed distribution rights in Japan and Korea.

Nike signed ten members of Brazil's soccer team along with Italy's, China's, and U.S.'s soccer teams.

In Latin America, Chile and Argentina joined the Nike-owned family.

Nike purchased Canstar Sports, Inc., (renamed Bauer).

1996   Tiger Woods signed on.

Nike's Equipment Division formed to produce hockey skates, in-line skates, protective gear, sport balls, eyewear, and watches.

Fact: In 1984, the first Air Jordans were banned by the NBA.

The Atlanta Olympics showcased the world dominance of Nike-supported athletes and teams.

Major League Soccer's inaugural season had five teams supported by Nike.

Brazil teamed with Nike in preparation for World Cup '98.

Tiger Woods won a record third consecutive U.S. Amateur title.

Revenues reached $6.4 billion.

1997   China became both a source country and a vital market for Nike.

Revenues reached $9.2 billion.

1999   Nike cofounder Bill Bowerman died.

2000   Nike sales slumped early in the year.

Withdrew donation of thirty million dollars to University of Oregon.

Nike admitted to worker exploitation.

Nike designed uniforms for Sydney Olympics.

2001   Revamped the company, bringing outsiders in for a new perspective.

The Casey Martin award was introduced to award people for challenging themselves in a sport despite physical, mental, or cultural differences.

2002   Nike partnered with Hurley International.

2003   Nike acquired Converse for $305 million.

LeBron James signed with Nike.

2004   May 24, Matthew Knight died in a scuba accident.

December 24, Knight stepped down as CEO, continuing as chairman of the board of directors.

William D. Perez became Nike's new CEO.

The Livestrong campaign was introduced to raise money to benefit the Lance Armstrong Foundation to help people with cancer overcome the disease.

Nike revenues rose above $12.3 billion.

2005   The twentieth edition of the Air Jordan was created.

RESOURCES

Brands, H. W. "Phil Knight: Just Do It." In *Master of Enterprise: Giants of American Business from John Acob Astor and J.P. Morgan to Bill Gated and Oprah Winfrey*, 256–266. New York: The Free Press, 1999.

Business Week Online Staff. The Best and Worst Managers of 2004. *Business Week Online*, January 10, 2005. (http://www.businessweek.com/magazine/content/05_02/b3915626.htm)

http://www.cdnn.info/safety/s040529/s040529.html.

D'Alessandro, David. *Brand Warfare: 10 Rules for Building the Killer Brand*. New York: McGraw-Hill, 2001, pp. xv, 14, 30, 71–73, 87–88.

Goldman, Robert, and Stephen Papson. *Nike Culture: The Sign of the Swoosh*. London: Sage, 1998.

Hauser, Susan. Must Be the Shoes. *People*, May 4, 1992, p. 139.

Hill, Robert L. Phil knows business. *Oregon Business*, February 1991, p. 83.

Katz, Donald R. *Just Do It: The Nike Spirit in the Corporate World*. New York: Random House, 1994.

Krentzman, Jackie. The Force Behind the Nike Empire. *Stanford Magazine Online*. www.stanfordalumni.org.

Lane, Randall. You Are What You Wear. *Forbes*, October 14, 1996, p. 45.

Lippman, John. Just Do Animation. *Wall Street Journal*. August 19, 2005, p. W3.

Los Angeles Times Staff. Nike's profit increases 32 percent; Sales of new lines of Shox sneakers and lower marketing costs boost results. *Los Angeles Times*. September 20, 2005. p. C.3.

Nattrass, Brian. *Dancing with the Tiger: Learning Sustainability Step by Natural Step.* Gabriola Island, BC, Canada: New Society Publishers, 2002, pp. 56–99, 212, 243.

Perseus Publishing Staff. *Movers and Shakers: The 100 Most Influential Figures in Modern Business.* Boulder, CO: Basic Books, 2003, pp. 231–233.

Rothman, Howard. *Companies That Changed the World: Incisive Profiles of the 50 Organizations—Large & Small—That Have Shaped the Course of Modern Business.* Franklin Lakes, NJ: Career Press, 2001, pp. 84–86.

Saporito, Bill. Can Nike Get Unstuck? *Time,* March 30, 1998, pp. 48–53.

Strasser, J.B. *Swoosh: The Unauthorized Account of Nike's Early Days.* San Diego: Harcourt Brace Jovanovich. 1991.

Trout, Jack. *Power of Simplicity: A Management Guide to Cutting Through the Nonsense & Getting Things Right.* New York. McGraw-Hill, 1998, pp. 51–52, 147–149.

Turner, Marcia Layton. *How to Think Like the World's Greatest Marketing Minds: Business Lessons from David Ogilvy.* New York: McGraw-Hill, 2000, pp. 21–36, 40.

Whipple, Julie. Phil Knight: After 24 years building Nike into a worldwide presence, Knight seeks to perfect his masterpiece. *Business Journal-Portland,* September 13, 1996, p. 5.

COMPANY INFORMATION

Nike World Headquarters
One Bowerman Drive
Beaverton, OR 97005
Phone: (800) 344–6453
www.nike.com
New York Stock Exchange symbol: NKE

AP Photo/Kirsty Wigglesworth, Pool.

Anita Roddick

Anita Roddick, the British businesswoman and founder, along with husband, Gordon, of the cosmetics phenomenon the Body Shop, started her first store in 1976. The Body Shop concept—based on environmentally friendly cosmetics and begun as a cottage industry—soon outgrew Roddick's first small store in Brighton.

Roddick expanded through franchises, a relatively new concept in the United Kingdom at the time, guaranteeing that the essence of the concept was duplicated. A high proportion of the franchisees were women, and Roddick can justifiably claim to have helped change the traditional male-dominated image of entrepreneurs in the United Kingdom. By 2005 there were over nineteen hundred stores in fifty countries, and Roddick was spending much of her time and energy championing social causes. Anita and Gordon Roddick were products of the sixties who entered the business world only because they had to find a way to support themselves and their children. First trying a residential hotel and a restaurant, they realized they needed more cash flow and more leisure time, especially since Gordon wanted to take two years off to ride a horse from the tip of South America to California. In 1976, they decided Roddick should open up a small cosmetics shop that would cater to politicized, "alternative" young women who preferred to avoid patronizing conventional stores.

The Roddicks had almost no discretionary income, which meant that they had to keep expenses very low. One way they did this was by buying in bulk and bottling the products themselves in reusable plastic bottles and jars. Many of the Body Shop's defining characteristics were decided at this early stage, though the decisions were often based on cost effectiveness rather than a strategic plan. The walls were painted green, not in anticipation of the Green movement but to hide water damaged patches. Product packaging was minimal and recyclable, and Roddick wrote the labels out by hand. She started the company while her husband was on his horseback riding trip, and when he returned, she had two successful stores running. She would continue to serve as the company's public figure, while Gordon took over the finances and worked behind the scenes.

Roddick got her initial ideas for products from the extensive traveling she did before she got married. She found herself in Tahiti and other places interacting with local women and noticing how they took care of their skin. She hired a chemist to help her create lotions made from the raw ingredients she observed, including cocoa butter and cucumbers, and bottled the product. She then set up a typesetter's tray of fragrant oils so customers could mix one of the initial twenty-five products with their preferred fragrance. Her strategy, which admittedly began mainly as a means to cut expenses, resulted in a company that had annual sales of over a billion dollars in 2005. Famous for creating a niche market sector for naturally inspired skin and hair care products, the Body Shop introduced a generation of consumers to the benefits of a wide range of products from Banana Shampoo to Peppermint Foot Lotion. It is estimated that the Body Shop sells a product every 0.4 seconds and has over seventy-seven million customer transactions through stores worldwide, with customers sampling the current range of over six hundred products and more than four hundred accessories. All this is done without spending any money on advertising. Roddick shunned advertising expense from the start, preferring to rely on public relations, franchising, and word-of-mouth.

Early on, when Roddick wanted to open a second store, she sold half of the company to a friend, Ian McGlinn, for his seven-thousand-dollar investment. Local banks refused to lend her more money because she had been in business for only a few months. In return for his investment in Roddick's business,

McGlinn received a share of the Body Shop's profits. Today, McGlinn's investment is worth over $240 million. Roddick says she has no regrets about giving away so much of the company's value. Without McGlinn's financing, she would not have been able to grow her company.

What makes Roddick unique is that she has demonstrated how social activism can be used to enhance the quality of a business. The Body Shop is well known for taking what it sees as its social responsibility seriously. It carries no products tested on animals. Recyclable packaging is used whenever possible. The Roddicks have used the Body Shop to promote political causes. Roddick has generated considerable controversy and has written two books about her trade and her views on management. In her latest work, *Business As Unusual: My Entrepreneurial Journey, Profits With Principles* (Anita Roddick Press: 2005), she claims that for many, management has made business "a jungle where only the vicious survive." She laments that for too many, managing a business is about sitting "in front of computer screens, moving millions of dollars from Japan to New York." She advocates for "a new view of business as a community where only the responsible will lead."

The Body Shop has grown in less than twenty years to become an international corporation with total employment of over nine thousand. The Body Shop International is the parent corporation for a network of franchises. It operates its own shops either directly or through subsidiary companies in the United Kingdom, the United States, and Singapore, as well as the major production outlets in Littlehampton, United Kingdom; Glasgow, Scotland; and Wake Forest, North Carolina.

The headquarters of the Body Shop International is located on England's south coast, in the seaside town of Littlehampton where Roddick grew up. In the past five years, the headquarters has grown from four hundred to fifteen hundred staff members and has become the focal point of the town. Each year about eighty thousand visitors from all over the world tour the corporate headquarters, the pagoda-like design reflecting the Roddicks' inclination for the unusual.

> *"I think that business practices would improve immeasurably if they were guided by 'feminine' principles—qualities like love and care and intuition."*
>
> Anita Roddick

THE EARLY YEARS

Anita Roddick attributes her success to her mother, Gilda Perella, an Italian immigrant to Littlehampton, the sleepy English coastal town where Roddick was born in 1942. She was the fourth of five children born to Gilda; the first child died early of meningitis. Roddick grew up with her older sisters, Lydia and Velia, and her younger brother, Bruno. Roddick says that she always

> *"By creating conversation, we let our customers spread our message by word of mouth."*
>
> Anita Roddick

felt special to her mother, but she didn't learn that there was a reason for that until she was eighteen. When Roddick was eight years old, her mother divorced the man she knew as her father, Donny, to marry Donny's cousin, Henry. Many years later she found out that Henry had been the love of her mother's life from the time before her arranged marriage to Donny. Henry, who lived in America, and Gilda began a long-distance affair several years into her marriage to Donny, and Henry fathered Gilda's two youngest children, Roddick and Bruno. Roddick has said that she never felt connected to Donny yet always felt a strong connection to Henry, so she was not surprised to learn Henry was her real father. She said later that learning that taught her to trust her instinct.

"On the whole businesses do not listen to the consumer. Consumers have not been told effectively enough that they have huge power and that purchasing and shopping involve a moral choice."

Anita Roddick

From her early years, Roddick had a sense of being different, an experience that was reinforced because the members of her family were the only Italian immigrants in a culturally homogenous community. Roddick's mother emphasized being different as a positive attribute. "My mum told me 'You are different! You are different! You can do whatever you want.' She pushed me to bravery in everything I did. She rejected every sacred cow."

Donny and Gilda owned a café in Littlehampton, the Clifton Café, in which Roddick spent her time after school and on weekends doing what she could to help. The family slept in one room, and they were, by Roddick's account, the stereotypical loud Italian family. After her divorce, Gilda married Henry in 1950, and he bought the café. He changed it to an American-style diner. Henry, however, had contracted tuberculosis by then and lived only eighteen months longer.

Roddick attended a Roman Catholic school, St. Catherine's Convent, where she learned how to trade the comic books and bubble gum Henry had brought from America. After Henry died, the family had to take over the café, and everyone worked long hours.

Roddick was not a great student in her younger days. When Henry came onto the scene, he encouraged her to read a lot, including the classics. However, she still failed her exam to get into a good secondary school. She ended up at Maude Allen Secondary Modern School for Girls, where she learned to love learning. She was encouraged here to be herself and was made to feel creative and special by the teachers. At the insistence of her mother who talked her out of pursuing acting as a career, Roddick applied and was accepted to Newton Park College of Education at Bath. The college had a strong bias toward art, music, and drama, and Roddick credits her education here for her appreciation of aesthetics.

At the end of her studies, Roddick won a scholarship to study in Israel for three months to complete her theses, "The Children of the Kibbutz" and "The British Mandate in Palestine." When she returned from Israel, she applied for a teaching job in a junior school and got it. She did not have to start work for several weeks, so she joined a friend in Paris. However, once in Paris, she knew she did not want to teach, so she quit the job. In Paris she worked at the *International Herald Tribune*. Once she returned to Littlehampton, she applied for a temporary job at her old school—the Maude Allen Secondary Modern School for Girls—and taught there for two terms. She found a permanent job teaching at a comprehensive school in Bitterne and set about making her classroom exciting, changing it every day, incorporating drama and music into her lessons, and going on field trips. Still with itchy feet, Roddick quit this job and headed to Greece for the summer. She then made her way to Geneva and talked her way into a job at the United Nations. After a year, she took her savings and bought a ticket on a boat bound to Tahiti, where she spent a month. During this time she made friends with local women, who taught her how they kept their skin so smooth. They showed her cocoa butter lumps that they rubbed on their skin. She moved onto Australia via New Hebrides and New Caledonia, where she became fascinated by the way in way local women took care of their skin and hair using the insides of pineapples or green mud. She soon moved on through Reunion, Madagascar, and Mauritius on her way to South Africa. Her stay in South Africa was cut short when she was kicked out of the country for breaking the apartheid laws by attending a jazz club on "nonwhites" night. She bought a ticket back to England.

CAREER PATH

After college, Roddick went from one job to another and one country to another until she came back to England, had children, and got married. Her husband, Gordon, worked as a laborer until he started a picture-framing business that Roddick helped with, but neither of them was very interested in the business. Looking for another business venture they could run together as well as a new home for their expanding family, they ran across a hotel that was for sale. Gordon took his limited savings, made an offer much lower than the asking price, and bought the St. Winifred's Hotel in Littlehampton. Together they did the repairs necessary and set up a bed and breakfast. They did well until the summer tourist season ended, and then they started losing money. They readjusted quickly, turning part of the hotel into a residential hotel. Most of the residents were quite eccentric, but the hotel started making a small profit. With the hotel running smoothly, the couple looked for another venture to occupy their time. With Roddick's café experience, they decided on a restaurant. After putting in a lot of time, money, and energy to create an Italian restaurant, they soon realized the theme was not going to be popular. Their restaurant was empty, and again they needed to adapt. They turned it into an American-style diner, and it became the most popular place in town. It was in the restaurant that the Roddicks began the practice of combining social activism with business. On top of the blackboard with the daily menu, Gordon would write political messages attacking the local council. As Roddick put it, "This was a foretaste of our belief that business should have a social conscience."

They became active in radical politics, starting the town's first Shelter group and occupying an empty office block in London to protest the plight of the homeless. Roddick's mother, Gilda, sold the restaurant she owned and became their devoted child-care provider, however, even with this help, the pressures of running both a hotel and a restaurant proved too much for the couple. Gordon, who was very much an adventurer and romantic, made plans to fulfill a dream of riding a horse from Buenos Aires, Argentina, to America. His wife supported his dream even though she wasn't thrilled by it, and they decided to sell the restaurant and go into a different business that would give them more money and time. Because the hotel did not support the family, they needed another venture that Roddick could do while Gordon was away. After some thought she came up with the idea of a cosmetics business with a difference: the use of natural ingredients sold in smaller quantities. She was irritated that she could not buy small quantities of lotions or cosmetics, as she could do with almost any other product.

While Gordon prepared for his trip, Roddick prepared the ideas for the shop. She decided on the name, having seen it used in the United States for auto body repair shops. She then went to the bank to ask for a loan, equipped with only her enthusiasm. She was soundly rejected and returned to Gordon hopeless. Gordon took control of the process and had a friend help design a business plan. They got the loan, putting their hotel up as collateral.

Roddick had known about twelve organic products used around the world for skin care because of her travels, so she first tried to create new products using these ingredients in her kitchen. She researched do-it-yourself cosmetics in the local library, but she didn't have much luck creating them. She went through the Yellow Pages and found a small manufacturing chemist, and they drew up a plan for products he would create with money up front. She then found a 300-square-foot retail space in a neighboring town that had a strong student culture, which she thought would better suit the product than the culture of her own town. She paid six months' advance rent for a rundown shop in a good part of town and fixed it up, using dark green paint to cover the water damage on the walls. Afraid she wouldn't be able to make the business work, she and Gordon made alternate plans. If in six months, it wasn't working, she would pack it all in and bring their children to meet him in Peru.

Roddick arranged the store with the twenty-five products she had commissioned. Lacking the finances to produce an inventory that would fill the shelf, she used different size containers, including the cheapest she could find—plastic bottles used by hospitals to collect urine samples. She made the shelves appear full of different products. She had a designer develop the logo and had friends help with filling bottles and hand-writing the labels for products whose names she created (i.e., Honey and Oatmeal Scrub Mask, Cucumber Cleansing Milk, Seaweed and Birch Shampoo, Avocado Moisture Cream, Hawthorn Hand Cream, Cocoa Butter Body Lotion.) A week before she was to open, two funeral parlors close by threatened to sue if she didn't change the store's name. They thought the bereaved would not want to use a funeral parlor next to a store called the Body Shop. Not knowing what to do, Roddick made an anonymous call to the newspaper telling them about the mafia of undertakers threatening a defenseless woman entrepreneur. Her public relations campaign not only quashed the suit but also generated a lot of publicity for her new business. This encounter established the company's principle of using media coverage rather than buying advertising to promote new shops and products.

On March 27, 1976, with her husband about to leave on his travels, the thirty-three-year-old Roddick opened the first Body Shop at 22 Kensington Gardens in Brighton. The store was packed on that first day. Roddick thought of new and creative ways to entice customers into the store in the coming weeks. She sprayed strawberry essence onto the pavement, creating a scented trail into the store. She put sandwich boards designed by local art students outside. To save money, she encouraged people to bring their old bottles back in and have them refilled. She also could not afford to put perfumes in the products, so she filled a typesetter's tray with a selection of perfume oils— musk, apple blossom, frangipani, honeysuckle, patchouli, jasmine, and so on—and let customer mix their own fragrance choices into the product.

She was quite passionate about the business and the products. She read as much as she could about natural ingredients. When she wasn't at the shop, she experimented at home mixing vodka with natural oils or went to local schools to talk about the products, selling products out of her van. Her focus at this time was solely on paying the bills, and if money was short, she would keep the shop open longer. Her mother was taking care of the children during this time while Roddick focused on the shop.

The business was an instant success. The Brighton store prospered, and Roddick was soon planning another in nearby Chichester. When the bank refused to finance a loan for the new shop, she lamented to a friend, Aidre. Aidre had a boyfriend who was interested in investing. The boyfriend, businessman Ian McGlinn, agreed to put up about seven thousand dollars for a half-share of the business. Roddick wrote to her husband asking for advice, but his response telling her not to give away half the business arrived too late. She had already done it. For McGlinn, it proved to be the investment opportunity of his life.

The Chichester shop opened in September 1976. It was a larger space than the store in Brighton, and Roddick needed other products in order to fill it. She brought in jewelry, scarves, cards, and books, in addition to the Body Shop products.

Early in 1977, a young herbalist, Mark Constantine, called Roddick to see if she would be interested in selling his herbal shampoos and products. She met with him because he mentioned that his uncle worked at a chocolate factory and so he had no trouble buying hard-to-get cocoa butter. He had a henna cream shampoo that looked and smelled like sludge and a lettuce lotion with bits of lettuce in it. He had a beeswax cleanser that had black specks caused by the dirt the bees carried in. Roddick was intrigued and thought they could create cards that went along with the products to explain why the products looked as they did. She placed the largest order she had yet placed and crossed her fingers. In less than a month, all of the product was sold, and she ordered more. Constantine's company is still the largest supplier of the Body Shop's products.

Gordon abandoned his trip in Bolivia after two thousand miles after one of his horses fell off a cliff and died. By the time he returned in April 1977, the Body Shop concept was unstoppable. With the company doing well, the Roddicks decided to sell the hotel and move into their own little house.

Roddick's friends and family ran the first few stores the company opened, but requests to set up branches elsewhere in the country were flooding in. To cater to the demand for stores, the Roddicks began franchising the concept in 1978, although the idea of franchising was still new in Britain at the time. Gordon called it self-financing. Potential franchisees would finance the business and agree to buy their stock from the Body Shop, and in return, would be licensed to use the Body Shop name. The Roddicks also gave their expertise and help in opening the new shops. Roddick interviewed many of the early franchisees herself. They originally had informal arrangements with the franchisees but subsequently developed formal agreements. For the first couple of years, there was no planning of where the shops would be. Wherever someone wanted to open one, they did.

In 1977, they also opened another company-owned shop in Reading, this time getting a loan from the bank. They started classes for their employees given by Mark Constantine about the products. In 1979, they opened their first international shops in Sweden, Stockholm, and Athens. The Body Shop began selling a kilo of perfume every couple of days.

They developed the popular Peppermint Foot Lotion in response to runners' complaints of sore feet just before the London Marathon began. They got permission to stand along the route and hand out free samples of the products, which generated a lot of publicity.

In 1980, the company took out another loan to move to a new warehouse and opened its new headquarters in October 1982. At this time, the Body Shop was opening two shops a day. Roddick told franchise holders that they could use their choices of three different shop styles, but she soon reversed this decision when she saw how different the shops were starting to look.

In April 1984 the company became publicly listed. The share price shot up on the opening day, and Roddick, her husband, and Ian McGlinn all became paper millionaires overnight.

Suddenly they had power and wealth, which they wanted to use wisely. Roddick had already been campaigning against animal testing of cosmetics; now she had the clout to make her voice heard. She and Gordon decided to use their shops to educate people about social and environmental issues. In 1985, they paid for Greenpeace, an environment preservation group, to put up posters protesting the dumping of hazardous waste into the North Sea. Customers could join Greenpeace at Body Shop stores. The next year, the Body Shop protested the slaughter of sperm whales for their oil. The Body Shop uses jojoba oil, a desert plant wax, instead of sperm oil in its products. Greenpeace designed posters and leaflets for the stores.

The Body Shop worked next with Friends of the Earth on campaigns that protested against acid rain and fostered awareness of the dangers to the ozone layer from aerosol sprays. They became involved with the American group of businesses, the Social Venture Network, which included Ben & Jerry's, Rhino Records, and Patagonia, among others, who all allocated a percent of their profits toward social programs.

"If you have a company with itsy-bitsy vision, you have an itsy-bitsy company."
Anita Roddick

The first U.S. shop opened in 1988, and almost instantly the company had twenty-five hundred applications for U.S. franchises. Before coming to the United States, the Body Shop had opened in thirty-three other countries. The Roddicks were unsure of the American market, where so many other British companies had failed, and so they waited until they knew they had the number of potential customers to make it worthwhile. They also had to deal with the problem of the name. Another company had the rights in the United States and Japan to the Body Shop name. It took a $3.5-million settlement for the Roddicks to acquire the rights.

Roddick, now one of the richest women in England, has been showered with awards as a result of both her business endeavors and her social conscience. Besides the titles of London's Business Woman of the Year and Retailer of the Year, she has received the United Nations' Global 500 environmental award and the Order of the British Empire.

Roddick is no longer CEO, and she doesn't sit on any executive committees of the company. However, she does spend much of her time coming up with new products and spearheading Body Shop campaigns. She actively participates on the board of several foundations, including the Body Shop Foundation; the New Academy of Business; the Ruckus Society, USA; and the Nuclear Age Peace Foundation, USA. In November 1999 she spoke out against the role of the World Trade Organization (WTO). She wrote her first autobiography, her second biography, *Business as Unusual,* in 2001. She edited *Take it Personally,* a collection of thought-provoking pieces to challenge the myths of globalization and the

"If you think you are too small to have an impact, try going to bed with a mosquito."
Written on the side of the Body Shop delivery trucks.

power of the WTO. She started her own communications company, Anita Roddick Publications, in 2003 publishing its first two books: *Brave Hearts, Rebel Spirits: A Spiritual Activists Handbook* and *A Revolution in Kindness*. She launched the website www.anitaroddick.com in 2001 to promote participation in her causes. She currently focuses on minimizing the negative effects of multinational corporations on sweatshop laborers.

PERSONAL LIFE

Roddick was very much a product of the social movements of the 1960s. She liked the hippie culture and the antiwar and other grassroots movements, although she was not fond of drugs, finding them disappointing. From the time she read a book about the Holocaust when she was young, Roddick has been very passionate about human and global issues.

> *"The kind of brain-dead, gum chewing assistant you find in so many shops drives me wild. I want everyone who works for me to feel the same excitement that I feel."*
>
> Anita Roddick

When she returned to England from her trip around the world, she was greeted enthusiastically by her mother. Before she had a chance to tell her mother about her travels, however, her mother announced that she had found the perfect man for her. Gilda had met him at her nightclub, El Cubana, and found him to be so much like her deceased husband Henry, Roddick's father, that she had taken him under her wing, cooking for him and mending his clothes. Gordon Roddick had been traveling around the world when he stopped at the club in Littlehampton. Roddick was feeling the need to have children and says that when she saw Gordon she knew instantly that she wanted him to be the father. She also says she didn't want to marry him, just have his children. Roddick's mother had been telling Gordon all about Roddick, so when they finally did meet, Gordon felt as if he already knew her well. They found they had very similar political views and both supported left-wing causes. After four days of talking, Roddick packed her bags and moved into Gordon's one-room apartment. She got a job teaching again but soon got pregnant and because she was unmarried, felt the social pressure of those days to quit her job.

In August 1969 she gave birth to her daughter, Justine, who was named after the heroine in Lawrence Durrell's *Alexandria Quartet*. She admits that the first few weeks of motherhood were harder than she expected; she didn't immediately take to her daughter for a couple of weeks. Roddick, Gordon, and Justine moved into a bigger apartment, and Gordon got a job as a laborer to make more money. Justine was only fifteen months old when Roddick found that she was pregnant again. Before her pregnancy was too far along for her to travel, they decided to visit San Francisco's Haight-Ashbury area. On the trip, they drove to Lake Tahoe in Nevada and continued on to Reno.

Here they decided on a lark to get married. Roddick says in jest that she still isn't sure if the marriage is considered legal in Britain.

The Roddicks' second daughter, Samantha, was born in July 1971, and the family needed a bigger home again. The search for a new place led to her first real entrepreneurial venture, the St. Winifred Hotel.

Roddick continues to travel extensively researching indigenous tribal customs. She is actively involved in philanthropic efforts through her company and says that she plans to leave her wealth to charity rather than see it pass to her heirs. Through the Body Shop she has supported campaigns by Greenpeace, Friends of the Earth, and Amnesty International, among others. Messages on shopping bags and vehicles express the Body Shop's support for these causes. Displayed on the side of the Body Shop vehicles is the sentence "If you think you are too small to have an impact, try going to bed with a mosquito." The phrase is one of Roddick's favorite quotations.

In 1998 she stepped down as CEO and remained as cochair with her husband Gordon until 2002, when she adopted a new role as creative consultant to the company. She is now a nonmanaging director. The fact that she now spends less time with the Body Shop allows her more scope to champion the causes she so passionately believes in. She also now has three grandchildren: Maiya Hopi, Atticus-Finch, O'sha Sophia Bluebell.

Body Shop Campaigns

2003–present
The Body Shop and Anita Roddick ran the Help Stop Violence in the Home Campaign and the Domestic Violence Campaign in partnership with Refuge

2001–2002
The Body Shop International and Greenpeace joined forces in 2001 to run the Choose Positive Energy campaign. This joint campaign helped highlight the importance of renewable energy in the fight against global warming.

2000
2000 saw the launch of the Body Shop Human Rights Award. This biennial award is unique in its focus across different areas of grassroots economic, social, and cultural rights activity across the world. The first award focused on the problem of the 250 million youngsters trapped in child labor. It highlighted the fact that education can make a real difference in freeing these children from poverty.

1998
1998 marked the fiftieth anniversary of the Universal Declaration of Human Rights. To celebrate, the Body Shop and Amnesty International joined forces to launch the world's largest consumer-based human rights campaign

ever—Make Your Mark for Human Rights. On December 10, 1998, the campaign culminated in a major international music concert in Paris. Customers were invited to "make their marks" for human rights in the world's first thumbprint petition. Over three million thumbprints were collected during the campaign in over fourteen hundred Body Shop stores. The thumbprints were used to create giant portraits celebrating each country's chosen defender.

The Body Shop produced "The Body and Self Esteem," the first publication in the Full Voice series. Distributed worldwide, this publication aimed to raise awareness of the issue of self-esteem and generate debate.

1997

The Body Shop launched a campaign based on Ruby, a doll representing real women: "There are three billion women in the world who don't look like supermodels and only eight who do."

1996

In 1996–1997 the Ogoni campaign shifted focus to the Ogoni Nineteen, who faced the same charges and fate as Ken Saro Wiwa and eight other Ogoni activists. This campaign was run by the Body Shop in seventeen countries. In September 1998 the Ogoni Nineteen walked free from Port Harcourt prison when all charges against them were dropped.

1995

In 1995 when Ken Saro-Wiwa and eight other Ogoni activists were sentenced to hang, the Body Shop was at the forefront of international efforts to save their lives. The Body Shop organized for Saro-Wiwa's son to attend the Commonwealth Heads of Government meeting in New Zealand to press leaders to act. Following the barbaric execution of Saro-Wiwa on November 10, 1995, the Body Shop redoubled efforts to bring about change in Nigeria.

The French testing of nuclear weapons systems in the middle of coral reef systems in the Pacific provoked international condemnation; the Body Shop ran the "Would they do it in Paris?" campaign.

During the fourth United Nations World Conference on Women, the Body Shop ran a "Women's Rights are Human Rights" campaign. Twenty-five markets collected over a million petitions for the cause.

1994

The "Thwart Thorpe" campaign adopted an antinuclear stance when the British government proposed to open yet another nuclear power plant. "No Time to Waste" was a home audit run from shops to encourage customers to think about their energy use and waste production.

The Body Shop ran a worldwide campaign demanding enforcement of the rules created by the Convention on the International Trade in Endangered Species designed to protect endangered species. Worldwide, the campaign was run in over thirty countries and collected over three million supporting signatures.

1993

The Body Shop began campaigning in support of Ken Saro-Wiwa and the Ogoni people of Nigeria, who were protesting against the economic exploitation and environmental destruction caused by the Nigerian military dictatorship and multinational oil companies such as Shell.

1991

The Body Shop cofounder Gordon Roddick brought the idea of a street newspaper back from New York to London and helped found the Big Issue, a newspaper to be sold by homeless people.

1989

The Body Shop ran a campaign with Survival International to highlight the plight of Brazil's indigenous Yanomami, threatened by destruction of their lands by mining and timber companies. The "Stop the Burning" campaign called for the Brazilian government to bring a halt to the mass burning of the tropical rainforests.

1988

The Body Shop launched its first international human rights campaign with Amnesty International.

1987

The Body Shop ran a six-part campaign to raise awareness amongst customers and staff on global environmental issues.

1986

The Body Shop ran a "Save the Whale" campaign with Greenpeace, launching a new raw ingredient, jojoba oil, that replaced the need for sperm whale oil.

LEADERSHIP LESSONS

According to her husband, Anita Roddick is a "volcano of creativity." She is a naturally enthusiastic salesperson, although she never pressures people to buy. She and Gordon were highly adaptive when things were not going well. They recognized their failures and dealt with them swiftly.

Roddick created the Body Shop's success without advertising and went against the tide of other cosmetic companies who promised youth and beauty to their customers. Roddick made no special claims for her

"Businesses which forego profits to build communities, or keep production local... risk losing business to cheaper competitors without such commitments, and being targeted for take-over by... corporate raiders."

Anita Roddick

products. In fact she didn't advertise, relying mainly on word of mouth to bring customers through the store doors. "Making products that work—that aren't part of the cosmetic industry's lies to women—is all-important," Roddick said in her autobiography, *Body and Soul*.

She has been an advocate of corporate social responsibility. In her latest book she is strongly opinioned about the role of her business. "[We make] sure we minimize our impact in our manufacturing processes, clean up our waste, put back into the community.... We go where businesses never want to be-cause they don't think it is the role of business to get involved." Roddick has been highly vocal in her beliefs about the causes she holds dear. Her enthusiasm and convictions help her to get media attention and avoid advertising, one of her fundamental business beliefs. Even though the Body Shop has avoided conventional advertising, it has promoted itself and its products vig-orously. Through the various types of initiatives in which the Body Shop is involved and through Roddick's high profile and her will-ingness to say controversial things, the Body Shop has always received a lot of publicity.

> *"If I had to name a driving force in my life, I'd name passion every time."*
>
> Anita Roddick

A key characteristic of the firm has been the importance of integrity and honesty in dealings with customers, staff, and suppliers. Roddick has said she tried to keep the company daring, brave, and fun, partly by protecting the firm from "big business." Roddick has said in her latest book, *Business as Unusual*, "You have to look at leadership through the eyes of the followers and you have to live the message. What I have learned is that people become motivated when you guide them to the source of their own power and when you make heroes out of employees. The Body Shop has always believed that business is primarily about human relationships. We believe that the more we listen to our stakeholders and involve them in decision making, the better our business will run."

Teach People

Roddick has likened the Body Shop stores to schools because she empha-sizes education so much. Sales people are trained to be knowledgeable but not forceful. If customers want information, they must ask for it, but there is plenty of information available. The containers clearly state the ingredients and purpose of the product. The stores also supply educational brochures, such as "Animal Testing and Cosmetics" and "What is Natural." The cus-tomers have access to a reference book called the Product Information Manual that provides backgrounds on everything the Body Shop sells. Roddick sought to establish credibility with her customers by educating them. She has shunned conventional advertising, at first because of the cost, but later because of the principle. Roddick believes that the cosmetics industry has manipulated women through advertising. In reference to the large cosmetics companies like Revlon and Estée Lauder, Roddick said, "What they were selling and the way they were selling it was the antithesis of my own beliefs."

Roddick has said that what helped distinguish the Body Shop when it began was her naivety and lack of business experience. She told customers the truth of what the products would and would not do in a simple, clear way. Instead of using a hard sell, she would dab some product on the back of her hand, and say, "Umm, I love the smell of this. Here, try it. What do you think?" The company began to grow quickly, especially after Roddick realized that it would sell even more products if she and her handful of employees were solicitous of customers, never pressured them, and tried to offer what they wanted to buy: high quality natural products marketed without all the frills and added expenses of the mainstream industry. When she set up the social campaigns sponsored by the Body Shop, she used the same method of keeping the message clear and providing plenty of easy-to-understand information to the Body Shop employees and customers.

Franchise

Soon after she started her first shop, other people wanted to open Body Shops of their own. After some glitches, a system was established which required franchisees to run their stores in a consistent manner. Franchising enabled many stores to open quickly, and Roddick's company supplied them all. More than half of her British franchisees are women. Roddick encouraged young women to follow in her footsteps and set up their own retail businesses. "Promote yourself, shout about your business," she told them. "And if necessary, be brilliantly devious." Each franchise carries an exclusive line of Body Shop products and a relatively standardized store design and franchise agreement.

In the other countries, the Body Shop International deals with head franchisers who are licensed to subfranchise with the owners of the retail outlets, and in some cases, the head franchiser also assembles particular products under license from the Body Shop International.

Be Fiscally Conservative

In spite of the Body Shop's radical image, its financial management has been very conservative in later years. Though the Roddicks financed the first shops and office building with loans, growth is now financed primarily from the company's earnings and capital raised from shareholders rather than from loans. The company is now completely free of debt. In early 1996, the Body Shop abandoned a plan to repurchase all outside shares and go private—a step that would have allowed the Roddicks to put the shares in trust and so ensure that the Body Shop's social agenda would be preserved beyond their tenure. The repurchase would have required extensive borrowing and would have limited the capital available for expansion. The Roddicks were concerned about that level of indebtedness to financial institutions. They worried that the company would be put in jeopardy. "The gap between success and failure was too narrow," Gordon states.

Be Passionate

Roddick uses emotions to encourage employees to join in the company's various community and political action projects. "Whenever we wanted to persuade our staff to support a particular project we always tried to break their hearts. At the next franchise holders' meeting we put on a real tear-jerking audio-visual presentation, with wonderful slides of the children against a background of Willie Nelson's version of 'Bridge over Troubled Water.' And to enable members of staff to experience what we had experienced, the next edition of 'Talking Shop,' the monthly video distributed throughout the Body Shop organization, was devoted to Boys' Town and what we could do there. The response was a joy. Everyone wanted to get involved in raising money and sponsoring boys, and from that moment onwards the International Boys' Town."

Roddick also encourages employees to use emotional expression for more conventional instrumental purposes; Roddick and other Body Shop employees frequently and consciously used emotion management techniques for instrumental organizational purposes. This strategy has created a close-knit, intimate community where employees are deeply involved with each other and passionately committed to their work.

Focusing on emotional values, Anita Roddick explained, "I am mystified by the fact that the business world is apparently proud to be seen as hard and uncaring and detached from human values. . . . The word 'love' was as threatening in business as talking about a loss on the balance sheet. Perhaps that is why using words like 'love' and 'care' is so difficult in today's extraordinarily macho business world. No one seems to know how to put the concept into practice. . . . I think all business practices would improve immeasurably if they were guided by 'feminine' principles—qualities like love and care and intuition."

Challenge the Status Quo

"Be daring, be first, be different," is Roddick's philosophy of business. In formulating the plan for the Body Shop, Roddick was driven by both a critique and a positive vision. The critique was of the cosmetics industry, which, she argues, "hypes an outdated notion of glamour and sells false hopes and fantasy."

Roddick claimed in her 1991 memoirs to employ a version of "democracy at work" that was a little difficult to implement. Although she made it clear that employees were to "challenge the rules, to question the status quo," she points out that this is not enough, that entrepreneurs would have to "encourage lèse majesté from your staff, by hollering and hooting, by what you wear, by the language you use, by taking the symbols of authority and challenging them all the time." Roddick chooses her employees carefully, hoping to find enough people who are nonconformist enough to be able to deal with "the idea of a company being quirky or zany or contemptuous of mediocrity."

Social Responsibility

Roddick is also very selective about choosing employees and franchise owners who make it clear they have the same philosophy toward environmental and social issues as the Body Shop. The company's mission statement begins by asserting that the company's reason for being is "to dedicate our business to the pursuit of social and environmental change." It goes on to affirm that the company will "passionately campaign for the protection of the environment, human and civil rights, and against animal testing within the cosmetics and toiletries industry." Body Shop headquarters staff are given one day a month off to work with disadvantaged children and the company takes on several social campaigns a year, with individual stores encouraged to do their own as well. "I pay my staff to be active citizens," Roddick has said.

Roddick set up a Department of Public Affairs and a unit called Values and Vision, consisting of thirty-nine people, many of whom were recruited from nonprofit agencies. Public affairs organizes social campaigns, often in conjunction with nonprofit agencies. The department's general manager reported directly to Roddick. The department also attempts to involve the Body Shop staff either in company projects or in community initiatives of their own choosing. Each employee of the company is granted one half-day of company time a month to participate in such projects. Over one-quarter of the employees typically volunteer for community activities and so contribute almost twenty thousand hours of work in total each year.

The Body Shop International's investment in its social agenda is considerable, but it is difficult to pin an exact financial value to it. In addition to its investment in its public affairs department and fair trade unit, the Body Shop International made charitable donations last year of over a million dollars. In addition, many shops donate profits, as does the Body Shop retail outlet in Harlem, New York, which donates 50 percent of its profits to the local community. When asked about the value of the company's giving, Roddick responded: "How do you measure time? How do you measure standing outside Shell for four hours and picketing with 50 or 60 of your employees? Gordon has been over in Brazil for the past four weeks [working with one of the Body Shop community trade suppliers]. How do you measure the time lost to the company? It's like breathing; it is so integrated."

The types of initiative taken on by the Body Shop fall into two broad categories: one-time campaigns on social issues, usually in association with other groups, and longer-term projects targeted at groups in need. It is the sociopolitical campaigns for which the Body Shop is best known that contribute directly to the company's public image. The Body Shop began its campaigning in 1985, assisting Greenpeace in lobbying against the dumping of hazardous waste in the North Sea. A year later, the company developed the prototype for many of its subsequent campaigns by using its retail outlets in the "Save the Whale" Campaign, also in conjunction with Greenpeace. This campaign also gave the Body Shop an opportunity to promote jojoba oil, one of its most popular products, which has properties similar to the oil from sperm whales. There was some resistance from franchise holders about being "too political," but Roddick said that this "was not an argument I was prepared to countenance." The Body Shop has conducted joint campaigns with Friends of the Earth on such issues as acid rain and ozone depletion. But as the company developed competence and experience with these activities and put in place its Environmental Projects Department, it started conducting its own campaigns.

Since the mid-1980s, when its campaigning practices started, the Body Shop has broadened the range of issues that it has addressed and strengthened its infrastructure for mounting campaigns. The campaigns involve animal welfare, environmental issues, and human rights. At any given time, dozens of the Body Shop campaigns are in operation. Many are initiated through the head office in the United Kingdom, but some come from the franchises in other countries. For example, the Body Shop in Australia and New Zealand initiated a campaign against nuclear testing by the French government named "Would They Do It in Paris?" The Body Shop International provided assistance. Such a campaign enjoyed broad support in Australia and New Zealand, but was much less popular in France, where there are a similar number of branches of the Body Shop. The Body Shop in Canada has initiated campaigns denouncing violence against women, a theme that has been picked up by the Body Shop International for promotion in other countries.

The Body Shop also has become increasingly adept at lobbying governments. When the Body Shop in Australia and New Zealand mounted its campaign against nuclear testing by France, the head office used its political clout in Europe to open doors so that influential politicians could be lobbied. The Body Shop also provides logistical support for social organizations such as Amnesty International, Greenpeace, and some lesser-known groups.

In addition to its issue campaigns, the Body Shop gets involved in longer-term projects that are of a lower profile. These are typically focused on groups in need both in the United Kingdom and internationally. In the United Kingdom, projects have included the Big Issue, a newspaper for the homeless that provides jobs for members of that group. The company built its soap factory in Easterhouse, a slum area in Glasgow, and it currently provides 130 jobs there.

The Body Shop also provides its expertise to various charities on an ongoing basis.

Internationally, the Body Shop has developed a program called Community Trade (formerly called Trade Not Aid), which involves paying a fair price for raw materials and accessories purchased from communities in need. Roddick traveled to Brazil to meet with tribal leaders. She lived with Brazil's Kayapo Indians, exploring how she could trade without destroying their culture. The Body Shop now buys brazil nut oil and vegetable dye beads from the tribe and is committed to helping them survive. Some other examples are products made from jute fiber from CORR The Jute Works, a trading organization of women's producer groups in Bangladesh, and the purchase of shea butter from a women's cooperative in the Tamale region of Ghana, massagers from India, and loofah products from Honduras. The Body Shop trades with over thirty-five suppliers from some twenty-five countries. The program has helped to support thousands of people in building livelihoods. Two of the longest-standing suppliers, Teddy Exports in India and Get Paper Industries in Nepal, have, with support from the Body Shop, set up AIDS awareness projects which now attract international funding.

The environmental campaigning attracted media attention as well as customers. Roddick has estimated that the publicity generated by Body Shop campaigns has been worth millions in free advertising. The Body Shop has been successful in promoting itself to consumers that identify with the issues that it raises. Nearly 80 percent of European customers claim that their purchases are influenced by the Body Shop's ban on animal testing, and a high percentage claimed to be influenced by natural ingredients, the company's environmental aims, and no wasteful packaging. People who buy the Body Shop's products can also feel a sense of solidarity with its concerns about the environment, animal welfare, and human rights.

> *"To run this business... you need ... optimism, humanism, enthusiasm, intuition, curiosity, love, humour, magic and fun, and that secret ingredient—euphoria."*
> Anita Roddick

Some campaigns have been highly successful. In 1989, the European Community proposed that all cosmetics be tested on animals. More than five million people signed the Body Shop's petition against this testing, and the proposal was withdrawn. More recently, a campaign for Amnesty International resulted in the release of fifteen political prisoners in response to letters from Body Shop customers. As Roddick said in a speech, "That is the relevancy of what business should be doing in the marketplace." Another important campaign was "Stop the Burning," which focused public attention on the destruction of the Brazilian rain forest.

Recognizing that businesses only succeed in being socially responsible after they first succeed in being a business, Roddick said, "I am not rushing around the world as some kind of loony do-gooder; first and foremost, I am a trader looking for trade."

Roddick believes that being socially active will help all businesses. "You couldn't do anything better for your business than align it with a charity dear to your heart. Not only will this be good for employee morale, help society, and reduce the government's burden, but being associated with charity attracts tremendous media attention and can help establish your business's name in your community." According to Roddick, "We must put back into society what we have taken out. And if we don't love our staff, our neighbors, the environment, we'll all be doomed."

Keep it Small

The Body Shop is very much a big business and growing larger. However, Roddick has always espoused an anti–big-business point of view, and in spite of the Body Shop's rapid growth into a large corporation, Roddick suggests that it is more like a "multi-local business" often operated by families. "The constant tension for me," she says, "is to keep a small company style in a bloody big company. I want myself to find escape routes to areas where intimacy can be encouraged. I constantly try to challenge the staff; I bring out a magazine from my office that comes straight from my heart. This is a desperate attempt to keep intimacy; getting them to come back to talk to me." She has

---

Estée Lauder

Estée Lauder's marketing techniques helped build one of the most successful cosmetic companies in the world.

Josephine Esther Mentzer, the daughter of immigrants, lived above her father's hardware store. She started her enterprise by selling skin creams concocted by her uncle, a chemist, in beauty shops, beach clubs, and resorts. In 1948 she persuaded the bosses of New York City department stores to give her counter space at Saks Fifth Avenue. Once in that space, she used a personal selling approach. In 1953 Lauder introduced her first fragrance, Youth Dew, a bath oil that doubled as a perfume. Instead of using their French perfumes by the drop behind each ear, women were using Youth Dew by the bottle in their bath water. In the first year Youth Dew sold fifty thousand bottles, and by 1984 the figure had jumped to 150 million.

Lauder gave her famous friends and acquaintances small samples of her products for their handbags; she wanted her brand in the hands of people who were known for having the best.

Even after forty years in business, Estée Lauder attended every launch of a new cosmetics counter or shop. She died of cardiopulmonary arrest on April 26, 2004, and was at least ninety-five years old. No one knows for sure—not even members of her family, who think she might have been two years older than that.

tried to run the business as a large family. The Roddicks still know most staff members by name. They give Christmas parties for them and gather managers together for summer weekend meetings in their garden.

Roddick used to try to visit every shop at least once a year, asking questions and offering support. She also still has an open telephone line for anyone to contact her.

POLITICAL INFLUENCE

Roddick's work through the Body Shop, which she sometimes referred to as a political movement all its own, was decidedly leftist. She still tackles a wide range of personal and political issues from self-esteem to human rights abuses, and she actively campaigns and demonstrates for the causes she believes in. She is very liberal and involved herself enthusiastically in the American culture wars, pounding the religious right. She campaigns for and financially supports leftist leaders who she believes will support her causes.

CRITICS

Sometimes calling her frenetic and self-righteous, critics are vocal about her perceived failings. They believe that she uses her causes to create more business. One critic doubts her explanation that she flies first-class only so she can "strike her blows for the People more effectively upon arrival." Others question her stance on unions and her interesting twist to the argument against them. While she has stated quite clearly that unions have no place in a nonexploitative workplace such as her own, Body Shop spokesmen have also responded to union demands for recognition by insisting that The Body Shop was simply too radical for unions.

As the Body Shop has grown in stature, it has been subject to criticism that its practices do not measure up to the standards it advocates for others. Roddick suffered damaging blows in 1994 when a series of articles pointed out that the company had behaved in most circumstances just like any other enterprise would, that its politics were mainly a "greenwashed" brand image meant to appeal to sensitive consumers, that in fact it sourced a smaller amount of its materials through its much vaunted "Trade Not Aid" program than customers might have believed. This criticism led to a spate of secondary commentaries in the media

> *"I sometimes wonder why we're not more outraged by the fact that three billion people live on less than $2 a day, while the wealthy have stashed away $8 trillion dollars in tax havens. They certainly don't seem to be picking up the tab on world poverty. Despite the astonishing wealth of the so-called 'long boom', a fifth of the human race is still living in absolute poverty without access to proper food or clean water."*
>
> Anita Roddick

and dumping of The Body Shop stock, with the consequence that at one point the share value was halved. Those who criticize Roddick are routinely dismissed by her as "cynics."

POSSIBLE FUTURE IMPACT

With the Roddicks' withdrawal from The Body Shop leadership, the company is likely to change some long-standing guidelines. It has begun to advertise in the United States and will likely not be as active socially and politically to the extent it was with Roddick at the helm. Although the Roddicks' share of ownership is substantial for a publicly traded company, they will be less involved, and the company will be more at the disposition of the large institutional investors.

With Anita Roddick Publications and her Web site, *www.anitaroddick .com*, Roddick will continue fighting for human rights and against economic initiatives and structures that abuse and ignore them.

The Roddicks do not intend to use the wealth that they have accumulated to ensure that the company continues under the leadership of their family. Before they die, it is their intention to place their wealth in a charitable foundation. "We believe it would be obscene to die rich," Roddick emphasized, "and we intend to ensure we die poor by giving away all of our personal wealth through a foundation of some kind."

TIMELINE

1942	Born in Littlehampton.
1950	Gilda Perella, Roddick's mother, married her father, Henry.
1960	Traveled to Israel on a study scholarship.
1969	August, Gave birth to her first daughter, Justine.
1970	Married Gordon Roddick.
1971	July, Gave birth to her second daughter, Samantha.
	Opened bed and breakfast business in Littlehampton.
1972	Opened restaurant.
1976	March 27, Opened first Body Shop store in Brighton.
	March, Gordon left for extended horseback trip in South America.
	September, Ian McGlinn's investment enabled second store to be opened.
1977	Met Mark Constantine, the herbalist who became the Body Shop's major supplier.
	First franchise was issued.
1978	First international franchise was given.

1982	The Body Shop moved into new headquarters.
1983	The Body Shop went public.
1984	Launched the first social campaign at Body Shop stores.
	The Body Shop is listed on the London Stock Exchange. Anita Won the Veuve Cliquot Businesswoman of the Year Award.
1985	The Body Shop assists Greenpeace in lobbying against dumping hazardous waste in the North Sea.
1987	The Body Shop is named the company of the year by the Confederation of British Industry.
1988	Launched franchise stores in the United States.
1990	The first shop in Japan opened.
1991	Anita Roddick's biography, *Body & Soul*, was published in ten languages.
	Stepped down as CEO and became the cochair with her husband, Gordon.
2002	Became creative consultant to the company.
2003	Started Anita Roddick Publications and new Web site.
2004	Became nonmanaging director.
2005	Released a book on leadership, *Business As Unusual: My Entrepreneurial Journey, Profits With Principles*.

RESOURCES

(Unless otherwise attributed, all quotes are from Roddick's *Body & Soul*.)

Adair, John. *Inspiring Leadership: Learning from Great Leaders*. London: Thorogood, 2003, pp. 292–293.

Biggs, Brooke Shelby. *Brave Hearts, Rebel Spirits: A Spiritual Activists Handbook*. West Sussex, England: Anita Roddick Press, 2003.

Chaston, Ian. *Entrepreneurial Marketing: Competing by Challenging Conventions*. New York: Palgrave Publishers, 2000, p. 86.

Fineman, Stephen (Editor). *Emotion in Organizations,* 2nd ed. London: Sage Publications, 2000, pp. 119–135.

Frank, Thomas. *One Market Under God: Extreme Capitalism, Market Populism, and the End of Economic Democracy*. Westminster, MD: Vintage Anchor Publishing, 2001, pp. 209–216, 235–236, 245.

Glancey, Keith S. *Entreprenurial Economics*. New York: Palgrave Publishers, 2000, p. 10.

Hauss, Charles. *Beyond Confrontation: Transforming the New World Order*. Westport, CT: Greenwood Publishing Group, 1996, pp. 203–205.

King, Roy. *Managing for Sustainability*. Broadstairs, UK: Scitech Educational, 2002, pp. 18–20.

Mariotti, Steve. *Young Entrepreneur's Guide to Starting to Running a Business*. New York: Crown Publishing Group, 2000, pp. 38, 57, 239, 251–269, 313–316, 361.

Perseus Publishing Staff. *The Big Book of Business Quotations.* New York: Basic Books, 2003, p. 14.

Perseus Publishing Staff. *Business: The Ultimate Resource.* Cambridge, MA: Perseus Publishing, 2002, p. 1134.

Quarter, Jack. *Beyond the Bottom Line: Socially Innovative Business Owners.* Westport, CT: Greenwood Publishing Group, 2000, pp. 119–133.

Roddick, Anita. *Body And Soul* New York: Crown, 1991.

Roddick, Anita. *Business As Unusual: The Triumph of Anita Roddick* London: Harper Thorsons, 2001.

Roddick, Anita. *Business As Unusual: My Entrepreneurial Journey, Profits With Principles* West Sussex, England: Anita Roddick Press, 2005.

Roddick, Anita. *Take It Personally: How to Make Conscious Choices to Change the World.* Berkeley, California: Conari Press, 2001

Roddick, Anita, Brooke Shelby Biggs, Robert F., Jr. Kennedy, and Vandana Shiva *Troubled Water: Saints, Sinners, Truth And Lies About The Global Water Crisis.* Vermont: Chelsea Green Publishing Company, 2004.

COMPANY INFORMATION

Global Headquarters
The Body Shop International
New City Court
20 St. Thomas Street
London SE1 9RG
UK
Phone: 44 (0)207 208 7600

The Body Shop International PLC
Watersmead
Littlehampton
West Sussex BN17 6LS
UK
Phone: +44 (0)1903 731500
Fax: +44 (0)1903 726250

The Body Shop International PLC
5036 One World Way
Wake Forest, NC 27587
USA
Phone: 919 554 4900
Fax: 919 554 4361
www.thebodyshopinternational.com
London Stock Exchange symbol: BOS

AP Photo/Laurent Rebours.

Howard Schultz

Howard Schultz, in an impressive entrepreneurial success story, took a small three-store coffee company and grew a business that became the largest specialty coffee retailer in the world and succeeded at the same time in creating a culture concerned for its employees, customers, and the global environment.

With over 11,000 locations, 40 million customers a week, 115,000 employees, and annual net revenues of $6.4 billion as of the end of 2005, Starbucks has fundamentally changed the way people around the world consume coffee. Before Starbucks came onto the scene, there were only a handful of premium coffee retailers around the United States. Coffee is now the second most-consumed drink in the world, after water. China's coffee consumption is growing by double digits, and in the United Kingdom coffee has now passed the tea consumption. Based on instinct and a single visit to Milan, where espresso stands abound, Schultz created a plan to turn Americans into coffee connoisseurs. Sales have climbed an average of 20 percent a year since the company went public, even though Starbucks uses virtually no marketing, spending just one percent of its annual revenues on advertising. Starbucks has stores around the United States, Asia, the Pacific, Latin America, Europe, the Middle East, and Africa and was named one of *Fortune*'s top ten most-admired companies.

It is hard to believe, especially given his current net worth of over seven hundred million dollars, that Schultz grew up with very few advantages in the federally subsidized projects in Brooklyn, New York. Using his athletic skill, he won a college scholarship that allowed him to escape poverty. His first serious job out of college was with Xerox, where he went through their renowned sales training program. A few years later, he went to work for Perstorp, a Swedish company that was planning to set up a U.S. division for its Hammarplast housewares. Schultz noticed that a small coffee outlet in Seattle was ordering a remarkable number of small coffeemakers. To satisfy his curiosity more than anything, Schultz flew out to Seattle to investigate. When he met the owners and took a tour of the coffee roasting plant, Schultz was immediately hooked. He knew he had to work in the coffee business and spent the next year begging the owners to hire him and put him in charge of marketing. They did, and although the business was almost entirely retail sales of whole coffee beans, Schultz set out to educate and enlarge the product's market.

When Schultz went on a business trip to Italy, he found a new niche he wanted to try in Seattle—the espresso bar. However, the original Starbucks owners did not want to go into the service business. When it became clear that no matter how much he tried to persuade them, they weren't going to budge, Schultz decided to open his own coffee shop. Starbucks was the first investor, wishing him well. His first shop, Il Giornale, opened in 1985, but Schultz was immediately planning for a major expansion that would launch seven more shops around Seattle. To do this, Schultz had to raise over $1.6 million, which he eventually did with thirty investors, including Bill Gates, after knocking on around three hundred doors. Soon after that, when three Il Giornale stores were netting five hundred thousand dollars, the Starbucks owners decided to sell the six stores they had, and Schultz went back to work to find another four million dollars in funding to buy them. Once he did that, he changed the Il Giornale stores to Starbucks stores, modified the logo, and created a plan to expand outside of Seattle. After the Chicago stores became successful, it was relatively simple to keep expanding into other cities. Originally opening thirty stores a year, the company now opens approximately five new stores every day worldwide.

With the memory of his father's life as an underpaid and unappreciated laborer burned into his psyche, it was natural for Schultz to lobby his investors for employee benefits. Starbucks was the first major company to offer health insurance and an employee stock ownership plan to part-time workers. As a result, Starbucks sees significantly lower turnover than other service companies. Schultz is adamant that employees be treated extraordinarily well, believing that if they're happy, they will make the customers happy.

Schultz has also passionately protected the Starbucks brand, which represents premium coffee. Although this has resulted in the delayed release of nonfat milk (which changes the coffee taste) and the frosty Frappucino blended beverage into the stores, the Starbucks brand has become well known around the world. Schultz has also lobbied for using premium and environmentally friendly products. At the same time, Starbucks has become one of the most generous corporate donors to CARE, with donations exceeding three million dollars.

Each Starbucks store is uniquely decorated and varies its peripheral product mix, but most carry coffee beans and coffee- and espresso-making equipment and accessories such as coffee grinders, coffee filters, storage containers, travel tumblers, and mugs. Starbucks is moving into the music business, as well, not only providing a selection of compact discs, but also launching Starbucks Hear Music media bars, where consumers can experience and acquire all genres of music through a service that offers custom CD burning. Starbucks has also launched its products into other distribution channels, including grocery stores, airlines, and other food service accounts.

THE EARLY YEARS

Howard Schultz was born in July 1953 to working-class parents Fred and Elaine Schultz. Fred never graduated from high school; he had quit school following the death of his father. He served as a medic in the Army during World War II and was stationed in the South Pacific, where he contracted malaria and yellow fever, which permanently weakened his lungs. After the war, Fred Schultz had a series of low-paying jobs, from factory worker to truck driver. "My father was a broken-down blue-collar worker," says Schultz in his memoir, *Pour Your Heart Into It*. "He was not valued and not respected, and it made him very bitter and angry. Schultz's mother, Elaine, or Bobby as she was known, was a strong-willed and powerful woman who stayed home with the three Schultz children full time during their childhood. Later in life she worked as a receptionist.

Schultz was three years old when his family moved out of his grandmother's house and into the federally subsidized Bayview Project of Brooklyn in 1956. Though at that time the projects were clean and new and there were a playground and paved basketball courts, they were definitely residences for the working poor.

Schultz's sister, Ronnie, was born soon after him. A difference of eight years separates Schultz from his younger brother, Michael. The larger age gap set Schultz up to serve as a father figure when the boys were younger, and he was able to insulate Michael somewhat from the harshness of their financial situation. Schultz referred to Michael as "The Shadow" when they were young, and they remain close today.

Growing up in the projects gave the Schultz children the opportunity to mix with a diverse group of friends. 150 families from a variety of backgrounds lived in their building, and neighborhood sports were a big part of Schultz's youth. His primary school was located on the grounds of the project, and after school and on weekends, hundred of neighborhood kids would meet for games. At times, Fred would also join in after work. Schultz became a fierce competitor because the poorer players had to sit on the sidelines for hours watching before being picked for another team, and he didn't want to do that. Luckily, Schultz was a natural athlete and liked to practice a sport until he achieved success. He loved baseball and went with his father and brother to numerous Yankees games to watch his idol, the Yankee slugger, Mickey Mantle.

Interestingly, Schultz's mother drank only instant coffee. When company came over, though, she'd buy some canned coffee and use the percolator, which was quite impressive to the young Schultz.

As Schultz grew older, he started to realize how tight his family finances were. He felt angry and ashamed when he realized it and soon started working to help the family as a paperboy. He later got a job behind the counter at the local luncheonette. At sixteen, he worked at a furrier in the garment district of Manhattan, stretching animal skins, and he spent one summer in a sweatshop, steaming yarn at a knitting factory.

Schultz credits his mother with giving him the courage to challenge himself. She believed in her children and gave them tremendous confidence, dreaming big dreams for them even though she herself had never finished high school. She would tell her children stories about people who had made something of their lives and insisting that they, too, could achieve anything.

By the time he got to high school, Schultz understood the stigma of living in the projects. To get to Canarsie High School, Schultz had to walk past regular homes, and he felt poor and looked down upon. He soon became a star quarterback at Canarsie High School even though the school did not have a football field. When he earned a letter for a letter jacket, his parents couldn't afford the jacket until they saved up enough money. To save embarrassment, Schultz borrowed money from his friend and hid the jacket from his parents. In the early 1970s, he earned his way out of the projects with a football scholarship to Northern Michigan University, the only offer he received.

Schultz wasn't as good as the other players on the team, and to stay in school he took out loans and worked part-time and summer jobs to pay for expenses. He had a night job as a bartender and sold blood at times. Schultz, a B student, majored in communications and took courses in public speaking and interpersonal communications. During his senior year, he also picked up a few business classes. After four years, he earned a BS degree and became the first college graduate in his family.

CAREER PATH

After graduating from college in 1975, Schultz didn't know what to do next, so he stayed in Michigan and worked at a nearby ski lodge. After a year, he went back to New York and got a job with Xerox, starting in their prestigious sales training program. The training helped Schultz develop sales, marketing, and presentation skills. After completing the course, he spent six months making fifty cold calls a day in Manhattan. He excelled as a salesperson, even though he never developed a passion for the product, and he was able to pay back his student loans and rent an apartment in Greenwich Village.

Three years later, in 1979, restless in his job, he applied to Perstorp, a Swedish company that was planning to set up a U.S. division for its Hammarplast housewares subsidiary. Perstorp hired him and sent him to Sweden for three months of training.

The company initially placed him in a building supplies division and moved him to North Carolina. He was miserable and found that he didn't have the passion for this product, either. After ten months, he told the company he wanted to quit. However, they wanted to keep him and transferred him back to New York with a promotion to vice president and general manager of Hammarplast housewares. He was in charge of the U.S. operations, managing about twenty independent sales representatives. His salary was seventy-five thousand dollars a year, and he was given a company car, an expense account, and unlimited travel, which included trips to Sweden four times a year. He had finally found a product line he liked (stylish Swedish-designed kitchen equipment and housewares,) and he was very successful during the three years he worked there.

In the meantime, Starbucks opened as a result of the motivation of Jerry Baldwin, an English teacher; Zev Siegel, a history teacher; and Gordon Bowker, a writer; who opened the first Starbucks Coffee, Tea and Spice store in Pike Place Market in Seattle in 1971, the same year that Schultz graduated from high school, with an investment of $1,350 each. The idea for Starbucks was born out of their experience with Peet's Coffee and Tea in Berkeley, California, a business established in 1966 by Alfred Peet, who had begun importing and selling exceptional coffees and teas, dark-roasting beans in a European tradition and teaching customers how to select and grind beans and to brew coffee at home for superior taste. The Starbucks name came as a result of a brainstorming session, but the partners were pleased to learn that it was also the name of the coffee-loving first mate in Herman Melville's *Moby Dick*. Starbucks was an immediate success. In the beginning, the three partners bought their beans from Peet, who mentored them in the art of coffee selection and roasting. Eventually, however, they set up their own roasting operations and developed their own roasting blends and flavors. In 1972 Starbucks opened a second location in Seattle, and by the early 1980s there were four stores that sold whole beans and coffeemakers.

In 1981, Schultz became curious about Starbucks when he noticed significant orders for a particular Hammarplast drip coffeemaker. He flew out from New York to Seattle to see the company and was immediately taken with the experience: the rich aromas of the coffee beans, the care with which the clerk ground and brewed a sample for him, and the philosophy behind the company that placed its highest priority on coffee quality. This dedication to quality began with selecting superior beans, carefully roasting, and educating customers so they could truly appreciate the qualities of the coffee. Schultz decided he wanted to be part of this company. He recalled in his memoir, "There was something magic about it, a passion and authenticity I had never experienced in business."

He met with Baldwin, Siegel, and Bowker and tried to break his way into the Starbucks family. He had a plan to take Starbucks across the country, but the founders didn't share his goals. However, after a year of tirelessly pursuing the owners to hire him, Schultz began work with Starbucks in September 1982, heading up marketing and overseeing the retail stores. He spent nearly all of his waking hours at the company, working behind the counters, tasting different coffees, and learning about all aspects of the coffee business from beans to roasting to retail.

In the spring of 1983, while attending an international housewares show for Starbucks in Milan, Schultz stopped into an espresso bar. He spent time going from one espresso bar to another—there were fifteen hundred of them in Milan alone—and all of them were packed. Schultz learned that they not only served excellent espresso, they also served as meeting places or public squares; they were a big part of Italy's societal glue, each with its own distinctive characteristics, but all with the common thread of a barista who made the rich espresso drinks and engaged the clientele in conversation. He returned to Seattle with the idea that recreating this experience could lead Starbucks in a new direction. He saw that in addition to providing superior coffee, like the espresso bars in Italy, Starbucks could provide a place for people to gather.

Despite his enthusiasm, however, Schultz found resistance to the idea when he returned to Seattle. Starbucks was about to purchase Peet's Coffee and Tea, and the original partners decided that the time wasn't right for trying out new ideas. It wasn't until April 1984, after a year of persuading the owners, that Schultz was able to test out the espresso bar idea inside a new downtown Starbucks store. It was an immediate success and within two months was serving eight hundred customers a day; customers lined up outside the store. Nevertheless, the Starbucks owners were still not comfortable with the idea, thinking of themselves as coffee roasters and not restaurant owners. Within a few months Schultz decided to leave Starbucks and to set up his own company based on the Italian espresso bar experience.

The shop was named Il Giornale, the word for newspaper in Italian. Jerry Baldwin, one of the Starbucks owners, became Schultz's first investor in the enterprise and a director of the new company, and Gordon Bowker, another Starbucks owner, served as a part-time consultant to help Schultz get started. One early investor was a physician, Ron Margolis, who was introduced to Schultz through their wives (the doctor's hundred-thousand-dollar investment eventually grew to be worth more than ten million dollars.) By the end of January 1986, Schultz had raised four hundred thousand dollars in seed capital. By the end of the year, he had raised $1.25 million in equity. He did this by calling around three hundred people in both the United States and Italy and doing numerous presentations. His experience in cold calling for Xerox helped him sustain the rejections, and he eventually found thirty willing investors. One of those investors was another rising entrepreneur, Microsoft founder Bill Gates. Dave Olsen, a competing coffee store owner, decided to join forces with Schultz, and they planned to open fifty coffee shops in five years.

The first Il Giornale store, staffed by baristas who made the coffee, opened in April 1986 in a 700-square-foot building and served three hundred customers on its first day. Six months later it served a thousand customers a day. Schultz then opened a second Il Giornale store in downtown Seattle and a third store in Vancouver in April 1987. By mid 1987, sales at the three stores had reached $1.5 million.

In March 1987, Baldwin and Bowker decided to sell the entire Starbucks operation (Siegel had left Starbucks in the early 1980s) including the stores, the roasting plant, and the name. Schultz raised the $3.8 million needed to acquire the company mainly by going back to his original investors. He completed the transaction in August 1987. In November of that year, Schultz brought in Lawrence Maltz, a seasoned executive who had been managing a beverage company.

Schultz then merged Starbucks and Il Giornale under the Starbucks name for operations totaling nine stores, and at age thirty-four, became president and CEO of the company. His vision was for Starbucks not only to become a national company but a company based on clear values and guiding principles. He wanted to build a company that would make the people who worked there proud, a company that would be both profitable and a good place to work. In 1988, the Starbucks board approved a plan to offer full health benefits to part-time employees, becoming the first private company to do so.

In 1989, Schultz hired Howard Behar to manage the process of opening stores. Schultz's original objective after the Starbucks acquisition was to open 125 new stores within five years. Finding it easier than he expected with Behar on board and the invention of the FlavorLock vacuum-sealed bag, which preserves freshness for months, he opened 150 stores by 1992. Despite posting losses for three consecutive years (1987, 1988, 1989) during this early growth period, Schultz was able to raise new venture capital ($3.9 million in 1988, $13.5 million in 1990, $15 million in 1991). By 1990 Starbucks became profitable, and its profits have increased by nearly 20 percent every year since then, excluding one-time write-offs in 2000 for Internet investments. In 1990 Schultz found Orin Smith, a Harvard MBA and budget director for the State of Washington to manage the more sophisticated financing. The management team of the two Howards and Orin Smith became known as H_2O.

On June 26, 1992, Schultz took the company public, and its initial public offering (IPO) turned out to be one of the most successful IPOs of the year. The capital infusion of $273 million supported the expansion of the store network. In 1992 and 1993, Starbucks developed a three-year expansion strategy and created zone vice presidents to oversee the development of each region. They bought a franchise of ten stores in Boston, the only time they have ever done that. Store launches became increasingly successful. In 1995, new stores generated an average of seven hundred thousand dollars in revenue in their first year, compared to $427,000 in 1990. Existing stores continued to post year-to-year gains in sales.

The company began to experiment with different store formats, with expanded product offerings, and with different partnerships such as the joint venture with Pepsico to create a bottled cold coffee drink, or with Dreyer's Grand Ice Cream to create a new line of Starbucks ice cream. In 1995, the company rolled out Frappucino, a frosty blended drink that Schultz fought against introducing, believing it would not fit with the Starbucks image of quality coffee. In 1996, however, Starbucks sold fifty-two million dollars' worth of Frappucino. The company's retail sales mix remained predominantly coffee beverages (about 61 percent) and whole bean coffees (15 percent) while it diversified into food items (16 percent) and coffee-related products and equipment (8 percent), and more recently, music. In addition, Starbucks now has alliances with Kraft Foods, Inc., Johnson Development Corporation, Albertson's, Inc., Horizon Air, HMS Host, Barnes & Noble, United Airlines, Starwood Hotel, Chapters, Inc., Safeway, Inc., Marriott International, Inc., Hyatt Hotels Corporation, Aramark, Compass, Sodexho, TransFair USA, SYSCO, HP, T-Mobile, TransFair Canada, White Wave, Inc., Bank One Visa USA, Hilton, Intrawest, Wyndham, Target, Kroger, Ahold, Fortune Brands, XM Satellite Radio, Borders, Westin, and Radisson.

In 1994, Schultz decided it was time to change his role: He was tired of managing day-to-day operations of a big company and wanted instead to experiment with creative ideas. In 1994, Orin Smith, who had been chief financial officer since 1990, was promoted to become president and chief operating officer, while Schultz remained chairman and CEO. In June of 2000, Smith became president and CEO. Schultz became chief global strategist and remains chairman of the board. Smith retired in 2005 and was replaced with current Starbucks CEO, Jim Donald, who had been running the North American operations for Starbucks. Previously, he spent five years running Wal-Mart's food operations.

The Starbucks Mission Statement

Establish Starbucks as the premier purveyor of the finest coffee in the world while maintaining our uncompromising principles as we grow. The following six guiding principles will help us measure the appropriateness of our decisions:

- Provide a great work environment and treat each other with respect and dignity.
- Embrace diversity as an essential component in the way we do business.
- Apply the highest standards of excellence to the purchasing, roasting and fresh delivery of our coffee.
- Develop enthusiastically satisfied customers all of the time.
- Contribute positively to our communities and our environment.
- Recognize that profitability is essential to our future success.

PERSONAL LIFE

As a Xerox salesperson, Schultz was able to pay off his college loans and rent an apartment in Greenwich Village. He had finally made it, and he had money for the first time. During one summer, eight of his friends rented a cottage in the Hamptons for weekends, and it was there on the beach during the July Fourth weekend in 1978 that he met Sheri Kersch. He recalled the meeting in his memoir: "With her flash of long wavy blonde hair and unflagging energy, Sheri attracted me with her impeccable style and class. She was in graduate school studying interior design and also spent summer weekends with a group of friends at the beach. She was not only beautiful but well grounded, with solid midwestern values, from a close and loving family. We were both starting our careers, without a care in the world. We began dating, and the more I got to know her, the more I realized what a fine human being she was." They bought their first apartment in Manhattan.

They were married in July of 1982 in East Hampton before moving out to Seattle, with the wedding photographed by Schultz's sister, Ronnie, a professional photographer. Schultz and his new wife took the summer off before starting their road trip out to their new life on the west coast. In 1985, just as Schultz was making plans to go out on his own with his Il Giornale coffee shops, they found out Sheri was pregnant. They made plans for Sheri to return to work after their son, Jordan, was born in January. Sheri supported the family until Schultz could get the new company off the ground. Their daughter, Addison, was born a couple of years after the acquisition of Starbucks.

Although Schultz's parents were very proud of him for achieving a level of success they had never known, they were also worried about his choices. He left a good career in New York to go to a small coffee company across the country, and when he left that to start his own company, they were more concerned. When his father had left jobs, it had caused a great deal of instability and disruption. But Schultz was willing to take the risk in order to get even further away from the struggles he had seen his parents go through. Unfortunately, Schultz's father died in 1988, before Starbucks had become a great success.

Schultz indulged his love of basketball by buying the Seattle Supersonics. He is also principal owner of the Seattle Storm of the WNBA, and he is seen at many of both teams' games. He also is a significant stakeholder in Jamba Juice.

Schultz has received a wide range of accolades for his work combining business with philanthropy, including the Botwinic Prize for Business Ethics from Columbia University, the International Humanitarian Award from CARE for his work to better the lives of individuals in coffee-producing countries, and the Jerusalem Fund for Aish HaTorah for making extensive contributions to better lives around the world.

Schultz has insisted that Starbucks adopt an environmental mission statement. This pledge commits Starbucks to buying only coffee that has been grown organically. The company also takes an interest in the farming communities that harvest the coffee beans. Starbucks has built schools, health clinics, and safe coffee-processing facilities. Starbucks makes charitable contributions through the Starbucks Foundation, which sponsors literacy programs, Earth Day clean-ups, and regional AIDS walks. The foundation is a direct-giving program in the communities in which it operates and in countries where its coffee is sourced.

> *"There's no long-term shareholder value if it isn't linked to building long-term values for your people."*
> Howard Schultz

LEADERSHIP LESSONS

In addition to the basics of business including, hiring excellent people, getting advice from smarter people, and in Schultz's case, looking for ideal real estate locations, the main lessons that can be drawn from Schultz's success are to dream big, use equity versus loans, control the quality of the product, and be socially responsible. "Don't be threatened by people smarter than you. Compromise anything but your core values. Seek to renew yourself even when you are hitting home runs. And everything matters," Schultz has said. His is a distinctive leadership style based on an idealism, though at first seemingly at odds with business principles, has lead to greater financial success.

Create a Vision

When Schultz on his trip to Milan saw all the espresso bars and the community they created, he immediately knew that he wanted to create that experience in the United States. Although he was not allowed to start creating it immediately, he kept the vision. When he tried a small version in a test at one of the initial Starbucks stores and found it an overwhelming success, he knew he had to pursue it on a much larger scale. He not only set about finding the capital to build one coffee shop, he also created a plan to open several shops and expand exponentially across America. He then shared this plan with potential investors and acquired the capital. If his plan had been to open only one store, he might not have received the needed investment.

Schultz found that by sharing a far-reaching vision with employees, they went above and beyond the call of duty to help. Schultz kept his strategic focus, and although he was also concerned with the performance of single stores, he was so because that impacted his ability to gather financing and secure success for his much larger goal. He visits thirty to forty Starbucks stores a week and believes that a corporate leader must share unbridled enthusiasm about the overall vision with his employees. He has said that the time he spends with people is "the single most important thing I'm doing."

When Schultz left Starbucks to create his vision of the type of espresso bars he saw in Italy, he had almost nothing to go on but his dream. He relied on his wife's salary to support his family while he went after it. He had a daunting task of securing a great deal of capital to start the business, but he persevered, and as he tackled each challenge, his anxiety was replaced by a growing sense of optimism. Schultz often encourages people now to dream big. "Most people can achieve beyond their dreams if they insist upon it. Just because it hasn't been done before doesn't mean you shouldn't try," Schultz said in his autobiography, *Pour Your Heart into It*.

Visions can expand as time goes on, as Schultz has found. Although he initially wanted to open fifty shops a year, that number turned into 125 and 365, and it is now over 500. He has also expanded his vision for Starbucks around the United States and now sees Starbucks shops all over the world. A few years from now, Schultz has said he wants Starbucks to be one of the most respected and recognized brands in the world. The important lesson in creating a vision, he believes, is to start with a big dream of how things can be and give that dream space to grow into more.

Use Equity

In creating his company, Schultz was never afraid to give away control of his company to investors. His options were to find numerous investors, grow very slowly, or take on debt. He stayed clear of debt, having learned when Starbucks bought out Peet's how debt hangs over a company and limits options. Growing slowly was not an option either if he wanted to accomplish his main goal of putting coffee shops around the country.

When Schultz was drawing up the documents to convince investors to back Il Giornale, Jerry Baldwin, a Starbucks owner, surprised him by offering one hundred and fifty thousand dollars of Starbucks money. Although Baldwin did not want to go into the coffee service business, he wanted to support Schultz. After that first investment, Schultz had more confidence that he could raise the money. This was short lived, however. With his short-term plans for the new business set, Schultz needed to raise $1.7 million, and the company he thought would give him the bulk of it declined. He had to go door to door, knowing that he would not be left with even 50 percent. He opted to give up some control in order for the company to grow rapidly. Even to open his first store, Schultz needed four hundred thousand dollars more. A physician husband of one his wife's friends gave him a hundred thousand dollars without looking at the financial projections solely because he trusted Schultz and was confident he would succeed in his own business.

He raised the rest of the four hundred thousand dollars by selling shares at ninety-two cents each to clients of Arnie Prentice, a cochairman of a financial services firm. He leased his first building, let Dave Olsen work on opening the store, and spent the bulk of his time the rest of the year trying to raise the next $1.25 million. He had no experience at the time with raising money or dealing with the people who had it and was often turned away with arrogance. He spoke to 242 people, and 217 refused him. He had to lower the price per share twice. He also faced a financial hurdle because although he continued to get commitments for the money, he could not use it until he met his impound number, a minimum amount an entrepreneur has to raise to gain access to the capital. His was set at nine hundred thousand dollars, so his first coffee shop had to struggle and all plans had to wait until he raised at least this much. It was likely more difficult for Schultz to gain investors' confidence and cash at the time he did because that was also the time that the technology industry was taking off, and there was certainly nothing as special about the coffee industry.

The main disadvantage of using equity to finance a business is that others can take the control away, and Schultz experienced the reality of this. When he found he had to raise an additional four million dollars to buy Starbucks when it went up for sale, he turned to his early investors again. One of these investors tried to prepare a separate plan to buy Starbucks, excluding Schultz from the deal and effectively turning him from a founder into an employee of the company. Bill Gates, another investor, went along with Schultz to a meeting with the shareholder who was trying to maneuver the company out from under Schultz. Schultz admits leaving the meeting angry and upset, sure that the other man was going to be able to do what he proposed. However, Schultz met with his other early investors, and within weeks was able to raise the $3.8 million he needed.

Using equity has its disadvantages, but Schultz found the trade-off worth it. Many investors were on his board of directors, and he became accountable to them for the success or failure of the stores. It seems that in Schultz's case, the board supported his decisions and acted more as advisors, most likely because once Starbucks started to make a profit after a large initial expense outlay, it kept making larger and larger profits. Schultz now says that entrepreneurs would be wise to focus on leading a company to perform well, and that is how they will keep control, whether their stake is more or less than 50 percent of the company. Nearly free of debt, Starbucks continues to grow and fuels expansion with internal cash flow.

Control the Quality of a Superior Product

From the time Schultz first walked into the Starbucks roasting plant, he was committed to high-quality coffee. When he started the Starbucks the world knows today, he created a plan that had high-quality coffee as its cornerstone. Starbucks today is committed to using only the finest whole bean coffees. To do this, they control all aspects of the product, from its purchasing to its roasting, packaging, and distribution to retail stores. Starbucks purchases green coffee beans from coffee-producing regions around the world and custom-roasts them.

Schultz had never wanted to give customers exactly what they asked for. He wanted to offer them a superior product and then educate them about its value. By doing this, although it would take longer and would not immediately satisfy a mass market, Schultz reasoned that he could create a sense of discovery and excitement and loyalty that would bond the customer to Starbucks. Their research and development efforts are led by food scientists, engineers, and chemists, and this team is responsible for the technical development of food and beverage products and new equipment. Starbucks spent approximately $10.5 million, $8.3 million, and $5.4 million during fiscal years 2005, 2004, and 2003, respectively, on technical research and development activities.

Dedication to high-quality coffee has led to significant price volatility for Starbucks and hinders exact cost management. Although most coffee trades in the commodity market, high-altitude Arabica coffee of the quality sought by Starbucks tends to trade on a negotiated basis at a substantial premium above commodity coffee prices, depending on the supply and demand at the time of purchase. Supply and price can be affected by multiple factors in the producing countries, including weather and political and economic conditions. In addition, green coffee prices have been affected in the past and may be affected in the future by the actions of certain organizations and associations that have historically attempted to influence prices of green coffee through agreements establishing export quotas or restricting coffee supplies. Any significant increase in the market price or any significant decrease in the availability of high-quality Arabica coffee could adversely affect Starbuck's business and financial results.

Cluster Expansion without Franchising

Schultz's strategy has been to cluster stores in particular areas. Although this means the outlets potentially poach customers from each other, Schultz believes that it also builds market share and enables the firm to dominate the local market. The Starbucks-everywhere approach cuts down on delivery and management costs, shortens customer lines at individual stores, and increases foot traffic for all the stores in an area.

All Starbucks stores follow a similar formula. This not only helps customers to know what to expect but also helps to strengthen and tighten the brand's identity in the public's mind. However, they have also allowed each store to have a different layout with a decor that matches the personality of the neighborhood.

Schultz has said that his model for expanding Starbucks is similar to that of McDonald's, with a few key differences. One is that Starbucks owns most of its stores, while McDonald's franchises.

Starbucks predominantly owns its stores and rejects a franchise model. By owning stores, Starbucks maintains greater control over the quality of the product and is able to nurture the company's values and culture. Schultz could have grown his business much faster if he had franchised, but he was concerned that if his company grew too fast, he would lose control over quality of the coffees and management of the brand name, which could hurt the company's reputation. His research told him that many franchise organizations have separate agendas, and he felt that this would be inconsistent with the Starbucks culture. He explained, "Over the short term these steps would drive up revenues and profits. But over the long term, they would be a giant mistake."

In recent years, the company has entered into a limited number of licensing agreements. When it comes to international expansion, initially, the company didn't have the ability to go into many markets. That drove Starbucks to the idea of partnering. Then that became its first and preferred choice for international expansion strategy. For instance, in Japan, Starbucks wanted a partner as well as capital and experience, so it created a 50–50 joint venture with Sazaby to launch Starbucks Coffee Japan in October 1995. Now the Japan company is split three ways, 40–40–20, because it has taken the company public. It currently operates more than six hundred stores throughout Japan. In other markets, Starbucks' ownership varies from 5 percent to 20 percent. It also has many situations with licensing arrangements.

Brand the Image

Schultz created the new Starbucks with the idea that the stores would serve as community gathering places. It is this emphasis on building emotional ties that defines the brand. Starbucks seeks to sell the idea of community as much as it does physical cups of coffee. This concept defines the brand as much as the product does. Though Schultz definitely believes the product is superior, he also realizes that most consumers don't believe that there is a huge difference between products. Starbucks doesn't have a patent on any coffee or coffee product it sells, but it has created an image to which the customer responds.

Continue to Innovate

Starbucks continues to expand its product line while staying true to its idea of quality coffee. Schultz has protectively guarded the product and brand, although he believes that it is important to embrace additional opportunities. "I was always willing to experiment on new things. I don't believe in holding everything close to the vest, it's not productive. It is far better to try something new, and fail if necessary," he said. In recent years, Starbucks has installed automatic espresso machines to speed up service, launched a prepaid Starbucks card, which is swiped through when you visit; this halves transaction time and has allowed for preordering and payment for coffee via the phone or the Starbucks Web site so that the coffee is waiting when the customer arrives. Starbucks has also introduced wireless Internet access, music CDs, and a downloading service.

Champion Employees

Whether Schultz realized that treating employees well would have a significant impact on the bottom line or whether he felt he needed to right the wrongs that were experienced by his blue-collar father is not known. Schultz has said that the saddest day of his life was when his father died: "He had no savings, no pension. More important, he had never attained fulfillment and dignity from work he found meaningful. As a kid, I never had any idea that I would one day head a company. But I knew in my heart that if I were ever in a position where I could make a difference, I wouldn't leave people behind."

The most profitable stores with the highest frequency of visits and customer satisfaction are the ones where the managers have been there one to two years, where they have developed relationships with customers. Howard Behar has said, "Starbucks is in the people business serving coffee." The baristas, or coffee brewers, are vital to the Starbucks experience. The relationships that are developed between baristas and their customers can be lasting and important to each party. Finding and keeping good baristas has been a challenge for the company as it has grown. From the beginning, Starbucks has tried to treat its baristas well—certainly better than most retailers or fast-food outlets treat entry-level workers. "It's an ironic fact," Schultz has said, "that while retail and restaurant businesses live or die on customer service, their employees have among the lowest pay and worst benefits of any industry." By relying on word-of-mouth based on its employees' service for marketing, Schultz has avoided the enormous advertising costs other retailers have faced. Starbucks spends just thirty million dollars annually on advertising, or roughly 1 percent of revenues, usually just for new flavors of coffee drinks and product launches. Most consumer companies its size spend upwards of three hundred million dollars per year.

Starbuck's success has largely been due to a balance of profitability and benevolence. Determined to build a company with "soul," as he described it, Schultz instituted benefits unprecedented in retail. Like most start-ups, Starbucks was not profitable. But Schultz managed to persuade its board of directors that none of its employees, not even part-timers, should go without health insurance. He argued that the additional costs would be offset at least in part because baristas would stay longer, reducing the costs of recruiting and training. Even though most baristas work part time, Schultz wanted to keep them happy and encourage them to sustain the connections that many had built with regular customers. "Treat people like family," Schultz has said, "and they will be loyal and give their all." Schultz insisted that all employees, even part-timers, get comprehensive health coverage—including coverage for unmarried spouses. Last year Starbucks spent two hundred million dollars on health care—more than it spent on raw materials to brew its coffee.

In 1991, with the achievement of the company's first profitable year, Schultz introduced "Bean Stock," a stock option plan for all employees who worked at least twenty hours per week. Schultz said, "I wanted to find a way to share both ownership of the company and the rewards of financial success with the people of Starbucks." His plan was to link shareholder value with long-term rewards for employees and to make the connection clear between the contribution that employees made to the success of the company and the growing value of the company. This was so unusual at the time that the firm needed permission from the Securities and Exchange Commission to grant stock options to more than seven hundred employees and still remain a private company under the law. When the Bean Stock program was introduced, Starbucks dropped the term *employee* and began referring to all of those who worked for the company as partners. In 1995, Starbucks also implemented an employee stock purchase plan. That first year, each partner was awarded options to buy stock worth 12 percent of his or her base pay.

Schultz instituted a comprehensive training program for his employees. Barista training involves twenty hours of online and in-store, on-the-job training. After entry-level training, advanced programs are also available online, including the recently introduced "black apron" training for baristas to achieve *Coffee Master* status. The management training program involves another ten weeks. Training for store development managers is conducted at headquarters in Seattle after the managers have worked for at least three months in a store.

These moves boosted loyalty and led to extremely low worker turnover, even though employee salaries were fairly low. "The power of your business lies in the power of your people," said Schultz, "Companies that don't recognize this won't thrive. It's not business as usual anymore. Customers are beginning to take cultural audits of your business practices. How you treat your people and what you give back to your community are what counts. You have to find ways to demonstrate the conscience of your business."

Besides the savings in employee turnover and advertising, Schultz's attitude also paid off in real terms in 1992 when the warehouse and roasting plant employees signed a letter stating they no longer wished to be represented by their union.

To ensure that the company lives up to its promises, Starbucks set up a mission review team and an internal system that enables partners to be in dialogue across the company and to provide feedback on what is and is not working. Employees are encouraged to report concerns to the team if decisions and actions are not consistent with the company's mission statement. As the company has grown, Starbucks has assembled a team of people from different regions to review employee concerns, seek solutions, and report back at the company's Open Forums, which are held biannually in every geographic region. Senior managers meet regularly with interested employees to provide updates, answer questions, and hear their concerns and grievances.

> *"Vision is what they call it when others can't see what you see."*
> Howard Schultz

Schultz has been lobbying the U.S. government, meeting with Senators and congressional leaders, to make sure every American has health insurance. He says that Starbucks has faced double-digit increases in insurance costs each of the last four years. "It's completely nonsustainable," he said, even for companies like his that "want to do the right thing."

Starbucks carefully tracks the satisfaction levels of its employees. Several years ago, when the company pushed people too hard to save money, it heard complaints and pulled back. "We squeezed to get margins and it was a mistake," Smith said. "We've learned from it and we don't do it anymore." In a 2004 survey, Starbucks found that about 87 percent of its workers were either satisfied or very satisfied.

Partner with Like-Minded People

With no barriers to entry, no technology, no extremely high startup costs, and no patents, Starbucks has only its people to differentiate itself. One of the biggest reasons that Starbucks has been able to create a niche in an industry

"Recognize the skills and traits you don't possess, and hire people who have them."
Howard Schultz

where there was none before is because of its partnering with like-minded people. Starbucks partners with customers, with vendors, with distributors, and with other people within the company. Its partnering philosophy cuts across all parts of the company.

Schultz commented on partnering, saying that "it wasn't only that I needed people with skills and discipline and business acumen that complemented my own qualities, but most important, I needed to attract and retain people with like-minded values. What tied us together was not our respective disciplines, and it was not chasing an exit strategy driven by money. What tied us together was the dream of building a company that would achieve the fragile balance of profitability, shareholder value, a sense of benevolence, and a social conscience." The key question that was in Schultz's mind was whether a potential partner has values that are aligned with the vision of Starbucks.

The competitive advantage that Starbucks created from its early years was to take a supplier contract, change it into something much more, and finally, develop it into a truly integrated alliance. This core competency led to the alliance competency that exists today in the company. An early relationship was with Costco Wholesale Corporation. The supply relationship became a huge cash-flow factor for the company, enabling it to increase its rate of retail store growth. One issue in most partnership discussions is the negotiation of price. However, in Starbuck's partnerships, the company manages to change the conversation so that it becomes much more about what would satisfy mutual customers rather than how low the price gets.

When Schultz decided to expand Starbucks internationally, the company initially didn't have the depth or numbers of talent to go into many markets. That drove Starbucks to the idea of partnering. Then that became its first and preferred choice for international expansion strategy. It could attract higher-caliber companies who wanted to do business with it because of success of the brand. When it comes to the partner selection process, it carefully evaluates potential partners, a process that can take eighteen to twenty-four months. It then narrows the selection and culls the list down to three or four companies. These three or four companies come to Seattle and make a presentation. What Starbucks looks for is a cultural fit. Potential partners meet with the most senior people at Starbucks, secretaries, and possibly someone from the Starbucks' plant. Starbucks looks at every interaction in order to determine if the applicants' actions match their talk. At the end of one negotiation, the potential partners and Starbucks managers went out for dinner. After a number of glasses of wine, the potential partner, relaxed and confident that the deal was made, made a racist comment. At that moment, the deal was off, according to the Starbucks managers: "We were unanimous: If the leader can't walk the talk, it was an easy decision for us that we could not live with that company as part of the Starbucks family."

Be Socially Responsible

Schultz has insisted that Starbucks adopt socially responsible programs. It has an environmental mission statement that commits Starbucks to buying only coffee that has been grown organically. The company also takes an interest in the farming communities that harvest the coffee beans. Starbucks has built schools, health clinics, and safe coffee-processing facilities. Locally, Starbucks has worked with stars like Magic Johnson to bring Starbucks stores to ethnically diverse neighborhoods across the country. The Starbucks Foundation sponsors literacy programs, Earth Day clean-ups, and regional AIDS walks.

> *"It would be very arrogant to sit here and say that ten years ago we thought we would be on the Fortune 500. But we dreamed from day one and dreamed very big."*
> Howard Schultz

From store design to energy consumption, Starbucks looks for ways to mitigate its impact on the environment. Most recently, it became one of the first retailers in the country to use a new green flooring option: a terrazzo made from 100 percent postconsumer recycled glass and colorful epoxy resins. The product, EnviroGLAS, combines environmental benefits and durability.

There's little question that Schultz's other recent innovation—buying a water company and contributing a nickel from every bottle sold to organizations who get clean water to children around the world—reinforces Starbucks's image of integrity. "This effort says a lot to our people and customers," explains Schultz. "It speaks to the heart of our company."

The company's Caring Unites Partners (CUP) Fund provides another example of ways it seeks to be a different kind of company. CUP is a financial assistance program that helps Starbucks partners in times of special need, such as illness not covered by insurance, death of a partner or family member, natural disaster, or other extreme circumstances. The CUP Fund is supported by partner contributions that are matched by the company.

Starbuck's mission is to go into a community and contribute something that community needs. In Seattle, Starbucks started a program around kids, literacy, and conservation. Children's books were collected in stores, and the baristas read to disadvantaged kids in the community. In New Zealand, Starbucks had a program called "Lend a Hand," in which the customer and barista select a local cause and participate in activities together. In the Philippines, the Starbucks Foundation and a local foundation took on a project to build a school in a particular area. In North Korea, Starbucks collected money for an orphanage.

POLITICAL INFLUENCE

Schultz has primarily contributed to Democratic candidates. Since 1997, he has donated $112,100 to Democrats and one thousand dollars to

Republicans. Starbucks has strived to present itself as a socially responsible and environmentally conscious operation. Schultz is an active voice in the debate on health care in the United States, meeting with congressional representatives and speaking about the need for affordable health care.

CRITICS

Although Schultz has done many things with a socially conscious view, he has still received a limited amount of criticism from some. The coffee industry has had a history of negative environmental impacts. In recent decades, farmers have found it more profitable to cut down as many trees as they could in order to grow coffee in the sun rather than in the shade, which affects bird sanctuaries and the habitats of other species.

In 1994, Chicago labor activists picketed stores, accusing the company of exploiting coffee growers in Guatemala. An open letter to Schultz accused Starbucks of exploiting growers. "The farmers who make you rich earn poverty wages," it said. "Sweatshops occur not only in the factory but in the field." Starbucks chose to make peace rather than resist the fair-trade pressures. Schultz supports the goal of the fair trade movement—to enable coffee growers to make a living and stay in business—and so Starbucks hastily negotiated a licensing agreement with TransFair USA. Days before protests were to begin, Starbucks announced its plans to launch a line of fair-trade certified coffee. Starbucks also started to work with Conservation International to save and regenerate endangered environments. Starbucks is now able to educate farmers on shade-grown organic coffee and provide them the market for the product.

Although Schultz was a pioneer in providing health care and stock options to part-time employees, not all employees were happy. Some felt overworked and undervalued, and several years ago a group that sued over unpaid overtime won an eighteen-million-dollar settlement.

Critics charge that the sayings printed on the Starbucks cups are too liberal. Although they aren't very inflammatory, critics say that the list of contributors is overwhelmingly liberal. Of the thirty-one contributors listed on the Starbucks Web site, only one, according to *National Review* editor Jonah Goldberg, offers a conservative viewpoint.

> *"You have to follow the path of doing the right thing by making decisions that are true to your mission and cause. You refer to your heart, conscience, and memory."*
> Howard Schultz

Starbucks' success has also brought critics. The clustering of so many stores so close together has become a national joke, eliciting quips such as a headline in *The Onion*, a satirical publication that said "A New Starbucks Opens in Rest-room of Existing Starbucks." Starbucks products are available in a lot of places, and many people now think of Starbucks as just another soulless big chain. Campus activists, neighborhood preservationists, and antiglobalization protestors have criticized the company. Critics say its method of flooding an area is undesirable because it forces out local competition.

The U.S. Organic Consumers Association also attacked Starbucks for using milk that is not certified free of the growth hormone rBST. Although this hormone has U.S. Food and Drug Administration approval, the U.S. Consumer Organic Association believes there are potential health risks associated with its use.

Starbucks is also criticized for the price of its coffee. Younger coffee drinkers say they feel uncomfortable in the stores; they either can't afford to buy coffee at Starbucks, or the only peers they see there are those working behind the counter. They find the Starbucks scene somewhat pretentious.

Starbucks has also been accused of using a predatory real-estate strategy by paying rents that are higher than the market rate to keep competitors out of a location.

POSSIBLE FUTURE IMPACT

Starbucks may be at something of a turning point in its development and faces a number of problems, including the danger that people will become bored with the brand, seeing it as tired and mature rather than as young and daring. Starbucks will most likely have to continue to innovate on a larger scale. It will also most likely do something to attract the younger customer. To address this, Starbucks is using an emerging entertainment business, which encompasses multiple music and technology based initiatives designed to appeal to the younger customer. Among these initiatives are strategic marketing and co-branding arrangements, such as the twenty-four-hour Starbucks Hear Music digital music channel available to all XM Satellite Radio subscribers and the availability of wireless broadband Internet service in the stores. Additionally, the entertainment business includes Starbucks Hear Music's innovative partnerships with other music labels for the production, marketing and distribution of both exclusive and nonexclusive music, music programming for Starbucks stores worldwide, and CD sales through the its Web site. Although their new Hear Music media bars, which let customers burn CDs at Starbucks shops from a library of more than one million digital tracks, have been disappointing, the company will likely continue to innovate in the music arena.

Starbucks' technology department could eventually see jobs migrate offshore. Like many corporate leaders, Schultz is still trying to work out this emotional labor issue.

TIMELINE

1953	July 19, Born in New York to Fred and Elaine Schultz.
1956	The Schultz family moved to the Bayview Project in Brooklyn.

1971	First Starbucks location opened in Seattle's Pike Place Market. Schultz graduated from high school.
1975	Graduated from Northern Michigan University.
1976	Started work as a salesperson for Xerox.
1979	Took a job with Perstorp.
1980	Made vice president and general manager of Hammarplast, a Perstorp subsidiary.
1981	Visited Starbucks for the first time in Seattle.
1982	Started working at Starbucks as director of retail operations and marketing. Starbucks began providing coffee to fine restaurants and espresso bars. Married Sheri Kersch.
1983	Visited Milan for a housewares show.
1984	Schultz convinced the founders of Starbucks to test the coffee-house concept in downtown Seattle, where the first Starbucks caffè latte is served. This successful experiment became the genesis for the company that Schultz founded in 1985. Left Starbucks and started his own company, Il Giornale.
1985	Jordan Schultz born.
1987	Bought Starbucks from the original owners and merged his company into the Starbucks company.
1988	Offered full health benefits to full- and part-time employees.
1991	Starbucks became the first privately owned U.S. company to offer a stock option program that included part-time employees.
1992	Schultz took Starbucks public.
1994	Resigned as president but stayed on as CEO and chairman of the board.
1995	Began selling compact discs as a result of an extremely popular in-house music program. Formed alliance with Canadian bookstore chain Chapters, Inc. Formed alliance with Dreyer's Grand Ice Cream to introduce Starbucks Ice Cream. Starbucks Coffee International formed joint venture with Sazaby, Inc., to open Starbucks coffeehouses in Japan.
1997	Established the Starbucks Foundation, benefiting local literacy programs in communities where Starbucks has coffeehouses.
2000	Schultz made the transition from chairman and CEO to chairman and chief global strategist.

RESOURCES

Baraban, Regina. Caffeinated Keynote. *Insurance Conference Manager*, January 1, 2003.

Cummings, Jeanne. Cautiously, Starbucks Puts Lobbying on Corporate Menu. *The Wall Street Journal,* April 12, 2005.

Daniels, Cora. Mr. Coffee: The man behind the $4.75 Frappuccino makes the 500. *Fortune,* April 14, 2003, p. 139.

Frost, Caroline. Howard Schultz: Profile, 6/8/06 http://www.bbc.co.uk/bbcfour/documentaries/profile/howard_schultz.shtml.

Gunther, Marc. *Faith and Fortune: The Quiet Revolution to Reform American Business.* New York: Crown Publishing Group, 2004, pp. 17, 93, 105–110, 116–120, 181.

Haig, Matt. *Brand Royalty.* London: Kogan Page, 2004, pp. 96–98.

Holmes, Stanley, with Drake Bennett, Kate Carlisle, and Chester Dawson. Starbucks: To Keep Up the Growth, It Must Go Global Quickly. *Business Week Online,* September 9, 2002.

Meyers, William. Conscience in a Cup of Coffee. *US News and World Report,* October 31, 2005, pp. 48–50.

Nattrass, Brian. *Dancing with the Tiger: Learning Sustainability Step by Natural Step.* Gabriola Island, Canada: New Society Publishers, 2002, pp. 100–139.

Price, Robert W. *Roadmap to Entrepreneurial Success: Powerful Strategies for Building a High-Profit Business.* New York: AMACOM, 2004, pp. 90, 167.

Schultz, Howard, and Dori Jones Yang. *Pour Your Heart Into It: How Starbucks Built a Company One Cup At A Time.* New York: Hyperion, 1997.

Segil, Larraine. *Measuring the Value of Partnering: How to Use Metrics to Plan, Develop, and Implement Successful Alliances.* New York: AMACOM, 2004, pp. 129, 238–239.

Smith, Richard. *Patterns of Extraordinary Careers: The Guide for Achieving Success and Satisfaction.* New York: Crown Publishing Group, 2005, pp. 180–182, 232.

Smith, Scott S. Grounds for Success. *Entrepreneur,* May 1998, p. 120.

Vrana, Debora. The Nation; Rising Premiums Threaten Job-Based Health Coverage, *Los Angeles Times.* September 15, 2005, p. A.1.

Warner, Melanie, with Jim Donald. Also Trying to Sell a Cup of Kindness. *The New York Times,* September 17, 2005, p. C-3.

COMPANY INFORMATION

Starbucks Corporation
P.O. Box 34067
Seattle, WA 98124–1067
(206) 447–1575
www.starbucks.com
New York Stock Exchange symbol: SBUX

George Soros

The world's most successful hedge fund manager, George Soros, is a self-made multibillionaire. Born in Budapest, Hungary, Soros studied in England at the London School of Economics (LSE) and held several unsatisfying jobs until he came to the United States in 1956 as a financial analyst. He made his fortune and helped significantly increase the fortune of many others when he started his own group of hedge funds, one of which is the notable Quantum Fund. His net worth reached a peak of an estimated eleven billion dollars, and today Soros is said to still be worth over seven billion dollars. He is no longer actively managing the funds on a day-to-day basis but has moved into the realm of helping to set economic and political policies worldwide. At age seventy-six, his influence is felt around the globe, although Soros himself remains a comparatively un-known figure in the world of business icons. Today he is chairman of the Open Society Institute and the founder of a network of philanthropic organizations that are active in more than fifty countries.

Soros first founded the international investment fund, Soros Fund Man-agement LLC, a private investment management firm that serves as principal advisor to the Quantum Group of Funds, a series of international investment vehicles, with Jim Rogers in 1969. The fund returned more than 4,000 percent over ten years, making Soros one of the world's richest men. In July 2000 Soros merged the Quantum Fund with the Quantum Emerging Growth Fund to form the Quantum Endowment Fund. The Quantum Fund is generally rec-ognized as one of the most successful investment funds ever, returning an av-erage 31 percent annually throughout its more than thirty-year history.

In 1992, Soros's Quantum Fund became celebrated for "breaking" the Bank of England and forcing it to devalue the pound. He did this by selling ten billion dollars' worth of British pounds sterling short, and in the process earning the fund a $1 billion profit. On September 16 of that year, the day dubbed Black Wednesday in England, Soros sold short the currency that the Bank of England refused to float; it also refused to raise its interest rates to match those of other countries participating in the European Exchange Rate Mechanism. Soros's actions forced the Bank of England to devalue the pound sterling. That move marked the beginning of a new era of market dominance over political con-siderations. Soros continued to look at foreign currencies to assess their real value and was a few years later, blamed for forcing sharp devaluations in Southeast Asian currencies.

Soros acquired the image of a daring pirate capable of roiling markets. The popular image of hedge-fund managers became that of swashbuckling risk takers who captured outsized profits or suffered horrendous losses. Indeed, his losses were staggering. He lost at least a billion dollars during the Russian market crisis in 1998. In another instance, he was jolted by a ricochet effect on international currencies and dropped $650 million for his clients in two days. Indeed, Soros was an incredible risk taker. Although he studied the markets intensely and saw patterns, when he bet on something he was generally so confident in his assessment that he bet millions more than the total value of his funds. That kind of action took an incredible amount of courage, and it usually paid off.

Soros spent his early years surrounded by what he remembers as an ad-venture. He and his family evaded capture by the Nazis by following his father's well-planned strategy. After surviving the Nazi occupation, the family also survived and escaped the Russian occupation. At seventeen, Soros left Communist Hungary by himself in 1947 to head for England, where he graduated from LSE. While a student there, Soros became familiar with the work of the philosopher Karl Popper, whose work on open societies had a profound influence on his thinking and later on his professional and philanthropic activities.

Soros is now a committed philanthropist and prodemocracy activist and has given away five billion dollars over the last twenty-five years through a network of foundations. He is now devoted to encouraging transitional and emerging nations to become open societies, both in the sense of freedom of commerce and tolerance of new ideas and different modes of thinking and behavior. Beginning in 1979, Soros's money enabled black students to attend the University of Cape Town in South Africa. Throughout the years, Soros has funded numerous nongovernmental organizations (NGOs) purportedly designed to aid in the creation of open societies, particularly in areas of the world where that concept seems miles from reality. These NGOs include the Human Rights Watch, Radio Free Europe/Radio Liberty, the International Crisis Group, and most notably, the Open Society Institute (OSI), for which Soros is chairman. Spending more than four hundred million dollars annually, the OSI develops and implements "a range of programs focusing on civil society, education, media, public health, and human rights as well as social, legal, and economic reform." All in all, Soros has been directly and financially involved in philanthropic organizations that reach more than fifty countries. Based primarily in Central and Eastern Europe and the former Soviet Union—but also in Africa, Latin America, Asia, and the United States—these foundations are dedicated to building and maintaining the infrastructure and institutions of an open society. In 1992, Soros founded Central European University, with its primary campus in Budapest.

The lines of philanthropy and politics are sometimes blurred where Soros is concerned. Indeed, it might be impossible to be to so involved in global activities and avoid being political. His support for the Solidarity labor movement in Poland, as well as the Czechoslovakian human rights organization Charter 77, contributed to the end of Soviet Union's rule in those nations. His funding and organization of Georgia's Rose Revolution was considered crucial to its success by Russian and Western observers, although Soros said his role has been "greatly exaggerated." In the United States he is known for donating large sums of money to efforts to defeat President George W. Bush's bid for re-election.

Soros is an intellectual who has remained a committed student of philosophy. He is also a prolific author, having written eight books: *The Bubble of America Supremacy: Correcting the Misuse of American Power* (2004), *George Soros on Globalization* (2002), *The Alchemy of Finance* (1987), *Opening the Soviet System* (1990) *Underwriting Democracy* (1991), *Soros on Soros: Staying Ahead of the Curve* (1995), *The Crisis of Global Capitalism: Open Society Endangered* (1998), and *Open Society: Reforming Global Capitalism* (2000). His articles and essays on politics, society, and economics regularly appear in major newspapers and magazines around the world.

THE EARLY YEARS

George Soros was born on August 12, 1930, in Hungary, as the second child of Tivadar and Erzebet Soros. His brother, Paul, had been born four years earlier.

Soros's father was by all accounts a strong and resourceful man. He was a great father who loved his sons passionately. The Soros family was originally the Schwartz family until Tivadar changed the name. Tivadar was trained as a lawyer but in 1914 enlisted in the Austro-Hungarian army because he thought it would be an adventure and would prove advantageous for a future legal career. However, he was caputred by the Russians and taken to a prison camp in Siberia, where he would stay until 1920, well after a treaty ended the war. It was in prison that he learned the Esperanto language, in which he would later write books. Tivadar was a strong influence on his boys. He pushed them into sports and taught them to be independent and adaptable to new situations, once sending a young Soros to travel on his own to another town. He didn't tell him until later that he had paid an adult to follow him. Tivadar had decided that he wanted to enjoy life to the fullest and set about only working a couple of hours a day, the rest devoted to appreciating what life had to offer.

Soros was drawing and skiing by the time he was four years old. The family was relatively well off because of the money his mother had brought into the marriage. They enjoyed a large apartment that faced the Hungarian Parliament building and a summer house on Lupa Island in the Danube. Soros was not a good student, doing especially poorly in math; however, he was well read and enjoyed the classics. Soros developed an interest in art and literature.

During the first years of World War II, there was little change for the Soros family. Gradually, changes began to affect Hungarian Jews. In 1938 Hungary passed a law that defined who was and who was not a Jew and limited Jewish participation in the professions. By 1941, Soros's school classes were segregated and his brother had to go to a newly formed Jewish school. Word of mass shootings and slave labor came, but few believed the stories were true.

When Soros was thirteen years old, the Germans invaded Hungary. Within days, Adolf Eichmann arrived in Budapest to oversee the destruction of the 750,000 Jews living in the country. He set up the Jewish Council, and Soros began working there as a courier. When he was given messages to deliver, he rode his bike home to let his father see the messages first. They were summonses that were being sent to lawyers in alphabetical order. Tivadar knew his time was limited. Soros deliverd the messages, but told the recipients they would be deported if they showed up. After he did this, Tivadar ordered him to stop working at the council.

Tivadar planned for the family to live as Gentiles to avoid the Germans, but Tivadar and Soros went out one day with the yellow patch sewn onto their clothing to see what people's reactions would be. Although this seemed like a fun reconnaisance mission to young Soros at the time, he was later troubled by the hatred he experienced that day. Tivadar used his connections to arrange for documents for his family. Some of these were borrowed, and some were forged. Tivadar obtained forged medical certificates stating that his boys had been circumcised because of the medical condition pymosis. Tivadar provided documents for others, as well. He decided that the family needed to live separately in case one of them was discovered.

Paul, under the name Janos Balazs, was sent away first to a room in the poor part of town. Soros, whose new name was Sandor Kiss, was sent to live with a man named Baumbach, an employee of the Ministry of Agriculture, whom Tivadar paid to let Soros pose as his godson. Soros later had to move because he was recognized by a classmate and went to where his mother was living at the lake resort. He called his mother Auntie for the next few months. Soros continued to read works of literature during this time and remembers this time as idyllic. He returned to the capital to move in with the Pohaszka family. In the capital, the reality of war was more pressing. Soros remembers seeing many corpses before the Russians took control on January 12, 1945.

The Russian occupation for Soros was a continuation of the exhileration he felt during the Nazi occupation. As he said later in life, "For me, this was the most exciting time of my life. For an adolescent to be in real danger, having a feeling he is inviolate, having a father whom he adored acting as a hero and having an evil confronting you and getting the better of it, I mean, being in command of the situation, even though you're in danger, but basically maneuvering successfully, what more can you ask for?" Compared to that, none of the risks he has taken as an adult have compared. Tivadar later wrote in his book *Maskerado* of his ordeal to survive fascist Hungary and help many people escape it.

It was during this time that Soros first was involved in financial transactions. His father would send him to the black market to trade money and jewelry because he would be less likely to arouse suspicion. His father's clients soon began giving him their money to exchange as well. Soros also gained broader economic insight. He noticed the very rapid inflation of the Hungarian pengo and the stability of the U.S. dollar and saw that inflation was being deliberately engineered by those in power. He deduced that the reason this was happening was because the Communists wanted to wipe out all the savings people had and buy up everything of value with the new money printed. Then, after the Communists had acquired what they wanted, they switched to a new currency and printed very little.

By March 1946, it was clear that the Soviets were not leaving and were going to make it difficult, and soon impossible, for anyone to leave Hungary. Tivadar asked Soros where he wanted to go, and he said he thought he might want to go to England because he had heard BBC Radio. Tivadar had a distant relative there, and he encouraged Soros to write him to see if he could help Soros get admitted to school there. So, when he was seventeen, in August,

1947, Soros left Hungary under the guise of participating in an Esperanto youth congress in the West. (Soros was taught to speak the language from birth and thus is one of the rare native Esperanto speakers.) He made his way to England, where he remained for nine years.

At first he lived with his distant relatives, the Franks, until he signed up for an English course and moved to a bed and breakfast in Islington. He failed the English portion of the test, however, that would allow him into LSE, so he enrolled instead at the Kentish Town Polytechnic, a commuter college without reputation. He was also very poor at this time and had to work multiple jobs, violating his visa. One of these jobs was as a farm worker picking apples. Another was a dishwasher at a diner, and another at a mannequin factory, where he attached wigs to the mannequin scalps; he was fired from this job for not doing it properly. He soon started to skip his classes at the Polytechnic and sneak into classes at LSE. He was kicked out of the Polytechnic when they found out what he was doing, but he took another set of entrance exams to LSE and passed. In fall of 1949, he began attending LSE full time. He graduated in 1952.

CAREER PATH

After graduating from LSE, Soros was introduced by a school friend to the owner of L. S. Mayer, a company that distributed handbags, souvenirs, and cheap jewelry. Soros went to work as an assistant salesperson and found the work "boring, demeaning, and meaningless," According to Michael Kaufman's biography. He was there for several years before he quit to work for a company that sold souvenirs and knickknacks to tobacconists. Soros got a company car and a territory around London. He did not do well and was assigned to another territory. He was depressed because he didn't like his job and had never really taken to England. He knew he needed to make a radical break and decided to try to get into a merchant bank.

He was finally hired by a firm whose owners also came from Hungary. However, the position still didn't fit him well. He didn't do well as a bookkeeper or clerk, but eventually he found himself interested in what the analysts within the company were doing. He liked what he saw, especially in arbitrage—buying in one market and selling in another—which required speed and risk. Just as he was getting to know what he liked, he was delayed on a trip back from Paris one weekend because of weather, and as a result, lost his job. The company gave him time to look for another job, and he found one from another of the firm's trainees—Robert Mayer. Mayer's father had a small brokerage firm in New York, where Soros's brother, Paul, was now living, and he needed an arbitrage trader.

While waiting to transfer, Soros had a great success at the company he was leaving. Ford Motor Company had gone public through an international distribution of shares. Soros realized that the demand for the shares in America would be higher than the demand in Europe. At his urging, the firm bought up Ford shares in London and sold them in New York. Soros got a percentage of the profits. As a result of this and his job offer in America, he was given a higher salary and more leeway in trading. As a result of his investing, he had about five thousand dollars when he left for New York in September 1956.

When Soros arrived in New York, he had a plan to earn enough money on Wall Street to support himself as an author and philosopher. He thought he would need about five hundred thousand dollars, which he planned to earn in five years.

F. M. Mayer was not a member of the New York Stock Exchange. It functioned as an over-the-counter trader, and Soros's job was to handle arbitrage in foreign securities. When the Suez crisis erupted into violence, Soros found luck by trading in oil shares with European contacts. When the feverish trade in oil shares subsided, he found a new market in what he calls internal arbitrage. A company seeking capital would sell bonds that had warrants attached to them. After a specified period of time, the warrants could be used to acquire shares. Soros came up with a scheme for trading both the bonds and shares independently by employing due bills. When he sold the bonds to a broker, the broker would give him back a due bill declaring that he would deliver the shares when they became detachable. Soros would then sell the due bills. Soros found markets for this type of trading in several industries, establishing relationships with the big investment houses.

Three years after starting with F. M. Mayer and still doing exceedingly well, Soros left the position because they questioned one of his decisions. He went to work for Wertheim & Company, a larger company and a member of the New York Stock Exchange. He was the assistant to the head of the foreign trading department. Here he focused or European securities and sought to make himself an expert. He looked at different European companies and tried to determine their real values, sometimes work backwards from their tax returns. One of the first bargains he found was Dresdner Bank, which had hidden value in its portfolio.

Soros's first setback, after a long string of incredible successes, was with the Studebaker. He had put a large portion of his savings into the car company, going both long and short on the stock. He thought he could manage the timing of his stock sales to take advantage of both, but he came very close to being entirely wiped out. During this time, in late 1962, he also had another setback at Wertheim with a Japanese insurance company. Although it turned out well in the end, Soros was upset with how his company treated him during this situation and left. He was soon working for Arnhold & S. Bleichroeder, after taking several months off to pursue philosophy and travel. While in Italy, he spent time analyzing Olivetti shares and bought shares for his soon-to-be employer. He sold them for a much higher price before he sent the cable advising Arnhold of the sale.

In July 1963, the government made it less lucrative for U.S. clients to buy foreign securities, effectively halting Soros's business. He stayed at Arnhold for the next couple of years with little to do and turned his attention once again to philosophy.

In 1965, Soros set up a model stock account with a hundred thousand dollars of the firm's money. He purchased sixteen stocks and tracked their progress. He learned a great deal from this exercise, and by 1967 had made the account profitable enough that the company established it as the First Eagle Fund and opened it up to clients, with Soros serving as the manager. It started with three million dollars in capital, and Soros invested his own money in it. Soros brought Jim Rogers aboard in 1968 to act as an analyst.

Soros set up a second fund two years later, the Double Eagle Fund, which, unlike the First Eagle mutual fund, was a hedge fund. Hedge funds had been around for a while before this, and the basic idea was to profit by going both long and short on shares of companies within a given industry. This way, the investor could hedge against industrywide macroeconomic factors while benefiting from the specific performances of individual companies. Hedge funds were exempted from government oversight and regulations. The investors also had no say in how their money was being managed in a hedge fund—it was up to the money manager. The First Eagle mutual fund was organized as an offshore account to give Soros more autonomy, and he did the same with the Double Eagle fund. The investors were limited to non-Americans who had tax-free status in the United States. In his dealings with these funds, Soros developed the idea of his theory of reflexivity, basically stating that the market is flawed and stock prices are not merely passive reflections of a company's value, they are part of a process in which both the stock price and the fortune of the company play a role. Soros believed that the discrepancy between the participants' expectations and the actual course of events was a factor in the process of stock valuation. These factors played off of each other, constantly changing the values as they interacted. They fit a pattern of boom and bust, which Soros just needed to recognize in order to profit. Though the boom–bust theory had been around for a while, Soros refined it by taking into account the fact that stock prices were agents of change rather than stagnant reflections of value.

In 1970, Soros and Rogers got involved with real estate investment trusts and made a great deal of money. In August 1973, they started their own business, amicably leaving the company with Double Eagle worth seventeen million dollars. They established Soros Fund Management on Columbus Circle in Manhattan. Many of the Double Eagle investors followed Soros. Starting with thirteen million dollars, Soros grew the investment to eighteen million in just one year. Those who followed Soros saw their overall investment for every $100,000 increase to more than $353 million by the end of 1997. Although known to his investors, Soros was not well known at all to the general investing public. In 1975 the *Wall Street Journal* ran a front-page article on the fund, however, noting the high earning it had gained for its foreign shareholders.

The fund was set up in Curaçao, Netherlands Antilles, and even Soros did not know who his investors were. He also set up Quantum Partners, a holding company, in the Cayman Islands, and Soros Fund Management in New York.

In 1978, Soros was charged with stock manipulation by the Securities and Exchange Commission (SEC). He signed a consent decree, which meant he neither admitted nor denied the charges, but agreed not to act in such a way in the future. The fund continued to see extraordinary growth, and by 1978, the value was beyond a hundred million dollars.

Soros and Rogers split in 1979, and Soros renamed his fund Quantum. He also decided to take more time off and began looking for a fund manager. In 1980, the fund grew by 102 percent to reach $381 million. Soros had been rich for a while, but now he was very rich. In 1981 Soros was in the June issue of *Institutional Investor,* which called him the world's greatest money manager. Ironically, he saw the fund's value drop by 26 percent that year, the first time it had dropped. He wrote a letter to his investors telling them he would be hiring out the fund management. Many investors defected, so many that the small number of American shareholders sanctioned by the SEC was coming close to exceeding the limit. The fund dropped in value from four hundred million dollars to two hundred million. By 1982 it was back up again by 57 percent, beginning another winning streak that would last fourteen more years.

In 1979, Soros also set up the Open Society Fund, and although he had been turning his interests toward open societies, his motives for setting up the fund were selfish. Setting up the trust was good business sense for tax reasons, he admitted. In apartheid South Africa, Soros started his charitable efforts by providing stipends to students at multiracial institutions. Soros was watching what was happening in Russia and countries affected by communism. He had thought he could make a difference in creating more open societies and set about educating himself further, attending weekly meetings at Helsinki Watch and international conferences. He contributed money to Helsinki Watch and Amnesty International as well as sending it to specific causes in South Africa. He thought of these investments as an adventure and experimented with them.

In 1987, Soros chose Stanley Druckenmiller to succeed him as Quantum's chief trader and strategist, although Soros continued to oversee the fund while Druckenmiller was there. Druckenmiller, with Soros's help, engineered a transaction that would make Soros instantly famous. On Black Wednesday, September 16, 1992, they sold short more than ten billion dollars' worth of British pounds sterling, profiting from the Bank of England's reluctance to either raise its interest rates to levels comparable to those of other European Exchange Rate Mechanism countries or to float its currency. Finally, the Bank of England was forced to withdraw the currency out of the European Exchange Rate Mechanism and to devalue the pound, and Soros earned an estimated $1.1 billion in the process. He was dubbed "the man who broke the Bank of England." In 1997, during the Asian financial crisis, then Malaysian Prime Minister Mahathir bin Mohamad accused Soros of bringing down the Malaysian currency, the ringgit.

In 2002, Soros was fined two million dollars by a court in France for insider trading, which Soros denied.

Soros continued to set up foundations, completely separate from government entities, in previously communist countries to encourage intellectual development. He thought that helping to create a robust civil society in lands emerging from communism or from poverty was far more likely to create a foundation for democracy than the mere opening of privatized economic markets or the import of a constitution. The Open Society Institute (OSI) was created in 1993 to support his foundations in Central and Eastern Europe and the former Soviet Union. Between 1994 and 2000, Soros's contributions to his foundations was more than $2.5 billion. Through OSI, Soros aims to shape public policy to promote democratic governance, human rights, and economic, legal, and social reform. On a local level, OSI implements a range of initiatives to support the rule of law, education, public health, and independent media. At the same time, OSI works to build alliances across borders and continents on issues such as combating corruption and rights abuses.

Despite large financial successes over a dozen years, when the Quantum fund fell by $7.6 billion, due in large part to the biotech boom and bust, Druckenmiller resigned. Today, Soros's funds are managed more conservatively and are worth approximately thirteen billion dollars. On the philanthropic front, the network of Soros foundations encompasses more than sixty countries, including the United States.

PERSONAL LIFE

Soros has been married twice, to Annaliese Witschak and to Susan Weber, but he is now divorced. He has five children: Robert, Andrea, and Jonathan with his first wife, Annaliese, and Alexander and Gregory with his second wife, Susan.

His marriage to his first wife, Annaliese Witschak, ended as a result of his desire for a more public life. She had always wanted a private life, whereas he hungered for more friends and a social life. His work took him away from his family, and he has openly conceded his failures as a father. At the time of the separation, Jonathan was nine, Andrea was thirteen, and Robert was fifteen. The day he moved out of his house, he played tennis; on the court next to him was Susan Weber, who would become his second wife. He moved into a small furnished apartment and didn't take much with him; he was by all accounts very generous in the divorce settlement. After twenty-five years together, Soros and his second wife, Susan, also divorced. She received roughly eighty million dollars in the settlement.

Erzebet and Tivadar came to live with Soros soon after he arrived in New York. His older brother, Paul, is an engineer and a well-known philanthropist, investor, and New York socialite. He is Jewish by birth, although his parents only practiced the religion in public in his early years to remain friendly with their community. Soros is an atheist. Concealing who he was at fourteen in Nazi Hungary had quite an effect. He developed a sense of shame because of this that inspired him to work harder to be successful, even beyond the point where he had so much he couldn't spend it all anyway.

Soros believed for most of his life that charity was a "misguided ego trip" and contributed very little. However, he has become one of the world's biggest philanthropists in the area. Combining his interest in philosophy, especially in open societies, and his knowledge of finance and economic policy, Soros has come to be a major player in the global development. It is estimated that he has given away over four billion dollars. He has been active as a philanthropist since the 1970s, when he began providing funds to help black students attend the University of Cape Town in apartheid South Africa and funding dissident movements behind the iron curtain. Soros's philanthropic funding in Eastern Europe mostly occurs through OSI and the Soros Foundations, which sometimes go under other names. The OSI says it has spent over four hundred

---

John Bogle of Vanguard

John C. ("Jack") Bogle is the founder and retired CEO of the Vanguard Group. Under his leadership, the company grew to be the second largest mutual fund company in the world. Headquartered in Malvern, Pennsylvania, Vanguard comprises more than one hundred mutual funds with current assets totaling about $550 billion. The Vanguard 500 Index Fund, the largest fund in the group, was founded by Bogle in 1975. It was the first index mutual fund. Bogle served as chairman and CEO until 1996 and senior chairman until 2000. *Fortune* named Bogle one of the investment industry's four Giants of the 20th Century.

Bogle was born on May 8, 1929, in Montclair, New Jersey. He attended Blair Academy on a full scholarship, earned his undergraduate degree from Princeton University in 1951, and attended evening and weekend classes at the University of Pennsylvania. Upon graduation he went to work for Walter L. Morgan at Wellington Management Company. After a distinguished career culminating with the position of chairman at Wellington, he founded Vanguard in 1974. He is famous for his insistence, in numerous media appearances and in writing, on the superiority of index funds over traditional actively managed mutual funds.

million dollars annually in recent years. Notable projects have included aid to scientists and universities throughout Central and Eastern Europe, help to civilians during the siege of Sarajevo, worldwide efforts to repeal drug prohibition laws, and Transparency International.

Soros has a keen interest in philosophy, and his philosophical outlook is largely influenced by Karl Popper, whom he studied under at the London School of Economics. His Open Society Institute is named after Popper's two-volume work, *The Open Society and Its Enemies.*

Soros has written eight books and has popularized the concepts of dynamic disequilibrium, static disequilibrium, and near-equilibrium conditions. His writings also focus heavily on the concept of reflexivity.

LEADERSHIP LESSONS

Essentially, a hedge fund, like the ones managed by Soros, is much like a mutual fund in that investors buy shares in the fund and invest those pooled funds. One important difference is the level of risk assumed. While most mutual funds simply buy stocks dollar-for-dollar with investors' funds, hedge funds use leverage. That is, they take a position several times that of the amount of funds invested with them. That can lead to spectacular returns—or spectacular losses. Another key difference is that the hedge fund may go aggressively "long" in one position and aggressively "short" in another. A short position involves borrowing an asset and then selling it. This shorting can also contribute to the leveraging of the portfolio. For example, a fund may borrow yen and pay a very low interest rate, say 1 percent. It may sell those yen and buy dollars, which it in turn uses to buy Treasury bills yielding 5 percent. Now, as long as the exchange rate between the dollar and the yen stays unchanged, the fund does extraordinarily well, making a profit of 4 percent on each yen borrowed. Because the fund is leveraged, this means a big return on investors' capital. A ten-to-one leverage position on that play will mean a 40 percent return to the investor. Of course, if the yen were to rise in value, it would be more expensive to pay back the borrowed yen, and the total return could fall rapidly. The fund might choose to cover or "hedge" that risk by making an offsetting investment in the foreign exchange market. Or the fund might choose to bet that the dollar would rise and the yen fall, leaving the fund's position unhedged. If the fund is right, it makes money both by "arbitraging" the difference between U.S. and Japanese rates and by making a correct guess on foreign exchange movements.

To be successful in this arena, Soros had to have some unique skills. He had to be able to manage a great deal of information. He also had to act very quickly on that information and take enormous risks. He had to be able to "pull the trigger," as he called it. He was very emotionally tied into how his funds did, despite his best efforts not to be. His keys to success lie in the area of information management, executing decisions, and of course, taking a healthy share of the profits. Soros's deal was 20 percent of the fund's yearly profits plus one percent of all assets under management.

Be Brash

"Invest first and investigate later," Soros would tell his fund managers. What's right at 9 a.m. might not be right ten minutes later, in his view. In making his billions of dollars, Soros knew that he had to be bold and take action quickly. He would bet large sums of money and encourage his managers to do the same. In the sales that earned him the title of "the man who broke the Bank of England," Soros listened to his manager, Druckenmiller, explain what he wanted to do, and then told him to do it on a much larger scale. In an act which he later indicated was primarily aimed at gaining him political influence with the U.S. and British governments, whom he did not believe were doing enough to promote reforms in the former communist countries of Eastern Europe, Soros took on the British pound on September 16, 1992, a day which was to become legendary in the financial markets. At the time, the British pound sterling was in the European Exchange Rate Mechanism (ERM), a semifixed exchange rate regime where currencies were only allowed to move against each other within quite tight bands. The system was intended to facilitate economic convergence among the member states of the European Union as a precursor to full monetary union. The ERM threatened to become unstable following the dramatic events leading to the reunification of West and East Germany and the costly burden of financing this reunion for the German government.

Because Germany was the largest and most influential economy in the European Union (EU), the German deutsche mark had been the peg upon which all other currencies hung. Any difficulties experienced by the German economy could therefore destabilize the ERM and have adverse consequences for all the economies of EU members. A public remark made to this effect by the president of the German Bundesbank drew the attention of Soros. At the time, it was also widely thought in Britain that the pound had gone into the ERM at too high a value in relation to the underlying performance of the British economy and that this value was unsustainable in the long term. British interest rates were high in order to help maintain the value of the pound by attracting financial investors and this was damaging the British domestic economy. Many economic commentators were calling for a withdrawal from the ERM in order to take the "squeeze" off the domestic economy and to allow sterling to fall to its true market level in a floating exchange rate regime. However, the British government had placed ERM membership as a centerpiece of its economic policy and had given strong guarantees that it would strongly defend its membership. Soros bet that the pound would not be able to hold its value against the other ERM currencies. He began short-selling sterling, pitting the might of his billions of dollars worth of funds against the Bank of England, which had to fight to maintain sterling in accordance with its ERM value by using its foreign currency reserves to buy the pound. Soros sparked a wave of selling of pounds and in a desperate move the British government eventually put interest rates up a total of five percentage points that day in order to attract investors, realizing that it could not realistically defend the pound in the currency markets given the extent of the selling activity. This did not deter the wave of selling as currency dealers increasingly realized the impact of Soros's actions and joined the bandwagon. Eventually the British government had to give in and announced that it was leaving the ERM. Soros earned a billion dollars, one of the most profitable currency dealings ever. Following its departure from the ERM, the price of the pound fell considerably. Sterling eventually picked up and settled in a price range well below its lowest permissible ERM value.

The way that Soros excelled was in executing his decisions. He bet that he was right, and he bet large amounts of money—many times the value of the funds that he held. One of the ways he is able to make bold decisions so quickly is by limiting the amount of staff he has on hand. No one prepares fancy reports for him or his investors. The information that is collected goes straight to Soros, and he ensures there is no bureaucracy to slow it down.

Soros has said that fortune favors the brave. If he has a chance to make a killing in a market, he is not afraid to put an important proportion of his chips into it.

Study the Market

After studying conventional economic theories of the market at LSE, Soros was highly critical of conventional wisdom and developed his own views of how markets operate, which he termed the theory of reflexivity.

His theory of reflexivity is based on the notion that people always act on the basis of imperfect knowledge, whether in the financial markets or everyday life, and although they seek the truth about the world they can never attain it because the very act of looking distorts the picture. People's perceptions about reality are therefore incomplete and can never be complete because their very actions change reality. Soros saw that in the economic and social world there is a neverending feedback mechanism between perceptions and reality, which is guided by human actions made on the basis of imperfect knowledge. This is the process of reflexivity.

Soros based this theory on a critique of conventional economic thought, both generally in terms of its impossibly objective view of human behavior and specifically in terms of its view of the way in which markets operate. He does not believe that market demand and supply are determined independently of each other and that they interact to set an equilibrium price and believes the market to be fallible and inefficient. Soros argues that actions are not based upon indisputable facts, which he believes cannot possibly exist, but upon people's expectations of what their actions will achieve. Soros therefore views all human action as being essentially speculative and actual outcomes may be different from expected outcomes because once actions are implemented they may create a different set of circumstances to those anticipated. Markets are therefore characterized by dynamic disequilibrium, where perceptions of reality may vary considerably from what is actually happening. Conventional economic theory is particularly inappropriate to the operations of financial markets because the price is primarily the cause of buyers and sellers actions and not merely the end result. He believes that characteristically fast changing circumstances, and widespread imperfect knowledge make dealing in the financial markets particularly speculative and thus open to arbitrage.

To understand as best he can the information he receives, Soros maintains one of the best global intelligence networks anywhere. Information flows in from a wide variety of contacts and analysts all around the world, including the companies in which the fund invests. Unlike the CIA, the foreign service bureaucracy, or even the staffs of central banks, this information network is subject to a test of profitability. If the fund doesn't make money, the information network gets pruned. His offices are designed for the information age, with computer screens dominating the desks and intermittent interruptions. When he was working only for his funds, Soros's entire life was devoted to it. He lived and breathed the developments of the market, and his focus was on market-breaking news that was intense and immediate. Information is extremely valuable in his industry, and to take advantage of it, Soros scans the globe for information. Much of the information flow is in the public domain but may not be universally known. Soros reads international journals and newspapers and receives valuable information from people around the world. Soros is also very familiar with the reporters who write the news stories. He can place the information provided in the proper perspective.

> *"An open society is a society which allows its members the greatest possible degree of freedom in pursuing their interests compatible with the interests of others,"* Soros said. *"The Bush administration merely has a narrower definition of self-interest. It does not include the interests of others."*
> George Soros

Understand the Interaction of Variables

The efficient market's hypothesis, particularly in its extreme form, holds that all information about the future is in the market at any given time. Supposedly, rational actors take the available information and price assets accordingly. However, Soros disagrees and wonders how any supposedly rational process could produce the kinds of price volatility that we have seen recently. While economists are predisposed to view markets as self-correcting and rational, Soros recognizes the volatility of markets and tries to exploit that. Part of Soros's theory of reflexivity is the economic parallel to the Heisenberg uncertainty principle in physics. Heisenberg held that simply by measuring

"How can we escape from the trap that the terrorists have set us? Only by recognizing that the war on terrorism cannot be won by waging war. We must, of course, protect our security; but we must also correct the grievances on which terrorism feeds. . . . Crime requires police work, not military action."

George Soros

something you affect it, and therefore it cannot have the same value that you measured. The name of the main Soros fund, Quantum, comes from that analogy to physics. Soros believes that there is reflexivity in financial markets because investors are always discounting future values. However, the future is not something that is out there independent of how an investor might discount it. So, Soros concludes that the present valuation of a stream of future earnings can vary in the present, not in response to what happens in the future, but simply by the act of discounting it today. As to the reason for his success, Soros says that he gets ahead because he knows there is nothing to be discounted. He does not look at the objective reality of a situation but rather on what he believes others are thinking.

POLITICAL INFLUENCE

Soros was not a large donor to U.S. political causes until the presidential election of 2004. In this election, Soros gave more than twenty-three million dollars to Democratic candidates. Soros's heavy criticisms of George W. Bush made him a figure of controversy. In an interview with the *Washington Post* on November 11, 2003, Soros said that removing Bush from office was the "central focus of my life" and "a matter of life and death" for which he would willingly sacrifice his entire fortune. Soros has loudly criticized Bush's policies.

Soros gave three million dollars to the Center for American Progress and committed five million to MoveOn.org, while he and his friend Peter Lewis each gave America Coming Together ten million dollars. On September 28, 2004, he dedicated more money to the campaign and kicked off his own multistate tour with a speech, "Why We Must Not Re-elect President Bush," delivered at the National Press Club in Washington, DC, on his crusade to defeat President Bush.

In addition, he has had a profound effect on other governments and has become known as something akin to a statesman. Most analysts claim that Soros played a crucial role in the collapsed of socialism in eastern Europe. From 1979, he distributed $3 million a year to dissidents, including Poland's Solidarity movement, Charter 77 in Czechoslovakia and Andrei Sakharov in the Soviet Union. In 1984, he founded his first Open Society Institute in Hungary and pumped millions of dollars into opposition movements and independent media.

His funding and organization of Georgia's Rose Revolution was considered crucial to its success by Russian and Western observers. Although Soros said his role has been "greatly exaggerated," he has been very influential in helping to create significant political changes around the world.

CRITICS

Soros has blurred the lines between finance and politics, and indeed criticism of his actions has focused on these areas, although the criticism, too, seems to blur. Critics claim that Soros has an undue influence on currency markets through Quantum Fund.

While he made billions from the Far Eastern currency crash in 1997, some observers suggest that he behaved irresponsibly by misusing his wide influence, most notably then Malaysian Prime Minister Mahathir bin Mohamad, who accused Soros of bringing down the ringgit, the Malaysian currency. He responded to accusations of being personally responsible for many financial collapses, including those in England, Eastern Europe, and Thailand, by saying that, as a market participant, he didn't need to be concerned with the consequences of his actions.

Soros made both money and a good deal of his reputation by his activities in forcing the Bank of England to leave the European exchange rate mechanism in 1992. Largely as a result of that decision, Britain has had the best economic performance of any of the European countries. In fact, Stan Druckenmiller, the fund's chief investment strategist, was given a certificate of knighthood for his service to the British economy. Soros believes that hedge funds force discipline on the central bank. But even if there are significant long-term benefits, Soros recognizes that the result can be a disastrous short-term event in financial markets.

Soros is one of his own biggest critics. Since childhood, he has analyzed himself to a great extent, reflecting on his shortcomings and mistakes to draw lessons from them. Even in his own mind, Soros is quite ambivalent about the role that hedge funds play in stabilizing the world economy. He acknowledges that on some occasions they provide a valuable service, when the institutions of government default. But by and large, he is not a fan of the role he plays when he exploits a central bank in a developing country. However, he also concludes that many of these countries do not have a proper democracy, with newspapers that can criticize which keep central banks honest, Soros believes.

Some critics charge that Soros's political and philanthropic activities are merely a mask for more selfish aims. They say that Soros appears to have no problem working to further his own self-interest economically, while at the same time lobbying for a drastic overhaul of the global financial system.

Soros has been criticized for his large donations, as he also pushed for the Bipartisan Campaign Reform Act of 2002, which was intended to ban "soft money" contributions to federal election campaigns. Soros has responded that his donations to unaffiliated organizations do not raise the same corruption issues as donations directly to the candidates or political parties.

Soros has many political critics amongst American conservatives and supporters of Israel. Supporters of the Bush administration dislike his contributions to campaigns against Bush. At a Jewish forum in New York City, Soros partially attributed a recent resurgence of anti-Semitism to the policies of Israel and the United States, and to successful Jews such as himself:

> There is a resurgence of anti-Semitism in Europe. The policies of the Bush administration and the Sharon administration contribute to that. It's not specifically anti-Semitism, but it does manifest itself in anti-Semitism as well. I'm critical of those policies. If we change that direction, then anti-Semitism also will diminish. I can't see how one could confront it directly....I'm also very concerned about my own role because the new anti-Semitism holds that the Jews rule the world....As an unintended consequence of my actions...I also contribute to that image.

Soros blames many of the world's problems on the failures inherent in what he characterizes as market fundamentalism. His opposition to many aspects of globalization has also made him a controversial figure.

POSSIBLE FUTURE IMPACT

Although Soros has made a fortune in the financial markets, he is now trying to change the system. He argues that the current system of financial speculation undermines healthy economic development in many underdeveloped countries. He feels that

> untrammeled intensification of laissez-faire capitalism and the spread of market values to all areas of life is endangering our open and democratic society....The doctrine of laissez-faire capitalism holds that the common good is best served by the uninhibited pursuit of self-interest. Unless it is tempered by the recognition of a common interest that ought to take precedence over particular interests, our system...is liable to break down.

Soros continues to work mainly with OSI to build free and open societies by making grants that strengthen civil society, reforming economic policy, sponsoring education at all levels, and advancing human rights, legal reform, public administration, media and communications, public health, and arts and culture.

TIMELINE

1930	August 12, Born to Tivadar and Erzebet Soros in Hungary.
1943	Nazi Germany invaded Hungary and the Soros family went into hiding.
1945	January 12, Russians took control of Hungary.

1947	Soros left his family to move to England.
1949	Began attending London School of Economics.
1952	Graduated from London School of Economics.
1956	Moved to New York to work for F. M. Mayer.
1959	Married Annaliese Witschak.
	Left F. M. Mayer and began working for Wertheim & Company.
1962	Left Wertheim & Company and began work for Arnhold & S. Bleichroeder.
1963	Robert Soros born.
1965	Andrea Soros born.
1967	Established First Eagle Fund.
1968	Brought in Jim Rogers as analyst.
1969	Set up Double Eagle Fund.
1970	Jonathan Soros born.
1973	Soros and Rogers left Arnhold to set up Soros Fund Management.
1979	Split with Rogers and renamed fund Quantum.
	Established Open Society Fund.
1983	Married Susan Weber.
1984	October 27, Alexander Soros born.
1987	Hired Stanley Druckenmiller to run Quantum fund.
1989	April 29, Gregory Soros born.
1992	Soros and Druckenmiller "broke" the Bank of England.
1993	Sets the Open Society Institute.
2004	Divorced Susan Weber.

RESOURCES

Camilleri, Joseph A. (Editor). *Democratizing Global Governance.* Gordonsville, VA: Palgrave Macmillan, 2002, pp. 67–68, 78, 83, 94–99, 123, 140.

Glancey, Keith S. *Entreprenurial Economics.* New York: Palgrave Publishers, 2000, pp. 64–68, 177.

Haseler, Stephen. *Super-Rich: The Unjust New World of Global Capitalism.* New York: Palgrave Publishers, 2000, pp. xv, 6, 124, 127, 167.

Kaufman, Michael T. *Soros: The Life and Times of a Messianic Billionaire.* New York: Alfred A. Knopf, 2002.

Lindsey, Lawrence B. *Economic Puppetmasters: Lessons from the Halls of Power.* Washington, DC: American Enterprise Institute for Public Policy Research, 1999, pp. 3, 4, 15, 132–133, 162, 169, 192.

Lowenstein, Roger. *When Genius Failed: The Rise & Fall of Long-Term Capital Management.* Westminster, MD: Random House, 2000, pp. 24–25, 41, 47, 112, 150–156, 177–180, 220.

Myers, Sondra (Editor). *Democracy Reader.* New York: International Debate Education Association, 2002, pp. xiv, 274–300.

Soros, George and Paul A. Volcker. *The Alchemy of Finance*. 1987. Hoboken, NJ: John Wiley & Sons, Inc.

———. *The Bubble of America Supremacy: Correcting the Misuse of American Power*. New York: Public Affairs (January 2004).

———. *The Crisis of Global Capitalism: Open Society Endangered*. New York: Public Affairs. 1998.

———. *George Soros on Globalization*. New York: Public Affairs. 2002.

———. *Open Society: Reforming Global Capitalism*. New York: Public Affairs. 2000.

———. *Opening the Soviet System*. New York: Public Affairs. 1990.

———. *Soros on Soros: Staying Ahead of the Curve*. New York: John Wiley & Sons, Inc. 1995.

———. *Underwriting Democracy: Encouraging Free Enterprise and Democratic Reform Among the Soviets and in Eastern Europe*. New York: Public Affairs. 1991.

COMPANY INFORMATION

Soros Fund Management LLC
888 Seventh Avenue, 33rd Floor
New York, NY 10106
Phone: (212) 262–6300
Fax: (212) 245–5154

Open Society Institute
400 West 59th Street
New York, NY 10019
Phone: (212) 548–0600
Fax: (212) 548–4600
www.soros.org

Courtesy of Photofest.

Martha Stewart

Martha Stewart, a "homekeeping" entrepreneur and cultural icon, has over-seen significant growth of the company she founded, Martha Stewart Living Omnimedia (MSLO). Her multimedia company, consisting of four business segments including publishing, television, merchandising, and Internet and direct commerce, saw revenues of almost two hundred million dollars in 2005. Stewart has become an icon of the entertaining and decorating world in large part because from early in her career she sought to establish and mine a brand identity. In Stewart's case, she is the brand. She has been able to leverage the well known Martha Stewart brand and extend that into new markets within the four business segments. Today, there are more than 2,800 Martha Stewart–branded products.

Although Stewart's high profile image is entwined with the brand, making the company reliant on her image, that did not seem to hurt MSLO in the initial years. For the company's first full year of operation as a publicly traded entity, the 2000 annual report listed revenues of $285 million.

In 2003, however, Stewart's business strategy was put to the test when she was indicted on on nine criminal counts, including securities fraud, obstruction of justice, and conspiracy, by the U.S. Securities and Exchange Commission. The charges stemmed from alleged insider trading related to the sale of 3,928 shares of ImClone Systems in 2001. Stewart resigned as CEO and chairman of MSLO on the same day she was indicted, but she remained on the company's board. Though the insider trading charges were thrown out, Stewart was found guilty of conspiracy, obstruction of justice, and two counts of making false statements, and she was sentenced to five months in prison. The losses were stunning. Stewart stepped down from the board of the company, and some analysts estimate that Stewart lost nearly four hundred million dollars in legal fees and lost business opportunities. The *New York Times* syndicate removed her name from her columns, and her TV program, which was broadcast on various CBS stations, was immediately dropped after the verdict.

Though the company has not completely recovered, there have been some promising signs. Stewart, though off the company's board, still owns about 60 percent of its stock. She is once again involved in the *Martha Stewart Living* family of magazines. Offerings of her products at Kmart have been expanded, and she is again the host of a daytime show, this one simply called *Martha*. She had another television show for one season, *The Apprentice: Martha Stewart*. In October 2005, Stewart released a new book called *The Martha Rules* that tells ten secrets of starting and managing a new business. Stewart also launched a twenty-four-hour satellite radio network with Sirius.

Stewart's continuing success despite her recent setbacks, can be credited to her ability to make the once tedious domestic routine, including cooking, cleaning, decorating, and sewing, fashionable again. Almost single-handedly, Stewart rejuvenated the field of "homekeeping," as she likes to call it, and built a hugely successful international business on the idea of style. Through virtually every media outlet, with her books, magazines, newspaper columns, television programs, catalog, and Web sites, Stewart has taught a mostly middle-aged, middle-class audience how to perfect domestic details.

> *"Without an open-minded mind, you can never be a great success."*
>
> Martha Stewart

Stewart's publishing venture consists of forty-eight titles, and in total her media properties reach more than eighty-eight million people a month. MSLO's publishing business, which provides 70 percent of the company's revenues, includes the magazines *Martha Stewart Living, Everyday Food, Martha Stewart Weddings, Body + Soul, Kids: Fun Stuff to Do Together,* and special-interest publications. Stewart's first book, *Entertaining,* has gone into thirty printings and has sold more than five hundred thousand copies. A series of books has been published in conjunction with Clarkson Potter and distributed by Oxmoor House and Random House. MSLO also publishes three weekly newspaper columns—*Living, Weddings,* and *Everyday Food*—through the *New York Times* Syndicate.

> *Martha Stewart Living* has received twelve Daytime Emmy Awards and sixty Emmy nominations since its debut, including three in 2005.

The television business segment includes the syndicated daily television show executive produced by Martha Stewart and Mark Burnett and distributed by NBC Universal Domestic Television Distribution. The *Martha Stewart Living* television show airs daily on the Style Network.

Through the merchandising business segment, Martha Stewart Everyday, the mass market brand, is distributed through Kmart in the United States and at Sears Canada, boasting sales of more than a billion dollars. Martha Stewart Signature indoor paints are made and sold by Sherwin-Williams, and several collections of bedroom, dining room, and living room furniture are created and sold in conjunction with Bernhardt Furniture Company. The Internet and direct commerce business segment consists of an online catalog, the company Web site, a Web site for ordering flowers, and another for ordering greeting cards.

THE EARLY YEARS

Born Martha Helen Kostyra on August 3, 1941, in Jersey City, New Jersey, Stewart was the second child of her Polish-American parents, Edward and Martha Kostyra. Edward was a high school gym teacher turned pharmaceutical salesman, and Stewart's mother was a homemaker.

When Stewart was three, her family moved to Nutley, New Jersey, her mother's hometown. Stewart and her five siblings grew up in a humble three-bedroom house, where Stewart gained many of her skills from her family. Her mother taught her and her siblings how to cook, bake, and sew, while her father passed along his fascination with gardening and design. At age three, Stewart began gardening with her father, and this chore forged a strong bond between them. She credits her father for much of her self-esteem and for teaching her that she could do anything. She also spent many summers with her maternal grandparents in Buffalo, New York, taking the train alone from age nine to get there. They taught her how to plant trees and flowers and how to can and preserve food.

Stewart was also very ambitious, stating at a young age her goal to be a nationally recognized personality. Friends marveled at her ability to juggle multiple projects. Stewart decided in grade school that she wanted to be a caterer, after learning what it was, and she opened her first business catering for friends and neighbors.

Stewart's youth was not idyllic, however. Her father was known to be an alcoholic who was demanding with his children. He was said to have blamed his family for holding him back from his dreams of being a doctor, and he felt blamed for the financial pressures the family had.

The family dynamics did not keep Stewart from excelling in school, though. She was an A student who participated in the school newspaper, the art club, and other after-school activities. Graduating with straight As, she was awarded a partial scholarship to Barnard College in New York City, where she studied European history and architectural art history.

While in college, Stewart decided to go to New York to get modeling jobs to help pay for her tuition. She began modeling for Bonwit Teller and doing ads for Tareyton cigarettes and Lifebouy soap. In 1961, Stewart was named as one of the Best Dressed College Girls by *Glamour* magazine. She was able to create a modeling portfolio by borrowing name-brand clothes from women she knew from school.

Debbi Fields

Debbi Fields is the founder and former chairperson of Mrs. Fields Cookies, a five-hundred-million-dollar company. Starting from scratch, she launched what has become one of the nation's most visible, successful dessert empires.

At age twenty and without any business experience, Fields convinced a bank to finance her business concept, and on August 16, 1977, Mrs. Fields Chocolate Chippery opened its doors to the public in Palo Alto, California.

Over the years, Fields's role expanded from managing one shop to supervising operations, brand-name management, public relations, and product development of the company's nine-hundred-plus company-owned and franchised stores around the United States and eleven other countries.

In 1989, she made Mrs. Fields, Inc., the first company in the food retailing business to use a state-of-the-art computer system to streamline operations and production schedules. The program is used as a model for business efficiency throughout the food industry and is used at Harvard Business School as an example of successful application of technology in business management. In building her company, she focused on product excellence, stated in her motto of "Good Enough Never Is," and excellence in customer service.

Fields has since sold her company and now serves as a consultant for Mrs. Fields Original Cookies and gives speeches around the country to companies seeking to achieve greater efficiencies. She wrote her autobiography, *One Smart Cookie: How a Housewife's Chocolate Chip Recipe Turned into a Multimillion-Dollar Business: The Story of Mrs. Fields' Cookies, The Mrs. Fields I Love Chocolate! Cookbook, Mrs. Fields' Cookie Secrets, Mrs. Fields' Best Cookie Book Ever!, Debbi Fields' Great American Desserts,* and her first cookbook, *Mrs. Fields Cookie Book: 100 Recipes From The Kitchen of Debbi Fields,* which has sold more than 1.5 million copies and was the first cookbook to top the *New York Times* bestseller list.

CAREER PATH

After graduation, Stewart, now married to Andy Stewart, continued a successful modeling career until 1965. In 1968, Stewart embarked on a new career as a stockbroker. She passed her broker exam and become one of the first female stockbrokers on Wall Street, working for a startup firm, Perlberg, Monness, Williams & Sidel, with which her husband had connections. In 1973, she decided to leave this career.

In 1974, Stewart decided to try her hand at catering. While growing up, she and her family always enjoyed entertaining large groups of people, so she thought this might be an appropriate business for her. She set up the business with a partner, Norma Collier, and they named the new venture The Uncatered Affair. They set up shop in Stewart's basement, using a kitchen next to the laundry room. She placed advertisements in local papers and TV stations. Her first official catering job was a wedding for three hundred. From there, word of her skills spread and business grew rapidly. Six months later the partners split contentiously. Collier has claimed that Stewart pushed her out of the business once she realized she had a future there. Stewart continued with her catering business and also added a little store called The Market Basket in Westport, where she sold pies and cakes. The company prepared meals for couples to pick up on their way home from work. These two ventures introduced many New York area families to the name *Martha Stewart* and began associating her with good food and trendy entertaining. Through word of mouth and some targeted local publicity moves, Stewart quickly gained a reputation as a talented caterer. She was profiled in the local newspapers. The business became such a success she outsourced some of it to other homemakers, who were interested in baking but not in running a business. On January 1, 1977, she incorporated her business as Martha Stewart, Inc.

At the same time that Stewart was seeing success as a caterer, her husband, Andy, made a career switch into publishing, giving her the impetus and connections that would make it feasible to consider writing her own cookbook. Andy had taken on the challenge of marketing an unusual book about fairies and gnomes. It would be one of his biggest hits, in part because of the tremendous revenue generated from ancillary products featuring the book's characters. The book, *Gnomes*, did very well, selling millions in its first year of publication. But the canvas book bags, ceramic figures, posters, notepads, and towels brought in significant additional revenue. Stewart immediately recognized the potential for extending a brand and set about applying the same principle to the various facets of her catering business.

In 1979, as a result of the buzz about her New York catering business, *People* magazine did a story on Stewart, positioning her as a lifestyle expert. Following the article's publication, Stewart was asked to submit occasional articles about food, gardening, entertaining, and decorating to such publications as *Good*

Housekeeping and *Country Living*. She was hired as freelance food editor for *House Beautiful*.

As a result of Stewart's lifestyle-expert status and the reputation she was gaining for staging parties, the Stewarts came up with the idea of publishing a book containing recipes and illustrations of food and home surroundings. Andy assisted Stewart in acquiring a publishing deal with Crown Publishing, and *Entertaining* was published in 1982. Cowritten with Elizabeth Hawes, *Entertaining* was a massive success and set the stage for Stewart to become a household name. In 1983 *Quick Cook* was published; in 1984, *Hors D'Oeuvres*; in 1985, *Pies and Tarts*; and in 1987, *Weddings*.

On July 6, 1987, Stewart signed a contract with Kmart, which had offered her a position as a spokesperson. Stewart was to receive two hundred thousand dollars a year for five years plus three thousand dollars for each thirty-day period in which she attended company-sponsored events.

By the late 1980s, Stewart had become considerably wealthy. She began purchasing land and houses throughout the east. She was promoted on shows such as the *Today Show* and *Good Morning America*. Another book was published, *Martha Stewart's New Old House*, and there were also shows being produced. Some of the videos were not successful, but her Christmas special, which aired on Lifetime, was a huge hit and was followed by another book, *Martha Stewart's Christmas*.

In October 2005, Stewart was denied entry to Canada under its "no-convicts rule" due to her status as a convicted felon. She had planned to attend a Thanksgiving festival in Nova Scotia's Annapolis Valley. Within two days of the story's breaking, Stewart was granted her work visa to enter Canada and attend the festivities.

Stewart went to many publishers with her idea and prototype for a new magazine. Finally, in 1990, Time Publishing Ventures agreed to run two test issues of *Martha Stewart Living,* which was distributed nationally. Stewart was on the cover and all over in the inside of the magazine. Though Time was skeptical of its success, test results came back in an overwhelming popular vote for the magazine.

Time's perception of the magazine completely changed. Once the demand for the magazine was recognized, advertisers jumped on board, including Kmart, which had initially decided against it. By May 1991, Time signed a ten-year deal with Stewart to publish a monthly magazine that she would edit.

It took a couple of years to convince a backer to support the idea; however, on January 19, 1993, Stewart signed a deal with Group W Productions, Inc., to produce a television show. By 1998, the *Martha Stewart Living* TV show had become a hit. It began as a half-hour cable show and was eventually was picked up by CBS. At about the same time, Kmart began selling a wide selection of Martha Stewart–brand merchandise that ranged from bath towels to garden trowels.

In 1995, Stewart incorporated MSLO and in 1997 purchased her magazine from Time Warner, Inc. She borrowed eighty-five million dollars at this time. On October 19, 1999, Stewart took the company public, and records indicate that she paid Time Warner only two million dollars for the magazine. The IPO of common stock began trading at eighteen dollars a share and raised $149 million in equity capital. The stock soon rose to thirty-six dollars in the euphoric securities market of 1999. Stewart became worth a billion dollars on paper.

PERSONAL LIFE

Stewart met her husband, Andrew, a law student at Yale University, on a blind date during her freshman year at Barnard. In July 1961, in her sophomore year and at the peak of her modeling career, they married. The following year, Stewart put her education and modeling career on hold to be with her new husband in New Haven. Andy acquired his degree in June 1962, and the couple moved back to New York. Stewart picked up where she'd left off at school and went back to modeling. She also spent time with her husband's mother, Ethel, who introduced Stewart to antiques and auctions.

In September 1965, Stewart's daughter, Alexis, was born, and Stewart ended her modeling career. Alexis claims they have always been close. During Stewart's incarceration, Alexis visited frequently, and later helped her mother on *The Apprentice: Martha Stewart*.

While Stewart was working as a stockbroker on Wall Street in the spring of 1971, she and her husband purchased and undertook a massive restoration of an 1805 farmhouse. The home at 48 Turkey Hill, known as Turkey Hill Farm, is still owned by Stewart and is featured in many of her books and television shows. During the restoration project, Stewart's passion for restoring and decorating was apparent. In her Turkey Hill home, Stewart began her catering business.

In 1987, after twenty-six years of marriage, Stewart's husband left her for her former assistant and filed for divorce on the date her best-selling *Weddings* book was released. The divorce was finalized three years later after a bitter separation.

Stewart is not known for generous philanthropy. In the sentencing portion of her trial in a bid for leniency, she revealed the amount she spent on charity; however, this was small compared with her other expenses. MSLO, Inc., has set up a nonprofit foundation to award grants that will help women turn their ideas into businesses. The company also sponsors three days per year for employees to volunteer their time.

After being released from prison, Stewart began to serve her home confinement at her estate in Bedford, New York. During the confinement she was permitted to leave her property for up to forty-eight hours a week to conduct business but was required to wear an electronic ankle bracelet transmitter to monitor her location at all times. On August 3 (her sixty-fourth birthday), Stewart's lawyers announced that her home confinement was extended for three weeks, until August 31, reportedly because she violated terms of the confinement.

LEADERSHIP LESSONS

Stewart has become a recognized expert at brand management. Business school students study her ability to grow her brand and continually market new products. She vigorously pursues publicity to generate enthusiasm for her products, surrounds herself with talented people, is on top of the uses of current technology, and is constantly looking for the next great idea.

Build on the Brand

When her husband generated millions of dollars of revenues with marketing a book and ancillary products, Stewart saw how successful branding in merchandise could be. Developing merchandising opportunities in the form of related products that can be packaged and sold under her brand name is the heart of her successful strategy. She concentrates on developing product ideas that can generate add-on sales.

> *"Life is too complicated not to be orderly."*
> Martha Stewart

In Stewart's case, she is the brand, readily linking her name to new media ventures and markets. The strategy worked extremely well until her legal trouble. Stewart has sold over 2,800 Stewart-branded products through retail outlets such as Kmart, Sears, and Sherwin Williams, her catalog (Martha By Mail) and the Internet via martha.com. Marthaflowers.com was launched in 2000 to extend her brand into the lucrative fifteen-billion-dollar floral industry. She has also launched an online greeting card business.

Stewart has become an icon of the entertaining and decorating world in large part because she grasped early on the importance of establishing and mining a brand identity. The company is now trying to move beyond the branding of Martha Stewart herself and move into product branding. MSLO's Sharon Patrick explains in a recent issue of *Advertising Age*, "Martha was the visionary and the driver of understanding the power of how-to content. Martha stands for what this brand is, and is instrumental in presenting it. It's moving from trusted personality to trusted products and services. The branded product becomes the next step." If the company can successfully do this, they can move beyond the brand personification and achieve more of a balance.

Focus on Quality

Stewart realized that in order for branding to be as successful as she wanted, she would have to focus on quality. She relentlessly pursued quality service as a caterer, spending a lot of time studying new recipes and ideas, using only the best ingredients, and striving to make her parties extraordinarily stylish. She continued focusing on quality and service as she moved into merchandising, writing, and managing an empire. Even everyday items sold through Kmart are of high quality, the packaging reflecting the brand. The company achieves this level of quality by comparing its products with others.

Pursue Positive Publicity

Part of the reason Stewart has become so well known is her strategy of doggedly pursuing publicity, which she defines as capturing the media's interest in the business. As her catering business was thriving, she set about writing articles for national publications in order to position herself as a leading expert in her field. The opportunity to write such articles provided Stewart with credibility and prestige, and the implied endorsement of such high-powered publications was priceless. Publicity is different from advertising, and though monetarily less expensive, it requires far more time and energy. Stewart has always been generous with information to media outlets. She cultivates friendships with people in the media, and even when she was starting out as a caterer, she courted reporters by hosting parties, donating food to charity events, and giving cooking lessons to young children. One of her public relations strategies is to pamper the press whenever possible.

"I want cotton. I want three-hundred thread count minimum, or this face doesn't sell these sheets. Just because Kmart sells inexpensive products doesn't mean they can't be beautiful. That's why I'm here: not to sink to your level, but to raise you to mine."

Martha Stewart

Using the exposure she received through her articles as a springboard, Stewart turned toward television, where she started with guest appearances on local television programs and on the *CBS Early Show*. This gave her the clout to pursue her own television show.

The day after her indictment, Stewart took out a full-page advertisement in *USA Today* and launched a Web site with an open letter of defense "to my friends and loyal supporters." She said, "I want you to know that I am innocent—and that I will fight to clear my name." She also used her Web site to tell her side of the story, give timely trial updates, and offer statements from Stewart's legal team and a library of different op-ed pieces written on her behalf. She also strategically timed interviews with Larry King and Barbara Walters.

Partner with Established Distribution Channels

While Stewart generates new products that she distributes through existing channels, she also continues to look for new distribution outlets. She strategically aligned herself with several well-established retailers with the power to push her products. The company has alliances with Kmart; Zellers, a Canadian mass market discounter similar to Kmart; Sears and Canadian Tire, which provide an entrée into the national department store arena; and Calico Corners and Jo-Ann Fabric and Crafts. On the manufacturing front, Sherwin-Williams produces a Martha Stewart line of paints, Fine Paints of Europe distributes branded paint, and P/Kaufman produces a line of decorative home fabrics.

Though many questioned her decision to lead her quality-focused company into a contract with Kmart, a mass merchandiser known for discounted prices, the strategy turned out to be effective. Kmart is Stewart's vehicle to deliver her products into homes across the United States. At the time of the arrangement, a staggering 70 percent of the country's population had shopped at the retailer.

Be A Trendsetter

Stewart always had a knack for being ahead of the curve in discovering and establishing new trends. Just as the market began to shift away from one fad, she was already onto something else. And her timing was impeccable with the publication of her first book, *Entertaining*, in 1982. She credits the ability to read the trends and adapt quickly to always consciously looking toward the future. Stewart is continually brainstorming new products with friends, employees, and managers, looking for the next big idea. She spends much of her time with other people who she considers great thinkers, and she says, "All we do is think and talk. Hashing and rehashing, going over plans and ideas." Stewart often takes pictures and notes when she is inspired and keeps track of her ideas, with help from her assistants, in over a thousand folders.

> *"I'm not a sponge exactly, but I find that something I look at is a great opportunity for ideas."*
>
> Martha Stewart

When she could not find the right colors of paint for a redecorating project, she and her staff sought about finding the colors in nature and having them created. This launched the company into the Sherwin Williams partnership.

Stewart has continued to redefine herself and her vision. When she saw significant success as a caterer, she might have been content to define herself as that. However, she expanded her idea of herself to expert at entertaining. This allowed her to create additional opportunities, starting with a career move as author with her book, *Entertaining*.

Embrace Technology

Staying ahead of trends requires that Stewart stay at the leading edge of information technology, which she claims makes it possible for her to accomplish as much as she does in a day. Investing in the latest and greatest technology for her homes, studio, and office enables information to be shared across her rapidly growing organization, keeping production schedules on course. "Technology makes it possible, so it's going to get done," she says.

Besides the ten phone lines in her Westport, Connecticut, home and her various computers and laptops, Stewart also uses a Sony MiniDiscRecorder to dictate instructions to her staff and to note ideas for stories. In the conference room of the MSLO offices, she has installed a state-of-the-art video teleconferencing system that enables her to attend out-of-town board meetings when she can't get away. Stewart was also one of the first corporate marketers to see the tremendous potential of e-commerce. She e-mails herself from her BlackBerry with reminders and ideas. Her use of technology as the head of MSLO is in stark contrast to her youth, when her family was the last one in the neighborhood to own a TV.

Her company's Web site, marthastewart.com, is frequently used as a case study of how to effectively grow an online business. The Web address is used often and effectively in all other media outlets the company uses. From the beginning, Stewart recognized that to attract and keep visitors coming back to the site, she had to give them information that was useful and could be acted upon. So, in addition to viewing a well-designed site that reflects the look and feel of the magazine, visitors can download recipes, check the program guide to learn what topics will be covered in upcoming TV shows, retrieve instructions on completing projects featured on TV, and access the Martha By Mail Web store, enabling them to purchase tools and accessories online. From the beginning, the site asked for the e-mail addresses of its visitors, giving the company the opportunity to contact those visitors with special offers and reminders. By providing their e-mail addresses, visitors gain access to online discussion groups, earn the chance to enter sweepstakes, and can receive a weekly bulletin from Stewart.

Hire Experts

Altogether, the MSLO staff consists of more than 650 people with bright ideas about cooking, crafts, holidays, weddings, babies, and other essentials. Though Stewart is the face of the company, it is led by a management team with a great amount of experience and talent. For some time before Stewart's incarceration, the company had been aggressively trying to reduce its reliance on her, both as a personality and as provider of information, and it continues to do this.

Whereas Stewart formerly developed all content ideas for the company, there are now in-house creative experts who have been hired to assume that responsibility. The company's reliance on Stewart's image is also being significantly reduced. The most obvious sign is that she no longer appears on the cover of the magazine. The management and officers are now assuming a more visible role in the various media outlets.

Some of the best experts are customers. MSLO has a letters department that reads and answers the five hundred thousand letters that come in annually. Stewart also reads many of these, unafraid of complaints. She uses customers' ideas, complaints, and compliments to modify or expand her products and services.

Repackage and Repurpose Information

Undoubtedly, one of Stewart's strengths is her ability to do several things at once. This is true in her personal life, where she is known as a dynamo who can't stand still, and at her company, where each piece of how-to information is used several times over in various forms. A magazine article is never just a magazine article. Nor is a TV segment just a one-time program. For example, an article on creating a festive holiday wreath can also be used as a chapter in an upcoming holiday decorating book and as a segment on a television show and a radio program. In addition, it can be mentioned in a syndicated newspaper column, listed as a program item on the Web site, and packaged as a do-it-yourself kit sold through Martha By Mail. Reusing and repackaging information in numerous forms is much more profitable than using it once and setting it aside, as so many media companies do. In fact, approximately 60 percent of the material presented in Stewart's books is culled from *Martha Stewart Living*.

Research Relentlessly

Stewart started her catering career by researching ideas into the late hours. She never considered time spent researching too much trouble and continues to be disciplined about research—even when thinking of the next big idea. Although she did not start her business by drawing up a business plan, she had a clear idea of what she wanted to offer.

In her latest book, *The Martha Rules,* Stewart promotes the idea of seeking out a variety of mentors in a variety of fields. Mentors do not have to be living or known personally, she believes, as long as they can provide information. She also acts as a mentor to her employees, providing guidance and advice to many of them.

The Martha Rules

1. Build your business success around something that you love—something that is inherently and endlessly interesting to you.

2. Focus your attention and creativity on basic things, things that people need and want. Then look for ways to enlarge, improve, and enhance your big idea.

3. Create a business plan that allows you to stay true to your big idea but helps you focus on the details. Then remain flexible enough to zoom in or out on the vital aspects of your enterprise as your business grows.

4. By sharing your knowledge about your product or service with your customers, you create a deep connection that will help you learn how best to build and manage your business.

5. Use smart, cost-effective promotional techniques that will arrest the eye, tug at the heart, and convey what is unique and special about your business or service.

6. Quality should be placed at the top of your list of priorities, and it should remain there. Quality is something you should strive for in every decision, every day.

7. Seek out and hire employees who are brimming with talent, energy, integrity, optimism, and generosity. Search for advisors and partners who complement your skills and understand your ideals.

8. When faced with a business challenge, evaluate or assess the situation, gather the good things in sight, abandon the bad, clear your mind, and move on. Focus on the positive. Stay in control, and never panic.

9. In business, there's a difference between a risk and a chance. A well-calculated risk may very well end up as an investment in your business. A careless chance can cause it to crumble. And when an opportunity presents itself, never assume it will be your last.

10. Listen intently, learn new things every day, be willing to innovate, and become an authority your customers will trust. As an entrepreneur, you will find great joy and satisfaction in making your customers' lives easier, more meaningful, and more beautiful.

POLITICAL INFLUENCE

Stewart has been a longtime supporter of various Democratic candidates and organizations. She donated $173,374 to Democratic candidates in 2004 and one thousand dollars to Republican candidates.

CRITICS

Critics have long been vocal regarding Stewart. The early criticism stemmed primarily from what was seen as her egotistical demeanor and her strong desire for control. She has been called aggressive, pushy, rigid, disorganized, short-tempered, demanding, greedy, self-serving, condescending, and dismissive by the press and people with whom she has worked. Stewart has agreed that she likes to control her environment and business. Her dealings with Kmart generated press coverage, and Stewart was portrayed as demanding and difficult to work with.

"Remember, I'm not Martha Stewart the person anymore, I'm Martha Stewart the lifestyle."

Martha Stewart

The main scandal in which she has been involved is the 2002 stock sale of almost four thousand shares of ImClone. ImClone had claimed they had an effective cancer drug, but the U.S. Food and Drug Administration (FDA) decided not to review the drug and the company stock price plummeted. By selling before the FDA announcement, Stewart saved approximately forty-five thousand dollars; however, she has claimed that she had a standing order to sell if the price dropped to below sixty dollars per share. Though the insider trading charges she was initially indicted for were thrown out, Stewart was found guilty of conspiracy, obstruction of justice, and two counts of making false statements. She was sentenced to five months in prison, five months of home confinement (which was later extended by three weeks), and two years' probation, and she was fined thirty thousand dollars. Although she is still appealing the verdict, she decided to serve her sentence and put the ordeal behind her. Although she had requested to be sent to the federal prison in Danbury, Connecticut, she was ordered to spend the five months in Alderson Federal Prison Camp, a low-security prison.

Life at Alderson for Stewart began October 8, 2004. She used the time to think about the future of her company, read, prepare a manuscript for her book *The Martha Rules*, and interact with other inmates. She has referred to the numerous friends that she had made during her time there. She also kept busy trying new recipes using a microwave oven, the only oven prisoners were allowed to use.

"M. Diddy": Martha Stewart's nickname at Alderson prison.

Stewart was sharply criticized for her reaction to the stock sale investigation. On June 25, 2002, she appeared on CBS's *The Early Show*, and when asked by Jane Clayson about the scandal during a cooking segment, she replied, "I just want to focus on my salad." Stewart dodged the same question several times. Stewart's response is shown in business schools and around the world as an example of how not to handle a direct question and a crisis situation. Stewart fell silent after the CBS episode, canceling public appearances and dodging reporters by using a private entrance and service elevator when they staked out a building where she was scheduled to appear. Critics took her silence to mean that she was guilty. Although she hired the Brunswick Group to handle damage control and help create a crisis strategy, it was too late, and much damage had been done to her and her brand. Until Martha Talks, the Web site used to give details about the trial, was unveiled, the media had no comment from Stewart.

Critics have also charged that Stewart has not given enough of her wealth away in the form of philanthropy. In a statement seeking leniency during the sentencing portion of her trial, Stewart did not show significant-enough philanthropic activities to justify a reduction in sentence. Prosecutors termed Stewart's claim that her charitable donations were significant as "specious," citing her submission that she "greeted new neighbors with freshly baked bread" and "gave cocoa to the parents of children appearing on her television show." Prosecutors pointed to the court documents showing her charitable contributions which amounted to less than the cost of one of her vacations. Indeed, absent from the submission for leniency were any statements from

---

Mary Kay Ash

Mary Kay Ash founded Mary Kay Cosmetics after her retirement. Ash worked for several direct sales companies from the 1930s until the early 1960s, achieving considerable success as a salesperson and trainer.

Ash started off by selling a child psychology book door to door and then worked as a sales representative and manager at the Stanley Home Products Company from 1939 to 1952. Later, she was national training director at the World Gift Company. Frustrated, however, at being passed over for promotions in favor of men, she retired in 1963, intending to write a book to assist women in business.

The book turned into a business plan for her ideal company, and in September 1963, Ash and her son, Richard Rogers, began Mary Kay Cosmetics with a five-thousand-dollar investment. The company originally operated from a storefront in Dallas but grew rapidly, particularly after Ash was interviewed for CBS's *60 Minutes* in 1979.

Ash was widely respected, if not always understood, for her unconventional approach to business. She considered the Golden Rule the founding principle of Mary Kay Cosmetics, and the company's marketing plan was designed to allow women to advance by helping others to succeed. Unfailingly supportive and enthusiastic, she advocated "praising people to success," and her slogan "faith first, family second, career third" expressed her insistence that the women in her company keep their lives in balance. At the time of Ash's death, Mary Kay Cosmetics had over eight hundred thousand representatives in thirty-seven countries, with total annual sales over two billion dollars.

---

any charities with which Stewart had worked, and she has not been actively involved publicly with any philanthropic cause.

Stewart faced more legal trouble in February 2004, when MSLO was sued by Kmart for allegedly "double-counting" royalty payments and advertising spending. On April 23, 2004, Kmart withdrew its lawsuit, having reached an agreement with the company to amend the terms of the June 2001 contract and to extend it through 2009.

POSSIBLE FUTURE IMPACT

Since Stewart's release from Alderson, she is more focused, centered, and relaxed. MSLO saw a increase in advertising pages and revenue in some of the company's magazines in 2005. Stewart's daytime television show, *Martha*, has grown in viewer numbers and is continuing to gain popularity. It finished in 2005 as the number-one new daytime show, increasing viewership by 10 percent over 2004. *Martha* has been sold to a wide range of leading broadcast station groups for its second season, including the NBC-owned and -operated stations, Hearst-Argyle, Gannett, Scripps-Howard, Viacom, Belo, Freedom, Young, Clear Channel, Meredith, and the Milwaukee Journal. She has also purchased and revamped another magazine, *Body + Soul*.

Stewart has many new projects in the works, including the establishment of Martha Stewart Everyday boutiques within Kmart's 2,145 stores, where the retailer is allocating approximately 4,500 square feet per store solely for Stewart to market and sell her branded products.

The company is also producing new theme-based video and DVD products using content from the television shows. The television segment also includes *Petkeeping with Marc Morrone* and *Everyday Food,* a nationally syndicated half-hour program on PBS. Stewart also produced a compilation holiday album in partnership with Sony Corporation.

With the launch of a twenty-four-hour satellite radio network with Sirius, Stewart plans to continue influencing consumers across multiple media outlets. Her daughter, Alexis, is also actively involved in the new station.

In 2006, Stewart partnered with developer KB Home to create a New England–style neighborhood of 650 houses in the affluent Raleigh suburb of Cary, North Carolina. Homebuyers in the community can choose from twelve models in townhomes and single-family dwellings, ranging from 1,300 to 4,000 square feet and with prices from $150,000 to $400,000. Three house designs are based on homes Stewart owns in Maine and New York, and floor plans and options for interior features in all models were chosen by Stewart and her design team.

She also plans to continue building her brand through new merchandise via existing distributors in the coming year, introducing a new housewares line for Kmart and exploring the possibilities for a gardening and outdoor product line. She has had meetings with Armstrong flooring and GE appliances regarding product development. It would not be a stretch to assume we will see more Stewart-branded products in both existing and new arenas in the future. It is likely that the company will attempt to brand more products, moving away from using the Stewart name and distancing itself from the persona of the founder. However, ultimately, it is the Stewart name that is branded and has significant meaning among consumers. It is possible that the Stewart name may become symbolic in the way that Betty Crocker is and last long after the person herself is gone.

TIMELINE

1941	Born in Jersey City, New Jersey.
1944	The Kostyra family moved to Nutley, New Jersey.
1959	Graduated from high school as a straight-A student.
	During high school, Stewart entered into modeling.
1960	Attended Barnard College.
1961	Married Andrew Stewart.
	Named "Best Dressed College Student" by *Glamour* magazine.
1965	Alexis, Stewart's only child, born.
1968	Passed broker exam and becomes a stockbroker.
1973	Ended her career as a stockbroker.
	Moved to Connecticut to the famous Turkey Hill Farm.
1974	Began catering with a business partner.
1975	Began catering on her own.
1977	Became incorporated as Martha Stewart, Inc.
1982	Stewart's first book, *Entertaining*, was published.
1987	Andrew and Stewart separated.
	Stewart's second book, *Weddings*, dedicated to her husband, was published.
	Signed contract to be a spokesperson for Kmart.
1990	Time Warner and Stewart partnered to create *Martha Stewart Living* magazine.
1993	TV show *Martha Stewart Living* began airing.
1999	Stewart went public with her company Martha Stewart Living Omnimedia.
2001	Signed an extended seven-year deal with Kmart.
	December, Sold four thousand shares of ImClone stock just before the stock plummeted.
2003	Indicted on charges related to the ImClone stock that was sold.
	June 4, Resigned as CEO the same day she was indicted.
2004	Found guilty of "misleading federal investigators and obstructing an investigation."

March 15, Resigned from the board of MSLO.

July 16, Sentenced to five months in prison.

October 8, Arrived at Alderson Federal Prison Camp to begin her five-month sentence.

2005   Early March, Released from prison.

September, *Martha* and *The Apprentice: Martha Stewart* air.

RESOURCES

Allen, Lloyd. *Being Martha: The Inside Story of Martha Stewart and Her Amazing Life.* Ashland, Oregon: Blackstone Audiobooks 2006.

Coleman, Calmetta. Grand Designs: Ms. Stewart's Advice For How to Improve Kmart: Ask Martha—Her Line a Hit, She Seeks More Clout at Retailer; It Flashes a Red Light—Homing In on a Board Seat. *Wall Street Journal*, May 1, 2000, p. A-1.

Gross, T. Scott. *Positively Outrageous Service: How to Delight and Astound Your Customers and Win Them for Life.* Chicago, IL: Dearborn Trade, 2004, p. 188.

Lamb, Larry F. *Applied Public Relations: Case Studies and Problem Solving.* Mahwah, NJ: Lawrence Erlbaum Associates, 2004, p. 132.

Michman, Ronald D. *Food Industry Wars: Marketing Triumphs & Blunders.* Westport, CT: Greenwood Publishing Group, 1998, p. 208.

Stewart, Martha. *The Martha Rules.* New York: Rodale Books, 2005.

Strauss, Steven D. *Eureka! How Business Innovators Get Great Ideas to Market.* Chicago, IL: Dearborn Trade, 2001, pp. 98–99, 219.

Turner, Marcia Layton. *How to Think Like the World's Greatest Marketing Minds: Business Lessons from David Ogilvy.* New York: McGraw-Hill Professional Book Group, 2000, pp. 51–64.

Wiley, Christopher Byron. *Martha Inc: The Incredible Story of Martha Stewart Living Omnimedia.* New York: John Wiley & Sons, Inc. 2003.

Williams, Timothy. Martha Stewart Signs Deal With Sirius Radio Network *New York Times*, April 19, 2005, p. C-4.

www.achievement.org

www.cnn.com

www.savemartha.com

COMPANY INFORMATION

Martha Stewart Living Omnimedia
11 West 42nd Street, New York, New York 10036,
Phone: (212) 827–8000
www.marthastewart.com
New York Stock Exchange symbol: MSO

Courtesy of Photofest.

Donald Trump

Donald Trump, arguably the world's preeminent real estate developer, has built his name into a brand that represents wealth and success around the world. The Forbes 400 list of 2005 estimated Donald Trump's net worth at $2.7 billion, which placed him in eighty-third place.

In New York City, the Trump signature is synonymous with the most prestigious addresses. Among them are the world-renowned Fifth Avenue skyscraper, Trump Tower, Trump Plaza, the Trump World Tower, and Trump Park Avenue. Trump also has partnered in property development in other locations, including Atlantic City, Chicago, Las Vegas, Los Angeles, Florida, Korea, and Canada.

Perhaps best known now for the television show he stars in and coproduces, *The Apprentice,* Trump had actually first considered going to Hollywood after graduating from high school. By the time he made it through Wharton Business School, however, his interest in real estate was cemented, and he got his early start in his father's New York real estate business. By the 1970s he had made himself a deal-maker in Manhattan. Taking a $350,000 loan from his father, he branched out into his first solo project in Manhattan, which was the conversion of the Commodore Hotel at Grand Central Station into the Grand Hyatt Hotel.

Over the years, Trump has owned and sold many grand buildings in New York, including the Plaza Hotel, which he renovated and brought back to its original grandeur, the St. Moritz Hotel, now called the Ritz Carlton on Central Park South, and the land under the Empire State Building. He completed the problematic Wollman Skating Rink, taking the project from the City of New York, which had struggled for years, pouring millions into it. At one time, he seemed to have a Midas touch and could do no wrong when it came to Manhattan or Atlantic City real estate.

However, the real estate market faltered, as did Trump's wealth, most of which was tied up in real estate ventures. After a debt restructuring in the early 1990s and another in 2004, Trump seems to have come back strong.

Outspoken and flamboyant, Trump garnered his share of press coverage. He has pursued a sense of style and glamour with vigor and has opened up his life and home to photographers and television shows. Until Trump, billionaires were almost always reclusive, unwilling to permit their privacy to be invaded, but Trump was eager to show off his wealth, which included the third-largest yacht in the world, an airline shuttle, and a private jet. Trump wrote candid memoirs, naming his friends and his enemies and illustrating the details of his winning negotiations.

Trump's solicitation of the media backfired during the break-up of his marriage to his first wife, Ivana, because of his affair with Marla Maples. He subsequently married and divorced Maples and is now married to Melania Knauss. He is the father of five children, two of whom work with him now.

Trump's first autobiography, *The Art of the Deal,* has become one of the most successful business bestsellers of all time, selling in excess of three million copies. He has coauthored six books in all. However, he is particular about what goes into print without his permission. He is especially sensitive to issues about his wealth. He sued *New York Times* reporter Timothy L. O'Brien and Warner Books, Inc., for saying that he was not a billionaire in the book *The Art of Being the Donald.*

"I like thinking big. If you're going to be thinking anything, you might as well think big."
Donald Trump

THE EARLY YEARS

Donald John Trump was born on June 14, 1946, in Queens, New York, the fourth of five children of Frederick C. and Mary MacLeod Trump, a native of Stornoway in Scotland. The Trump children were, in order, Maryanne, Fred Junior, Elizabeth, Donald, and Robert. The family lived in Jamaica Estates on Long Island at the time of Trump's birth.

Frederick Trump was a successful builder and real estate developer who came to specialize in constructing and operating middle-income apartments in Queens, Staten Island, and Brooklyn. Ultimately, Fred was one of the largest landlords of New York's outer boroughs, and when he died in 1999, he was worth two hundred million dollars. Mary was very interested in living with a sense of style and glamour.

Trump was strongly influenced by his father, who was strict, although able to enforce his edicts without resorting to physical threats. He was a domineering presence in the Trump household. Fred insisted that all of his children work, and Trump chose to go into his father's business. He would hang around with his father, eager to absorb information. He watched his father negotiate with contractors and micromanage his business. His father had a lot of energy and ambition, as the younger Trump saw it, and he wanted to follow in his footsteps. His father encouraged Trump to go into the real estate business. His mother had no specific dreams for him, he recalled, other than for him to be happy.

Trump was an energetic, assertive child, who rebelled against authority. He was, in his own words, according to Robert Slater in *No Such Thing as Overexposure,* "very assertive, aggressive . . . with words. I was a little wise guy, a little brat." He would throw chalk and erasers in class and even once punched a music teacher. The teacher received a black eye, and Trump was nearly thrown out of school. He was not interested in academics, preferring his own ways.

When he was thirteen, his parents sent him to the New York Military Academy (NYMA) on the edge of Cornwall-on-Hudson, next to West Post, fifty-five miles north of New York City, hoping the discipline of the school would channel his energy in a positive manner.

At NYMA, Trump was singled out as a problematic new student who needed extra attention. The leaders used physical force to intimidate the students, but Trump later said the he simply let them know that he was not intimidated. The discipline he experienced there led him to channel his competitiveness and aggressiveness into more positive actions. He started doing better academically, even becoming an honor student and receiving the school's highest grade in geometry. He did especially well in sports, becoming one of the school's star athletes. The school stressed the value of winning in everything, and Trump was an eager participant and vowed to be the best in whatever he did. Though he met girls only at mixers as a teenager, he acquired a reputation for knowing how to attract women. His classmates voted him "Ladies' Man."

Promoted to cadet captain during his senior year, he had charge of the honor guard. As a reward for his excellence, Cadet Captain Trump, then seventeen years old, led the NYMA up Fifth Avenue in the 1963 Columbus Day parade.

During the summers Trump worked with his father in the real estate business. By the time he graduated from the NYMA in 1964, he thought he wanted to go to Hollywood to become a movie producer because he liked the industry's glamour. Before doing that, though, he decided to go to college.

He considered enrolling at the film school at the University of Southern California, but then a friend, experiencing great difficulty in finding a suitable apartment, asked him about real estate and, commented on his astute answers. When Trump tried to explain why he preferred going into movies instead of real estate, he didn't have a good answer. He abandoned his thoughts of Hollywood and spent the next two years at Fordham in the Bronx, near enough to his Long Island home for him to commute daily. He would wear nice clothes to school and arrive in his sports car. Even in college, though, Trump would not drink or smoke.

After two years at Fordham, Trump spent his final two years of college at the Wharton School of Business at the University of Pennsylvania in Philadelphia. Wharton had turned out some leading entrepreneurs and had one of the few real-estate departments. Most of the department's students came from families that had worked in real estate. The curriculum called for visits to neighborhoods to check out demographics. Trump loved the school and did very well.

At one point in his studies, Trump put his learning into practice. He and his father purchased a bankrupt apartment complex called Swifton Village in Cincinnati, Ohio, for less than six million dollars. They obtained financing above the purchase price so they could do the necessary remodeling and eighteen months later sold it for twice the price.

After graduating in 1968 with a degree in economics, Trump had decided upon a career in real estate development, but his goals were much larger than those of his father. "There's something about Mother Earth that's awfully good," he said in a 1990 interview, "and Mother Earth is still real estate.... Real estate is something solid. It's brick, mortar" (quoted by Robert Slater, *No Such Thing as Overexposure*).

Trump had wanted to expand into the Manhattan real estate market and tried to convince his father to go there, but his father was reluctant and tried to steer Trump away from it. The risks seemed too great in Manhattan. A property in Manhattan that cost thousands of dollars per square foot cost Fred only thirty cents in Brooklyn, so Manhattan made no economic sense to him. Because he couldn't afford to go into the market on his own just then, Trump decided to wait a while and work for his father while he looked for opportunities.

Trump's brother, Fred Junior, initially followed their father into real estate, but found he did not like it. He then became a pilot for Trans World Airlines, but he died at the age of forty-three of alcoholism. Trump's sister Maryanne started out as a housewife but later went to law school and eventually became a judge on the U.S. Court of Appeals for the Third Circuit. His sister Elizabeth married and lives in Palm Beach, Florida. His brother Robert helped him run their father's business after Fred Trump died in 1999. They later sold it, and Robert is still involved in real estate.

CAREER PATH

Trump started his career in an office he shared with his father in Sheepshead Bay in Brooklyn. He worked with his father for five years, learning a tremendous amount about every aspect of the construction industry; from him, Trump was able to finance an expansion of the company's holdings by convincing his father to be more liberal in the use of loans based on the equity in the Trump apartment complexes.

Trump hoped all along to succeed in Manhattan, however, even though the real estate community there was in the hands of a few players. One of them was Harry Helmsley. Trump and the much older Helmsley got along well. Before her public feud with Trump, Leona, Harry's wife, used to call Trump "the young Harry Helmsley." It was important to Trump that he make it on his own and not stay at his dad's company forever. His dad was well known and successful, and Trump wanted to get out from under his shadow. According to Richard Slater in *No Such Thing as Overexposure*, Trump said to himself, "I'm his son; I can do things, too. It's not just because of my father."

The way to do that, he decided, was to make a name for himself in Manhattan. To Trump, Manhattan represented the big league, and it was an area where Fred Trump didn't play.

Finally, in 1971, Trump rented a small, dark, and dingy apartment on 75th Street and Third Avenue with no view. He got to know the city, and he began to search for good properties. He was still commuting back to work in Brooklyn, but he had established a foothold.

He figured that he was not going to get very far in Manhattan without the right connections. He had to start breaking into society, so he sought to join one of the most exclusive clubs in New York City, Le Club, a members-only restaurant and nightclub on East 54th Street, founded in 1960 by society columnist Igor Cassini. After calling the club didn't work, Trump called the president and asked to become a member. The president invited him for a drink at 21. Trump didn't drink, but he sat with the president while he did. On their second meeting, the president had decided to propose Trump for membership. The membership didn't help much, but he did meet the celebrity attorney Roy Cohen, who helped him get connected. Cohen had first gained national attention as the assistant to Senator Joseph McCarthy, the Wisconsin senator chased who alleged that there were subversives within the federal government. Cohen had been indicted a number of times on charges of bribery, conspiracy, and bank fraud, though he was never convicted. He knew the New York social scene well and took Trump under his wing.

In the 1970s, New York City was going through an economic downturn, and Trump was finding it difficult to break into the real estate market there. He had no track record. To negotiate deals, to acquire properties, he had to convince others purely on the basis of his energy and enthusiasm, not on his abilities. Trump also had big dreams. He wanted to build large buildings. To do this, though, he needed a track record; without a track record it was hard to find a project. However, after looking diligently, he found something he could undertake.

In his search for cheap properties, he learned that the bankrupt Penn Central railroad, which owed six million dollars in back taxes, was interested in dumping the money-losing Hotel Commodore. At the time, the entire area around Grand Central Station on 42nd Street was deteriorating. The hotel, along with the rest of the neighborhood, had a run-down look that had driven customers away. It was filthy inside and out, but thousands of middle- and upper-middle class commuters emerging from Grand Central Station and the underground subway stations passed by it on their way to work.

He could probably afford to do the project, and he would gain a lot of recognition for reviving one of the city's great landmarks. His father helped get him started by providing him with $350,000 that he used for his expenses.

What Trump proposed was to make a deal with Penn Central to buy the land under the building, to ask the city to forego taxes and take only a share of the profits, to induce a major hotel operator to buy in and operate the refurbished hotel, and, finally, to convince a bank to lend him more than sixty million dollars. No one, not even his father, believed he could do all of that, but his enthusiasm made it possible.

He asked for a tax abatement scheme from the city of New York amounting to tens of millions of dollars—without having first obtained financing for the project. Getting those tax breaks, Trump was convinced, would bring the banks around.

Hoping to create a 1.5-million-square-foot hotel that would be the most spectacular hotel project since the building of the New York Hilton, he knew he had to have a big-name hotel chain as a partner. Hyatt was eager to create a flagship project in New York City, and Trump managed to secure a deal with Hyatt boss, Jay Pritzker, to become equal partners. Trump was to build the hotel, and Pritzker's Hyatt was to manage it. They announced their new partnership at a joint news conference on May 4, 1975.

Meanwhile, Trump was attempting to develop one of the most valuable pieces of property in Manhattan, the 76-acre riverfront area along the Hudson River between 59th and 72nd streets that became known as Riverside South.

Though civic activists had hoped the property would be developed as a major urban waterfront park, Trump bought the 76 acres in 1974 with other things in mind. He was torn between building offices and apartments, but he later opted for apartments because for a riverfront property, apartments seemed more appropriate. He held several meetings with community activists, but he ended up selling the property and focusing on the hotel.

When the media reported that Penn Central was nearing a decision to board up and close the hotel, the city decided to give Trump the tax abatements he had wanted. They were afraid that the eastern part of 42nd Street would turn into the same kind of eyesore as the western part. On May 8, the Board of Estimate voted to give Trump a forty-year tax abatement program. He was granted an option to purchase the land from the railroad for twelve million dollars.

The project made Trump a player in Manhattan. Despite his youth and inexperience, he could make connections and make things happen, although he was still unknown to the general public at that time. Though few had faith that he would succeed in getting the project through, he did it in a grand way. He erected a completely new building; rejecting the limestone-and-brick facades of the nearby buildings, he chose to put up a wall of highly reflective glass on the hotel's exterior, producing a mirror effect that enabled passersby to see the reflection of the Grand Central Terminal, the Chrysler Building, and other buildings in the Grand Hyatt. Inside, he made a magnificent lobby with brown Paradisio marble and brass railings and columns. And, even more impressive, he brought the project in on time and under budget.

The Grand Hyatt opened in September 1980. Trump asked his wife, Ivana, to oversee the interior decorating. An instant success, generating thirty million dollars of profit a year, the new hotel jump-started Trump's career. He now had his first solid body of work.

In 1978, while the Grand Hyatt was in development, Trump began planning an apartment-retail complex designed by Der Scutt at 57th Street and Fifth Avenue that was meant to shake the very foundations of New York real estate. Until then, the buildings along Manhattan's most famous shopping boulevard lacked an exciting modern design. Trump wanted to change that. Acquiring the site of the former Bonwit Teller building for twenty-five million dollars, he also negotiated for the air rights so that he could build a sixty-eight-floor residential tower on one of the great locations in Manhattan. The budget was put at two hundred million dollars.

When the building opened in April 1983, it became one of the city's most recognizable, heavily visited, and unique attractions. The six-story pink marble atrium with its eighty-foot waterfall became its instant signature. The pink marble certainly caught everyone's attention. Trump boasted that he had bought the "whole damn mountain" after Ivana had suggested that the color pink made people look better. The luxurious building attracted well-known retail stores and celebrity renters such as Johnny Carson, Paul Anka, Liberace,

Steven Spielberg, Sophia Loren, and Andrew Lloyd Webber. Trump moved into the top three stories, where he installed rare marble in the bathrooms, gold fixtures, a fountain in the center of the living room, and white carpet.

Trump's first instinct was to call it the Tiffany Tower because nearby Tiffany's was the premium name in high-quality jewelry and had broad brand recognition. But then he had a brainstorm. He had never named a building after himself. It was the kind of bold step that he loved to take. Yet it was very risky. If the building failed, his name would forever be associated with that failure. But not only did he name the building Trump Tower, but he put the name in two-foot-high gold lettering on the outside above the front door.

While Trump Tower was in construction, Trump repurchased the Riverside South property in 1982. He also started investigating the profitable casino gambling business. In 1980 he was able to acquire a piece of property in Atlantic City and brought in his younger brother Robert to head up the complex project of acquiring the land, winning a gambling license, and obtaining permits and financing. Holiday Inns Corporation, the parent company of Harrah's casino hotels, offered a partnership, and the $250 million complex opened in 1982 as Harrah's at Trump Plaza. Trump bought out Holiday Inns in 1986 and renamed the facility Trump Plaza Hotel and Casino.

In 1985, he bought the St. Moritz for seventy-two million dollars (he sold it for $180 million in 1988.) That same year, he also purchased a property in Palm Beach, Florida. For ten million dollars, Trump bought Mar-a-Lago, a hundred-and-eighteen-room Hispano-Moorish-Venetian castle built in the twenties by Marjorie Merriweather Post and E. F. Hutton, set on 17.5 acres extending from the ocean to Lake Worth. Ever since, his meticulous restoration and literal regilding of the property have been a work in progress. The winter of 1995–1996 was Mar-a-Lago's first full season as a commercial venture, a private club with an initiation fee that is quoted at more than seventy-five thousand dollars.

NBC, with its four-thousand-strong work force, was threatening to leave New York, so Trump in early in 1985 designed Television City for his Riverside property. He planned to build the world's tallest building, along with a good deal of studio space for NBC. His announcement of the building was a lead story on Dan Rather's *CBS Evening News* that night. Trump also wanted to build six thousand to seven thousand apartments in six seventy-story towers, a rooftop park, a two-million-square-foot suburban mall, and a six-thousand-car garage underneath. Critics remarked that he was, in effect, building a three-story-high wall fourteen blocks long that would divide the city from the river. The wall would cast a huge shadow across the West Side, they argued, blocking out light and wrecking the ambiance of the neighborhood. The neighborhood groups hated it. Mayor Ed Koch was also no fan of the project and, in the spring of 1987, turned down Trump's proposed Television City. Trump said that he thought Koch's decision had something to do with his embarrassment over Trump's bailout of the Wollman ice skating rink.

By 1986, Trump had watched as the City of New York had spent seven years trying to rebuild the Wollman rink in Central Park while he was rebuilding a major hotel and constructing a sixty-eight-floor residential tower. The city had spent twenty million dollars on the project, to its great embarrassment. Realizing that he could play the part of the hero, Trump plopped down three million dollars, and within four months the rink was open—on November 14, 1986, just in time for the winter skating season. He came in $750,000 under budget.

In February 1988, Trump acquired the Plaza hotel for $407 million, and spent $50 million refurbishing it under his wife Ivana's direction. He also bought the Eastern Shuttle for $365 million, which he promptly renamed the Trump Shuttle. Trump also purchased a Hilton Hotels casino-hotel in Atlantic City when the corporation failed to obtain a gambling license and renamed the $320 million complex Trump's Castle. Later, while it was under construction, he was able to acquire the largest hotel-casino in the world, the Taj Mahal at Atlantic City, which opened in 1990.

In the fall of 1989, *Forbes* noted that Trump was worth $1.7 billion.

However, things were about to change for Trump. The real estate market was declining, reducing the value of and income from his holdings. His own net worth plummeted to five hundred million dollars over the course of a year. In addition, he was spread thin and not paying attention to much of his developing empire. The construction of the billion dollar Trump Taj Mahal casino had been running behind, and the key executives who were getting the job done for him were killed on October 10, 1989, in a helicopter crash in New Jersey. Trump was said to be despondent.

In 1990 the Trump organization required a massive infusion of loans to keep it from collapsing, a situation which raised questions as to whether the corporation could survive bankruptcy. Trump owed the bankers nine billion dollars. The personally guaranteed portion was around one billion. A debt restructuring began in the spring of 1990, when Trump called his bankers together for a meeting in his conference room and admitted that he was in serious financial trouble. He told them that he needed another sixty-five million dollars to stay afloat and that he needed a five-year breathing space. No bank could lay claim to him until June 30, 1995. That meant the banks had to defer all interest and principal on loans for that five-year period. Trump put additional teeth into his argument by threatening to tie up his lenders in court for years with litigation. He would, of course, drop the legal threat if they agreed to the sixty-five-million-dollar line of credit.

The banks, knowing that they had limited recourse, agreed to Trump's terms. Years later, Trump called the agreement one of the best deals he ever made because it provided him with the liquidity to pay the banks and make other good deals. Though the banks insisted that he live a less lavish life, both publicly and privately, they let Trump decide which parts of his luxury life to retain and which to scuttle. He sold a number of properties, including the

Plaza Hotel, the Trump Shuttle, a twin-towered thirty-two-story condominium building near West Palm Beach, Florida, his 282-foot yacht, and his Boeing 727. Appraisers inventoried the contents of his Trump Tower home. Liens were attached to just about everything, but he was able to keep most of his businesses alive and functioning. He kept the casinos, the West Side Riverside project, and many other assets. Trump understood from his bankers that he needed to appoint a chief financial officer, and he named Steve Bollenbach to the CFO post. The media reported at the time that Trump had to limit his personal living expenses to $450,000 a month in 1990, $375,000 a month in 1991, and $300,000 a month for 1992, although Trump has insisted that this report was inaccurate and he was never put under any expense constraint.

Trump began plotting his comeback before the rest of the world fully grasped the direness of his situation. To bail himself out, Trump converted his casinos to public ownership, despite the fact that the constraints inherent in answering to shareholders do not come naturally to him. Inside the Trump organization, for instance, there is talk of "the Donald factor," the three to five dollars per share that Wall Street presumably discounts Trump Hotels & Casino Resorts by allowing for his braggadocio and unpredictability. The initial public offering in June 1995, raised $140 million, at fourteen dollars a share. Less than a year later, a secondary offering, at thirty-one dollars per share, brought in an additional $380 million.

By 1994 Trump had eliminated a large portion of his nine-hundred-million-dollar personal debt and reduced significantly his nearly nine billion dollars in business debt. Trump was reported to be worth close to two billion dollars in 1997.

In 1998, the stock price of Trump Hotels and Casino Resorts had fallen into single digits as the company remained profitless and struggled to pay just the interest on its nearly two billion dollars in debt. Under such financial pressure, the properties were unable to make the improvements necessary for keeping up with their flashier competitors.

In 1998, Trump sold his half of the Grand Hyatt for $242 million to the Pritzker family of Chicago, his longtime and long-estranged partners in the property. Most of the proceeds weren't his to keep, but he walked away with more than twenty-five million dollars. The chief significance of the Grand Hyatt sale was that it enabled Trump to extinguish the remnants of his debt. When Forbes published its annual list of the four hundred richest Americans, he just made it (at number 373) with an estimated net worth of $450 million.

In 1999, the Trump International Hotel and Tower opened its doors to the world. This fifty-two-story, mixed-use, superluxury hotel and residential building is located on the crossroads of Manhattan's West Side, on Central Park West at Columbus Circle. It is designed by the world-famous architect Philip Johnson and has gotten the highest sales prices and rentals in the United States. It is one of only three hotels in the United States that has received five stars from Mobil for both the hotel and restaurant. It has also received the Five Star Diamond Award from the American Academy of Hospitality Services.

In 2001 Trump completed Trump World Tower, a seventy-two-story residential tower across from the United Nations complex. That same year, he began construction on Trump Place, a multibuilding development along the Hudson River. Trump also has an undisclosed stake in Trump International Hotel and Tower, a forty-four-story mixed-use (hotel and condominium) tower on Columbus Circle.

In 2002, Trump purchased the fabled Delmonico Hotel located at 59th Street and Park Avenue. It has been developed into a state-of-the-art luxury thirty-five-story condominium to be named Trump Park Avenue. Another of Trump's new ventures in 2002 included the six-hundred-million-dollar Trump Grande Ocean Resort and Residences in Miami Beach, Florida, in partnership with a large local development company, and a superluxury sixty-story condominium tower on the Las Vegas strip.

In 2002, Trump entered into an exclusive agreement with NBC to become equal partners in the Miss Universe franchise. As part of the agreement, NBC and Telemundo became the U.S. broadcasters of the Miss Universe, Miss USA, and Miss Teen USA competitions for five years beginning in 2003. Trump had initially entered a partnership with CBS for Miss USA but switched to NBC.

In late 2003, Trump, along with his siblings, sold their late father's real estate empire to a group of investors that included Bain Capital, KKR, and LamboNuni Bank for a reported six hundred million dollars. Trump's one-third share was two hundred million dollars, which he later used to finance Trump Hotels & Casino Resorts.

Problems loomed for Trump's casino resorts. In a May 28, 2004, *Wall Street Journal* article, Trump said the spectre of bankruptcy bothered him "from a psychological standpoint," but added, "it really wouldn't matter that much." On October 21, 2004, Trump Hotels & Casino Resorts announced a restructuring of its debt. The plan called for Trump's individual ownership to be reduced from 56 percent to 27 percent, with bondholders receiving stock in exchange for surrendering part of the debt. Since then, Trump Hotels has been forced to seek voluntary bankruptcy protection to stay afloat. As a result of his company filing for Chapter 11 protection, in May 2005 Trump relinquished his CEO position to Stephanie A. Plumpy.

In 2004, Trump became the executive producer and host of the NBC reality show *The Apprentice,* in which a group of competitors battled for a high-level management job in one of Trump's commercial enterprises. The other contestants are "fired," or eliminated from the game. The winner of the program is "hired" into the Trump organization with a one-year "introductory" contract with a salary exceeding $250,000. At the end of each episode, Trump eliminates one contestant by telling them, "You're fired." For the first year of the show Trump was paid only fifty thousand dollars per episode, but following the show's initial success, he is now paid a reported three million per episode, making him one of the highest-paid TV personalities.

In 2004, Trump became the headliner at the Learning Annex Real Estate Wealth Expo in New York. He was reportedly paid a million dollars for his one-hour seminar. Since then he has appeared at six more expos for the Learning Annex.

In 2005, Trump launched Trump University, an online university offering business, real estate, and entrepreneurial courses. In 2006 he started Trump Mortgage, a mortgage firm, as well as Go Trump, an online travel website.

On June 15, 2006, Trump was scheduled to speak in the Minneapolis Convention Center to host the Trump Think Big Expo.

PERSONAL LIFE

Trump married Ivana Zelnickova Winklmayr, a fashion model who had been an alternate on the 1968 Czech Olympic Ski Team, in 1977. Ivana had been married once before to a Canadian skier, which had allowed her to emigrate out of Czechoslovakia.

Married life for the Trumps began smoothly and with much joy. Shortly after the marriage, their first child, Donald Junior, was born on December 31, 1977. Within five years, two other children followed, Ivanka (born October 30, 1981) and Eric (born January 11, 1984).

After the birth of the first of the couple's three children in 1978, Ivana began to work for Trump Industries, first as a decorator and later managing one of the properties. Ivana spoke five languages, although Trump frequently criticized her English.

Trump was known for being a ladies' man throughout his marriage to Ivana and has acknowledged having numerous affairs. When he had an affair with Marla Maples, a fledgling actress, though, it was widely reported in the press after Maples confronted Ivana with the news in Aspen in view of many reporters.

The subsequent divorce proceedings in 1992, Ivana's thinly disguised memoir novel, and her battle cry of "Don't get mad—get everything," made her a popular figure, while Trump was villainized in the press.

On October 13, 1993, another Trump daughter, Tiffany, was born to Marla Maples. Two months later the couple was married. Trump filed for a highly publicized divorce from Maples in 1997, which became final on June 8, 1999, allowing Trump to avoid a clause in the couple's prenuptial agreement that would allot Maples substantially more than the two million dollars he would have to pay if they were divorced earlier.

On January 22, 2005, Trump was married for a third time in a highly publicized wedding to Slovenian model Melania Knauss. They were married at Bethesda by the Sea Episcopal Church on the Island of Palm Beach, Florida, followed by a reception at Trump's Mar-a-Lago estate. Guests at the wedding included Bill and Hillary Clinton, Kathie Lee and Frank Gifford, Star Jones, Shaquille O'Neal, Barbara Walters, Billy Joel, Tony Bennett, Simon Cowell, Matt Lauer, Rudolph Giuliani, Kelly Ripa, Chris Matthews, Don King, Katie Couric, Regis Philbin, Heidi Klum, Pat O'Brien, Mark Burnett, and many others.

Melania gave birth to a boy, Barron William Trump, on March 20, 2006.

Trump is popularly known by his nickname "The Donald," given to him by ex-wife Ivana. He doesn't drink or smoke and claims he's never even had a cup of coffee. Due to his outspokenness and media exposure, he is an easily recognizable public figure whose distinctive comb-over is the subject of humor by comedians. He is also well known for not liking to shake hands, although he does that frequently anyway, washing his hands afterwards. He is six-foot-three, drinks a lot of Diet Coke, and lives in the top three stories of the Trump Tower, a fifty-three room apartment that has been widely photographed and featured on *Lifestyles of the Rich and Famous*. It has twenty-nine-foot ceilings in the living room decorated with neo-Romantic frescoes; the living room also has an erupting fountain. Together with the two-story dining room, which has carved ivory frieze ("I admit that the ivory's kind of a no-no," Trump said), the onyx columns with marble capitals that had come from "a castle in Italy," the chandelier that originally hung in "a castle in Austria," and the African blue-onyx lavatory combine to solidify Trump's reputation for living lavishly.

Trump has had his share of sorrow, however. His brother, Fred, Junior, an alcoholic, died at age forty-three in 1981. Trump called his death "the toughest situation I've had." Because of his brother's alcoholism, Trump himself never drinks. In 1999, Trump's father died.

LEADERSHIP LESSONS

Through the years, whether in up times or down, Trump has shown a fairly consistent working style. One of his primary character traits in business is that he is beyond all doubt optimistic. He believes that what he sets out to do, on the grandest of scales, really can be done, despite what experienced others say. He is also known to be quite direct. He says what's on his mind, using colorful language to underline his bluntness. He has always been busy, keeping a lot of irons in the fire because he never knows when one project might not go through. When that happens, he simply turns his attention to something else.

His father gave him a formula for doing business in real estate that he adhered to: "Get in, get it done, get it done right, and get out." Trump has always focused on the quality of his projects, making sure they were done the best they could be, even if that meant that he had to micromanage. In fact, his autocratic style, trying to take on everything himself, and inherent dislike of technology (he doesn't use a computer and insists that e-mails are for wimps), went against most of what he was taught in business school, but it has worked for him.

He is known to usually be in the office. He doesn't like to travel and is afraid he'll miss an opportunity if he's not there. He believes in self-promotion, negotiates with a vengeance, pays attention to details, and uses the media as much as he can to further his business goals.

He knew that none of his promotion or grand schemes or other strategies meant anything if he couldn't get the job done. "You can't con people, at least not for long," he wrote in *How to Get Rich*. "You can create excitement, you can do wonderful promotion and get all kinds of press, and you can throw in a little hyperbole. But if you don't deliver the goods, people will eventually catch on."

Negotiate

Trump's father and brother, Fred Junior, taught him a lot about real estate. Fred Junior did not enjoy the business, especially dealing with suppliers and contractors, and he did not deal with them in a way that gained his father's respect. Trump was quick to learn that he had to be tough in business negotiations. He loved them and thought of the negotiation as an art form.

His primary rule in negotiating with contractors is to know exactly how much they need to spend to get the job done. He then solicits several bids and then further works the bidders against each other.

Trump also visits his properties very often and constantly intervenes. He admits that it is much easier now that he has celebrity status to get concessions, but he always tried to get everyone down as far as he could. In addition to the cost savings in getting a low price, he admits he also found negotiation fun.

Trump learned his negotiation skills from his father and the contractors who worked for his father's business. In Brooklyn and Queens, he found he had to negotiate with developers for every penny.

Think Big

Trump's reasoning was always that if he was going to do the work, he might as well make it the biggest and best he could. He reasoned that only by acting boldly would he have any chance of attracting the financial resources required and get the attention of the media.

In contrast with many other real estate developers, he understood from this early stage in his career that it took no more time, no more effort to organize a large project than it did a much smaller one. It was that insight that gave him the incentive to think big initially. This became the common theme of every building project he undertook.

Use Other People's Money

For Trump to realize his grand-scale ambitions, he knew he would have to use other people's money. In fact, he made sure to invest as little of his money as possible, relying instead initially on big-name financial partners to foot the bills. Such partners solidified his own standing with the banks once he sought them out for financing of other projects.

In 1988 when he bought the Plaza Hotel for four hundred million dollars, Trump put up no equity, borrowing more than the necessary amount, $125 million of which he personally guaranteed. Although Trump owned some very valuable properties, he was also deeply in debt, but that was part of his strategy. He leveraged heavily and convinced his father to do more of that in his own business.

Trump preferred borrowing to selling stock when he needed to raise money to build a new casino or buy a hotel because he did not want to give up managerial control. Because of his reputation, banks were willing to lend him a great deal of money.

Trump has said, "Leverage is an amazing phenomenon. I love leverage." Trump was not bothered at all by owing vast amounts, up to nine billion dollars at one time.

Micromanage

From working with his father, Trump knew that his big dreams for his properties would mean nothing if they were not implemented efficiently. When he started out doing well by building the Grand Hyatt, he was micromanaging every step along the way. When he got into trouble, he believed that he was responsible for his undoing because he lost track of the details of his business. Now he monitors the tiniest detail, negotiating even small contracts and meeting the members of the building teams. For many projects, he even signs every single check.

He has taken a helicopter out to check out a paint color in one of his properties that he heard was too pale. He takes close look at plans and has been known to cross out trees and other small items on a drawing. Trump hires the best architects and the best engineers and then monitors most of their moves.

Of course, this micromanaging comes with a downside. "Part of my problem," Trump said, "is that I have to do a lot of things myself. It takes so much time."

Promote Thyself

Trump, unlike his father, had an incredible desire to publicize his work and his worth. He got his first real taste of publicizing himself during the renovation of the Wollman skating rink. That project put him in front of the media on a continuing basis, for doing something positive—even heroic, some thought.

"We ran a news conference every two minutes," said Howard J. Rubenstein, president of Rubenstein Associates, Inc., the prestigious New York–based public relations firm that handled Trump's media relations at that time. Rubenstein expands in Robert Slater's book, *No Such Thing as Overexposure,* "Donald was brilliant....Every single step of the way, we held a news conference. And they gave him the front pages and back pages. The *New York Times* would write one or two stories, but television kept coming back for more and more." They staged press conferences for everything during the project: when Trump announced it, when he broke ground, when he showed his plans, when he laid out the ice, when the ice was ready".

After his success with the rink, Trump contemplated how in a larger sphere he could advertise himself as a doer and deal-maker. One stunt involved orchestrating an "invitation" from the federal government to examine the Williamsburg Bridge, which was falling apart. Trump had no real interest in the job, but by putting on a hard hat and taking a stroll on the bridge for the cameras he stoked the fantasy that he could rebuild the city's entire infrastructure.

After his troubles in the early 1990s, Trump came back, and since 1993 he has issued statements to the effect that the previous year was "the most successful year I've had in business." A spate of Trump-comeback articles appeared in 1996, including several timed to coincide with his fiftieth birthday.

In interviews when he is showing journalists his projects, he commonly says something about the project being "the greatest building ever built." About his apartment: "This is the greatest apartment ever built." About 40 Wall Street: "This will be the finest office building anywhere in New York. Not just downtown—anywhere in New York." On a successful venture in Atlantic City, he took out an ad, announcing "The Most Successful Condominium Tower Ever Built in the United States." Trump even has a term for his penchant for saying these sorts of thing. He calls it "truthful hyperbole."

"You want to know what total recognition is?" Trump asked an interviewer David Remnick, "I'll tell you how you know you've got it. When the Nigerians on the street corners who don't speak a word of English, who have no clue, who're selling watches for some guy in New Jersey—when you walk by and those guys say, 'Trump! Trump!' That's total recognition."

To further promote himself, Trump has succeeded in marketing the Trump name on a large number of products, including Donald J. Trump Men's Collection, Trump Ice (bottled water), Trump Vodka, and *Trump Magazine.*

Use the Media

To fully promote himself, Trump turned to the media, always open to interviews and any chance to do so. This has backfired occasionally when the media printed things about his finances he didn't want known, but mainly he has quite deftly used them to his advantage. When one interviewer from *The New Yorker* questioned him, he sometimes answered by saying that his response was "off the record, but you can use it." The interviewer understood that Trump wanted the comment printed and pressed Trump on it. Trump explained, "If you have me saying these things, even though they're true, I sound like a schmuck."

Trump uses media outlets as much as possible with the idea that it will improve his business. He seeks news conferences often and often appears as himself in movies. He appeared briefly in *Home Alone 2: Lost in New York*, for instance. Kevin, the main character, asks him where the main lobby is; Trump says "Down the hall and to the left." He did a cameo appearance on the *Drew Carey Show*: Trump ended up giving Drew and his friends excellent seats at a Yankees baseball game while also giving them directions through New York City. His name was often mentioned in the sitcom *Just Shoot Me*, and he played a cameo role in *Zoolander*, commenting on his approval for for the title character, played by Ben Stiller. In the video game *Grand Theft Auto III* there is character named Donald Love, who is a real estate mogul and entrepreneur—an obvious spoof of Trump. Trump also guest-starred on an episode of *The Fresh Prince of Bel-Air*, when he almost buys the family's mansion for his nephew. A Muppet Donald Trump also appears in an episode of the thirty-sixth season of Sesame Street, alongside grouch Muppet Donald Grump.

Trump guest-starred as the father of Waldo in *The Little Rascals*. In 1995, Trump also appeared as a guest star on *The Nanny*. He hosted an episode of *Saturday Night Live* on April 3, 2004, spoofing his own show, *The Apprentice*, in some of the skits. Trump has also been included in numerous television commercials over the years, obtaining a million-dollar fee for a Pizza Hut commercial in the 1990s, a three-million-dollar fee for a Domino's Pizza commercial in 2005, and a five-million-dollar fee for his Visa Card commercial the same year.

At the 2005 Emmy Awards, he sang the theme song for the classic TV series *Green Acres*. He wore a farmer's outfit and held a rake in his hand while singing the song. He won the award for "Best Emmy Idol" for his performance, which he shared with *Will and Grace*'s Megan Mullally. He was referred to on the broadcast as "Diva Donald."

On March 30, 2005, he was cohost (in the absence of Kelly Ripa) with Regis Philbin on *Live with Regis and Kelly*. On September 27, 2005, Hollywood Records released *The Regis Philbin Christmas Album*, on which Trump and Philbin sing a duet of "Rudolph the Red-Nosed Reindeer." On October 24, 2005, Trump starred as himself on *Days of Our Lives*. On the show, he gave a donation to the Horton Foundation. On February 27, 2006, Trump made an appearance on the game show *Deal or No Deal*, advising the contestant to take the banker's deal—the contestant initially refused Trump's advice, and ended up winning much more money after being advised again by Trump.

"Money was never a big motivation for me, except as a way to keep score. The real excitement is playing the game."

Donald Trump

Trump is also very aware of his image and how he is portrayed, especially in print. In January of 2006, Trump filed a five-billion-dollar libel suit against biographer Timothy O'Brien and publisher Warner Books for claiming that he was only worth $150–$250 million, instead of being a billionaire.

POLITICAL INFLUENCE

Donald Trump has twice seriously attempted to run for president of the United States. In 1996, he ran in the Republican primaries before dropping out. On October 7, 1999, Trump announced the formation of an exploratory committee to inform his decision of whether or not he should seek the Reform Party's nomination for the presidential race of 2000. He then quit the Republican Party, in preparation for a presidential campaign as a Reform Party candidate. Trump eventually decided against running in the 2000 campaign after the Reform Party disintegrated into factionalism.

Trump's political views are largely centrist. He is prochoice regarding abortion and supports gay rights, Social Security privatization, and tax cuts. In 2004, Trump expressed opposition to the Iraq War but claims to have still voted for Bush due to his tax cut policy. Trump has contributed to both Republicans and Democrats, having donated slightly more money to Democratic candidates. In the first six months of 2005, he gave almost twenty thousand dollars to political campaigns, all but two thousand dollars of which went to Democrats. Senators he has recently supported include Hilary Clinton and Chuck Schumer of New York, Frank Lautenberg of New Jersey, and John McCain of Arizona. He also refused to favor one candidate over the other in the 2004 U.S. presidential election, giving two thousand dollars each to George W. Bush and John Kerry.

In late 2005, New York State Republicans attempted to win back Trump and put him forth as the Republican candidate for governor in 2006. However, Trump refused and in a shocking move endorsed Democrat Eliot Spitzer, who holds a huge lead over all his potential Republican opponents.

Trump has interacted with world leaders. The list of superpower leaders and geopolitical strategists with whom Trump has engaged in frank and fruitful exchanges of viewpoints includes Mikhail Gorbachev, Richard Nixon, Jimmy Carter, Ronald Reagan, George Bush, former Secretary of Defense William Perry, and the Joint Chiefs of Staff.

CRITICS

Donald Trump has had more than his fair share of critics, although most of them harp on his penchant for exaggeration. Alair Townsend, a former deputy mayor in the Koch administration, once quipped, "I wouldn't believe

Donald Trump if his tongue were notarized." In time, this quote became misattributed to Leona Helmsley, who was happy to claim authorship.

After Evander Holyfield upset Mike Tyson in a heavyweight title fight, Trump claimed that he'd collected twenty million dollars by betting a million on the underdog. This prompted the *Post* to make calls to some Las Vegas bookies, who confirmed that nobody had been handling that kind of action or laying odds close to 20–1. Trump never blinked when confronted with the facts. He just moved on.

Many of the other critics Trump has focus on his financial strategy of using leverage. This financial strategy works well only when business is very good. When business is slow, debt payments are more difficult to meet and Trump's creditors got stuck with the debt even though he was able to walk away relatively unscathed. Of course, he argues, that's the nature of business. When he did very well, so did his creditors.

Even Warren Buffett got into the fray:

> The big problem with Donald Trump was he never went right. He basically overpaid for properties, but he got people to lend him the money. He was terrific at borrowing money. If you look at his assets, and what he paid for them, and what he borrowed to get them, there was never any real equity there. He owes, perhaps, $3.5 billion now, and, if you had to pick a figure as to the value of the assets, it might be more like $2.5 billion. He's a billion in the hole, which is a lot better than being $100 in the hole because if you're $100 in the hole, they come and take the TV set. If you're a billion in the hole, they say 'hang in there Donald.' . . . Donald Trump wanted to get rich. That might not be a great qualifier. What would you do to select that one person out of this whole crowd here, because there will be a huge difference in results here. There's not a huge difference in IQ. But there will be a huge difference in results. You would probably relate it to a lot of qualities, some of which would be straight from Ben Franklin—I would suggest that the big successes I've met had a fair amount of Ben Franklin in them. And Donald Trump did not. . . . I've seen more people fail because of liquor and leverage—leverage being borrowed money. Donald Trump failed because of leverage. He simply got infatuated with how much money he could borrow, and he did not give enough thought to how much money he could pay back.

Some have charged that Trump lives a fairly shallow life, not bothering to examine any of life's complexities. David Remnick in *The New Gilded Age* said that Trump acts as the

> perpetual seventeen-year-old, they say, who lives in a zero-sum world of win-ners and "total losers," loyal friends and "complete scumbags"; the insatiable publicity hound who courts the press on a daily basis and, when he doesn't like what he reads, attacks the messengers as "human garbage"; the chairman and largest stockholder of a billion-dollar public corporation who seems unable to resist heralding overly optimistic earnings projections, which then fail to

materialize, thereby eroding the value of his investment—in sum, a fellow both slippery and naïve, artfully calculating and recklessly heedless of consequences.

For a fairly long time, Trump was parodied in Berke Breathed's long-running political cartoon strip, Bloom County. In this incarnation, he had been hit by an anchor. With his body damaged, his brain was placed inside the body of Bloom County's most disgusting character, Bill the Cat. As a penniless cat, his relationship with Ivana became long-distance and he continually searched for new ways to make money—even redecorating Roach Hotels. By the end of the series, he had bought the entire strip and fired all of the rest of the characters, replacing them with cartoon versions of Ivana and himself.

Trump has had an ongoing battle regarding how wealthy he is. Although he is very open with most aspects in his life, he has not shown a detailed report of his finances, of which over 90 percent are private. He has argued with *Fortune* over the size of his estate so he can be ranked higher (although the magazine says that most people call in to try to stay off the list).

POSSIBLE FUTURE IMPACT

Trump will undoubtedly continue to develop real estate in Manhattan and elsewhere. Plans for a Trump International Hotel and Tower on Waikiki Beach Walk have been announced that include a 350-foot tower with about 460 hotel-condo units.

He is also planning on writing additional books. Robert Kiyosaki, author of the Rich Dad, Poor Dad series, and Trump are teaming up to write *More Important Than Money,* a book about investing that the duo will self-publish under Kiyosaki's Rich Press imprint.

Trump will no doubt have a few surprises, as well.

TIMELINE

1946	June 14, Born in Queens Frederick C. and Mary MacLeod Trump.
1959	Sent to New York Military Academy.
1964	Graduated from New York Military Academy.
	Enrolled at Fordham.
1966	Switched schools to attend Wharton School of Business.
1968	Graduated from Wharton.
	Went to work in father's real estate company in Brooklyn.
1971	Moved to Manhattan and commuted to Brooklyn.
1975	Announced a 50–50 partnership with Hyatt and plans to buy his first property in Manhattan, the old Commodore Hotel at Grand Central Station.

1977   Married Ivana Zelnickova Winklmayr.
            December 31, Donald Trump, Jr., born.
1978   Plans made to build the Trump Tower at 57th street and 5th
            Avenue.
1980   The Grand Hyatt opened and was an immediate success, gen-
            erating thirty million dollars of profit per year.
            Acquired land in Atlantic City and formed partnership with Hol-
            iday Inn Corporation.
1981   October 30, Ivanka Trump born.
            Brother Fred Junior died of alcoholism.
1983   Trump Tower opened.
1984   January 11, Eric Trump born.
1985   Bought St. Mortiz and Mar-a-Lago.
1986   Redid the Wollman ice skating rink in Central Park, coming in
            $750,000 under budget.
1988   Acquired the Plaza Hotel and Eastern Shuttle, which he renamed
            the Trump Shuttle.
1989   *Forbes* put Trump's wealth at $1.7 billion.
            Three top executives were killed in a helicopter crash.
1990   The Taj Mahal opened in Atlantic City.
            Told banks to whom he owed nine billion dollars he needed
            sixty-five million more and that he needed to restructure his debt;
            the banks agreed and all payments were deferred for five years.
1992   Divorced Ivana.
1993   October 13, Trump's daughter with Marla Maples, Tiffany, born.
            December, married Maples.
1994   Eliminated most of personal debt.
1995   The IPO of Trump Hotels & Casino Resorts occurred, raising
            $140 million.
            Second stock offering brought in an additional $380 million.
1998   Stock price fell to single digits.
            Sold his share of the Grand Hyatt for $242 million.
1999   Trump International Hotel and Tower opened.
            Trump and Maples divorced.
2001   Completed the Trump World Tower.
2002   Purchased Delmonico Hotel.
2003   Sold father's real estate company to a group of investors for six
            hundred million dollars.
2004   Trump Hotels & Casino Resorts went into Chapter 11 bank-
            ruptcy.
            The Apprentice debuted.
2005   Relinquished role of CEO of Trump Hotels & Casino Resorts.
            Launched Trump University, Trump Mortgage, and Go Trump.
            Married Melania Knauss.

2006   Spoke at the Trump Think Big Expo.
            Broke ground on Las Vegas Trump casino.
            March 20, Son Barron William born.

RESOURCES

Binkley, Christina. Ideal Apprentice Holds Key to Trump Hotels; While Mogul Pursues TV Career, Butera Talks With Bondholders, And That's Fine With Everyone. *Wall Street Journal* May 28, 2004, p. C.1.

Buffett, Warren. Three Lectures to Notre Dame Faculty, MBA Students, and Undergraduate Students. Spring, 1991. http://www.tilsonfunds.com/BuffettNotre Dame.pdf.

Craig, Michael. *Best (And Worst) Business Deals of All Time.* Franklin Lakes, NJ: Career Press, 2000, pp. 74, 108, 153–158, 178–180.

Danziger, Pamela. *Let Them Eat Cake: Marketing Luxury to the Masses—As Well As the Classes.* Chicago, IL: Dearborn Trade, 2005, pp. 88–89, 155, 233.

Good, Steven L. *Churches, Jails, and Gold Mines: Mega Deals from a Real Estate Maverick.* Chicago, IL: Dearborn Trade, 2003, pp. 34, 205–218, 227–228, 231–235.

Mariotti, Steve. *Young Entrepreneur's Guide to Starting and Running a Business.* New York: Crown Publishing Group, 2000, pp. 116, 256–269, 263, 275.

Remnick, David (Editor). *The New Gilded Age: The New Yorker Looks at the Culture of Affluence.* New York: Modern Library, 2000.

Slater, Robert. *No Such Thing as Overexposure.* Upper Sadde River, NJ: Pearson Education, 2005.

Trump, Donald, and Meredith Mciver. *Trump: How to Get Rich.* New York: Random House, Inc., 2004.

Trump, Donald, and Tony Schwartz. *Trump: The Art of the Deal.* New York: Ballantine, 1987.

COMPANY INFORMATION

The Trump Organization
725 Fifth Avenue
New York, NY 10022
Phone: (212) 832–2000
Fax: (212) 935–0141
www.trump.com
Trump Entertainment Resorts Incorporated
New York Stock Exchange symbol: TRMP

Ted Turner

Ted Turner built a communications empire and almost single-handedly changed the way news is perceived and presented. Before Turner built the Cable News Network (CNN), news was reported after the fact in small summaries. Today, news is what is happening at the moment, and it is reported twenty-four hours a day. Turner capitalized on new technology, recognizing that satellite-based broadcasting was the future of television. He built up a library of existing content that he bought outright and to which he sold the rebroadcast rights. Very few people saw the potential that Turner saw and even fewer attempted to capitalize on it. For his success in changing an industry, Turner was honored as *Time Magazine*'s Man of the Year in 1991.

Turner's father handed him a very successful billboard advertising company, and Turner could have retired at any moment in his career. His drive to succeed and his competitive need were seen not only in his business successes but also in his sailing achievements. Turner successfully defended the America's Cup in 1977 in his yacht, *Courageous*.

When Turner bought his first television station, almost no one but him saw its potential. Many advisors adamantly cautioned against going into what they saw as a losing battle. Over several years and while losing millions of dollars, Turner bought content for the station and a tower to beam microwave signals beyond his range to five neighboring states. He bought the Atlanta Braves, along with the contract that he could broadcast sixty games a season. When he successfully arranged to take advantage of satellite technology, his Channel 17 became the Turner Broadcasting System Superstation, the first station to broadcast nationally. He later acquired the entire MGM library of film and television properties, paying $1.5 billion in 1986. In 1991, he bought the rights to and the library of Hanna-Barbera Cartoons and later launched his Cartoon Network.

He is probably most well known for starting CNN, the first around-the-clock, all-news television station. Critics derided the idea of a nonstop news network. Turner thought differently and pursued his vision relentlessly. He went on to start CNN Headline News, which offered updated newscasts on the half-hour, and made an unsuccessful bid to buy CBS. Later, other stations would mimic the CNN template, but that would not occur for almost ten years, leaving Turner's network as the only player in a lucrative market.

"All my life people have said that I wasn't going to make it."

Ted Turner

Turner is also quite well known for his political and philanthropic efforts, most notably his billion-dollar pledge to the United Nations. He financed the first Goodwill Games, which were held in Moscow in 1986. His social life has been quite active.

Turner is divorced now after being married three times, most notably to his last wife, actress Jane Fonda. He has five children with his first two wives. He is known as much for his outspokenness and gregarious personality as for his successes. Stories of his egregious excesses have long been around. He is by all accounts complicated and contradictory but very charismatic.

CNN no longer belongs to Turner. The media mogul stepped down as vice chairman of AOL Time Warner in January 2003. In subsequent interviews, he claimed that the poor performance of AOL Time Warner's share price had cost him seven or eight billion dollars ("How I Lost $8 billion, by Ted Turner," *The Guardian*, February 6, 2003). In 2006, he left the board of AOL Time Warner. Still worth an estimated 2 billion dollars even after unloading most of his Time Warner AOL shares, Turner was listed as one of *Forbes*'s World's Richest People in 2005. He is also the largest private landowner in the United States.

THE EARLY YEARS

Edward Turner III was born in Cincinnati, Ohio, on November 19, 1938, to Florence Rooney and Edward Turner II. His younger sister by three years, Mary Jane, contracted lupus cerebritis while Turner was in college, a debilitating disease that gave her violent fits and agonizing pain for five years before she finally died.

> *"I've never run into a guy who could win at the top level in anything today and didn't have the right attitude, didn't give it everything he had, at least while he was doing it; wasn't prepared and didn't have the whole program worked out."*
>
> Ted Turner

Turner grew up lonely and unloved. He was tormented by an abusive, alcoholic father who hoped to provoke his son to greatness by beating him. His mother, who graced Turner with her own good looks and ebullient, outgoing personality, eventually left his father after twenty-two years—in great part, she said, because of her husband's severe treatment of their only son.

Ed Turner always treated his daughter very well, however, and showered praise and love on her.

After the Japanese launched the attack on Pearl Harbor, Ed Turner enlisted in the navy. For the next four years Ed would trundle his wife and young daughter off with him to a long succession of Gulf Coast posts. He left three-year-old Turner behind in Cincinnati with his grandmother, Florence Sicking Rooney until Turner was sent away to boarding school at the age of six. Turner would spend all but one of the next fifteen years living away from his family. When he did come home during that time, he spent much of his time with Jimmy Brown, a seventeen-year-old boat handler from West Africa whose first job had been to take care of *Thistle*, the forty-foot Great Lakes schooner Ed sometimes kept down in the Bahamas. He later came into the Turner household as cook, chauffeur, and caretaker for Turner. Turner said that he loved Brown as a father.

After the war, Ed Turner brought his family, minus Turner, back to Cincinnati, where, with a little help from his mother-in-law, he set himself up in his own billboard company. Turner Advertising was hardly an overnight success since Ed chose to locate the new business across the Ohio River in Covington, Kentucky, outside the lucrative but intensely competitive Cincinnati market. Once he signed up one of Cincinnati's bigger breweries, however, Turner Advertising was in business for real.

Ed remembered a sleepy old billboard company in Georgia that had caught his eye during the war, and it took him just one visit to convince the retiring owner of Price & Mapes, Savannah's only billboard operator, to merge with Turner Advertising. Once again Ed gathered up his wife and daughter and took them south. Noting that his boy, now nine years old, was in continuous hot water at his Cincinnati boarding school, Ed decided a little dose of military discipline might now be in order. Accordingly, Turner was packed off to spend the fourth grade at a stark, forbidding institution called Georgia Military Academy.

By 1948, Ed Turner was ready to settle down in Savannah. He bought a large five-bedroom house at 3204 Abercorn Street, just a few blocks from the city's historic old Oglethorpe Square district. For the first time in his life, Turner would have a room under his parents' roof. His father made him work for Turner Advertising on labor gangs that did everything from erecting new billboard sites to creosoting signboards and pasting up sixteen-sheet posters. Turner had to give back part of his earnings to his father for room and board. Jimmy Brown also came to live with the family. Ed allowed Turner to live at home during one school year and bought his son a new Penguin sailing dinghy. It was Jimmy Brown, however, who first took Turner out on the Skidaway River and taught him how to read the wind and water. Sailing was a way that Turner could bond with his father. Ed enjoyed watching Turner compete in junior regattas at the Savannah Yacht Club. The following year, Ed made Turner enter McCallie, an exclusive boy's school in Chattanooga, Tennessee. Turner was never a great student, much preferring the outdoors to schoolwork.

In 1956, Turner went to Brown University and decided to study classics, a choice his father ridiculed. He was expelled from Brown in his junior year for having girls in his dorm room. After turning to the Coast Guard for a brief time, Turner and a friend who had also been kicked out of Brown went to Atlanta to work for Ed Turner. Turner became an account executive and did well for the company.

A little more than a year after his divorce from Florence, Ed surprised everyone by marrying Jane Dillard. Jane had a son from her first marriage, Marshall Hartmann, and he came to live with his mother and Ed Turner until he graduated from McCallie in 1962, six years behind Turner. Marshall looked up to Turner as an older brother and was even a witness at Turner's marriage to Judy Nye. Once his father married Jane, however, Turner backed away from his stepbrother and has never publicly acknowledged their relationship.

In 1962, his father bought out part of a competitor for four million dollars but later tried to negotiate out of the contract because he felt that he had gotten in over his head. In March of 1963, Ed Turner committed suicide, making his son, Turner, the company's president and chief operating office, and leaving him a modest fortune.

"The media is too concentrated, too few people own too much. There's really five companies that control 90 percent of what we read, see and hear. It's not healthy."

Ted Turner

Turner would always be heavily influenced by his father, even after his death. He kept the silver .38-caliber revolver that his father used to kill himself in his desk. Once, while giving a lively speech, he waved a well-thumbed copy of the latest issue of *Success* magazine and stopped suddenly and showed the cover, which featured a picture of himself. Turner's loud voice suddenly trailed off to a whisper. "Is this enough?" he beseeched plaintively as he stared up at the rafters, holding the magazine high over his head. "Is this enough for you, Dad?"

CAREER PATH

After his father's suicide, Turner took over the reins at Turner Advertising. He immediately reversed his father's nearly completed sale of the failing business. Interestingly, the *Atlanta Constitution* of Wednesday, March 6, 1963, carried a front-page story headlined "Billboards Restricted by Senate," detailing the passage by the Georgia State Legislature of a controversial new law limiting the number of billboards on interstate highways. The article appeared only a few columns away from the newspaper's announcement of Ed Turner's suicide.

> *"The world and life have been mighty good to me. And I want to put something back."*
> Ted Turner

Once he took control of Turner Advertising, Turner soon discovered that the billboard business was a tax-depreciable revenue stream that threw off enormous amounts of cash with almost no capital investment. Most outdoor advertising companies, Turner's included, were basically monopolies that could be sustained through mergers and acquisitions. The significant economies of scale achievable in outdoor advertising meant that the larger companies could generally operate at higher profit margins than smaller ones and could therefore price their competition out of business. Once he learned that lesson, Turner moved quickly to expand into new markets. He bought out competitors in Knoxville and Chattanooga and began to consolidate his hold on the entire South.

Turner hired James C. Roddey, who became the first and last president of his company, away from Rollins Company, where Roddey had been in charge of Rollins's interests in radio, television, and the new business of cable television. With Roddey on board, Turner turned to purchasing a radio station in Chattanooga, Tennessee, WAPO. Turner's outdoor billboards were consistently generating lucrative profits, but turnover among advertisers always left a number of his signs unsold. Rather than spend money maintaining those empty boards, Turner saw them as the perfect way to promote his radio station. Over the next two years Turner Communications acquired a second station in Chattanooga, two in Charleston, and one in Jacksonville, Florida. With the promotional assistance made possible by Turner's billboards, every one of those underperforming stations was soon turning a handsome profit. He renamed the company Turner Communications Group.

Radio proved to be no more interesting to him than the billboard business. Now that Turner was moving into the major leagues in ocean racing and consorting with kings and princes, he was yearning for more of a reach in business. He decided that breaking into the big time would be infinitely easier if Turner Communications were a public company.

On October 18, 1968, Robinson Humphrey Company, Inc., an Atlanta-based securities firm, sold 130,000 shares of Rice Broadcasting stock. The net proceeds were immediately consumed by Rice Broadcasting's sole operating asset—WJRJ, a lackluster UHF (ultra-high-frequency) television station that had total revenues that year of only $411,000 and accumulated losses well in excess of $800,000. If Robinson Humphrey had not initiated an immediate, all-out effort to sell WJRJ-TV, it would almost certainly have risked watching the company go under. Turner knew nothing about ultra-high-frequency television and couldn't even pick up WJRJ, Channel 17, on his own TV. In 1968 fewer than half the sets in the area were able to receive a UHF signal. WJRJ's own research showed that the station was viewed by fewer than five percent of the households in greater Atlanta.

Turner knew television was growing faster than any other medium and assumed it wouldn't be long before TV started to cut into his outdoor advertising profits. The license to own a TV station, Turner was convinced, could be worth a fortune in a few years. In the meantime, billboards would continue to throw off enough profit to help him get the station into the black.

On January 26, 1970, the merger of Rice Broadcasting into Turner Communications Corporation was announced. The transaction consisted of a tax-free exchange of stock, with Rice shareholders swapping 3.6 shares of Rice Broadcasting for one share of Turner Communications stock. No cash was involved. Turner Communications became the surviving entity and a public company in the bargain by virtue of having reverse-merged with Rice. Turner controlled the combined companies in a deal that valued WJRJ at about $2.5 million. For an additional $180,000 in Turner stock, Turner acquired WJRJ's 1,093-foot broadcast tower in a separate transaction with a real estate partnership controlled by Rice's former owners. By the end of 1970, Turner Communications, which had before always been profitable, posted a net after-tax loss of over seven hundred thousand dollars.

WJRJ was the weaker of two UHF independents in the Atlanta market. Turner ordered Jim Roddey to have the station's call letters changed to WTCG (Turner Communications Group). Turner found another UHF station for sale in Charlotte, North Carolina. The company accountant and longtime aide to his father quit the company and took Roddey with him over this, and the board vetoed the Charlotte station. Turner bought the station on his own by borrowing $250,000 against his signature just as the sheriff was about to begin liquidation proceedings. He assumed nearly three million dollars in station liabilities in order to close the deal, securing the debt with his Turner Communications stock. Later he would have to borrow from his company to keep the Charlotte station on the air. He promptly renamed the station WRET, in honor, he said, of his father. To avoid an obvious conflict of interest, he also assigned Turner Communications an option to acquire the station in exchange for forgiving any funds it lent him.

By early 1971 Turner Communications was severely undercapitalized. The Federal Communications Commission reported that 99 of 146 UHF stations reporting in 1970 were operating in the red. Turner hired Will Sanders to manage the crisis. Sanders was able to buy back enough shares to push Turner's ownership over fifty-five percent. Turner Communications stock had slid from five dollars a share all the way down to one dollar, but Sanders was banking on an independent appraiser's estimate of the company's true market value. The appraisal confirmed Turner's belief that his company had doubled in value since the merger. Despite WTCG's operating loss, Turner Communications was now worth at least twelve million dollars on the open market.

The Atlanta market was the tenth largest in the country, and UHF penetration was exploding. On March 31, 1971, without any warning, his competitors, WATL's owners, United Broadcasting Corporation, decided to pull get out of the Atlanta market, leaving Turner's station as the only UHF station there. WTCG went from fifth of five television stations to fourth of four in Atlanta. As the only remaining independent, Turner now had plenty of room to maneuver.

In the first two years Turner owned WTCG, his potential audience had grown from five percent of Atlanta's households to nearly fifty-five percent and climbing by promoting the station on billboards and concentrating on acquiring content to show.

WTCG broadcast almost nothing but old black-and-white movies and stale reruns, but the station continued to post impressive revenue gains. Turner bought whatever movies and television show content he could, often overpaying. Most television stations, particularly financially strapped independents, typically licensed films for a limited number of showings. The rights then reverted back to the owners. Turner went against conventional wisdom and bought films outright whenever he could. That way he could run them as often as he wanted, prorating the purchase price over hundreds of airings. Few realized the significance of his approach, which necessarily limited him to the oldest, cheapest programs on the market; but by owning the product whenever possible, Turner gained the leverage that would ultimately make WTCG the single most profitable television station in the country. WTCG often broadcast older reruns of *Lassie*, *Leave It to Beaver*, *I Love Lucy*, *Father Knows Best*, and *Petticoat Junction*. Turner promoted his station as being one of family values.

In moves that would later be ironic given his success with CNN, Turner capitalized on the viewers who did not watch the news. The networks fed their evening news shows to their local affiliates, but the ABC station in Atlanta chose instead to fatten its ratings by counterprogramming entertainment fare. When ABC finally came down hard on its affiliate and insisted it carry the network news, Turner rushed into the breach with old *Star Trek* reruns. It wasn't long before WTCG had captured a big portion of the evening audience. NBC's affiliate, WSB, was perpetually number one in the Atlanta market. When WSB declined to carry several network offerings in favor of more profitable locally produced shows, Turner pounced again and picked up a package of five NBC sitcoms from the network, eager to have any outlet in the growing Atlanta market. To satisfy the FCC requirement that a station broadcast at least seven hours of news or public affairs programming a week, Turner scheduled his station's news hour at three o'clock each morning, knowing that he couldn't compete with the other stations. Turner installed Bill Tush, a weatherman he'd inherited when he acquired WTCG, as the station's news director, anchor, and incipient local celebrity. Tush would "rip and read" the news from wire service dispatches and, sometimes, straight from the *Atlanta Constitution* newspaper. He occasionally livened things up by introducing a German shepherd as his coanchor and outdoor editor. He would also deliver the news from behind a mask of Walter Cronkite. During the Atlanta Braves' six-year sojourn in the National League cellar, Tush even delivered the baseball scores with his head in a paper bag. Local insomniacs tuned in just to see what Tush would do next.

An old girlfriend of Turner's who had married one of Atlanta's top professional wrestling promoters persuaded her husband to move his matches from the local ABC affiliate to WTCG. Soon Channel 17's tiny little studio housed a full-size wrestling ring. Wrestling helped WTCG's anemic ratings begin to edge upward and first brought home to Turner the pulling power of professional sports. The Atlanta Braves had arrived in Atlanta from Milwaukee in 1962. Their parent company, LaSalle-Atlanta Corporation, had lost nearly a million dollars a year ever since, although part of that loss was defrayed by WSB, which paid LaSalle two hundred thousand dollars a year for the right to telecast twenty Braves road games. The arrangement had not been particularly satisfactory for either party. When Turner offered six hundred thousand dollars a season for the next five years, the Braves took it without caring about the fine print in the Turner contract, which allowed WTCG to broadcast sixty Braves games a season.

Turner resold his Braves' broadcast rights to twenty-four other stations across six southern states. Almost without realizing it, Turner had created the largest "mini-network" in the country. Considering WTCG's other offerings, Braves games also quickly became WTCG's highest-rated broadcasts.

In 1971 WTCG lost more than five hundred thousand dollars. By 1972, however, the station was breaking even, and it earned over a million dollars the following year. Turner soon turned the Atlanta and Charlotte stations into two of the most successful independents in the country. Turner had a growing library of several thousand old movies and broadcast rights to Atlanta's major league baseball, basketball, and hockey teams.

In a new ruling intended to benefit struggling independent television stations, the FCC in 1972 allowed cable television operators to "import" distant signals from certain stations in the top one hundred markets across the country. Turner conceded shortcomings in the new FCC ruling but, in his 1972 report to shareholders, suggested that "stations like WTCG are the ones most likely to benefit from these new regulations." From that moment on Ted Turner knew his real market was an ever-expanding audience beyond Atlanta. He began by co-opting the television-starved citizens of Georgia's rural hill country, where television reception of any kind without cable was all but impossible.

Turner managed to begin sending WTCG's signal via microwave into more than a hundred thousand new homes beyond the reach of the other Atlanta stations. Soon he would stretch his signal to Macon and Columbus and then down to Tallahassee.

In late 1975, Home Box Office (HBO), a Time-Life pay-cable subsidiary, announced that it planned to use a Satcom I transponder to deliver its movies to participating cable system head ends nationwide. Systems that purchased a television receive-only (TVRO) antenna could now carry a pay-cable service, charge subscribers an additional fee, and share the proceeds with HBO. When HBO paid the nine million dollars required for a long-term lease on an RCA satellite, there were only two earth stations in the entire country that could receive its signal. Turner read about the deal in *Broadcasting* magazine. Where others saw enormous risk, however, Turner saw the chance of a lifetime. The cable industry was quick to see the satellite as its only means of survival. Teleprompter Corporation, then the largest operator of cable systems in the country, endorsed satellite delivery at the outset and, by announcing in early 1976 that it would order earth stations for each one of its systems, provided the impetus satellite technology needed. Within weeks other large multiple-system owners followed suit. Their endorsement of satellite distribution helped push down the price of receive-only earth stations from a hundred thousand dollars to twenty-five thousand dollars three years later. The "uplink" facility needing to get a signal up to the satellite, however, still cost over $750,000. Turner approached RCA, hoping to pick up one off the shelf. He was told that satellites were not for "private" use and were intended to provide established networks like ABC, CBS, and NBC with an economic alternative to the expensive AT&T telephone lines they had been using to tie their network affiliates together. Turner tried AT&T, which by now had also entered the satellite business. The telephone company had no interest.

Then Turner found Ed Taylor, Western Union's youngest vice president, who had already spent nearly ten years in the satellite business. Taylor also served on the industry task force in 1967 that recommended satellite communication over any other system. Turner went back to RCA, with Taylor on board, and was finally able to induce them to grant him a long-term transponder lease on their newest satellite, on two conditions: Turner must provide his own earth station transmitter, and he would have to secure FCC approval. With calls to a few wealthy sailing friends in New York, Turner raised enough to cover the down payment on an earth station. Another friend, Sidney Topol, president of Scientific-Atlanta, Inc., sold him a Series 8000 Satellite Earth Terminal. Then Turner took off again for Washington to get FCC approval.

What Turner was doing wasn't exactly illegal; he was just setting precedent. In less than a week a full-blown earth station transmitter/receiver some thirty feet tall had been installed at the bottom of a sparsely wooded hollow near

Cobb Creek in Douglasville, Georgia, its ten-meter dish pointed toward the sky, its ten-ton white electronics trailer tied nearby, its microwave antenna pulling in WTCG's signal loud and clear from the downtown Atlanta studios about ten miles away. Turner had set up his earth station as a separate business, Southern Satellite Systems, Inc., but he was not allowed to own any part of the new company, since Southern Satellite would in all likelihood be construed by the FCC as a common carrier, and broadcast license holders could not own common carriers. Turner sold Southern Satellite to Ed Taylor for one dollar. Then Taylor went to RCA, which acquired Southern Satellite from Taylor in exchange for Turner's agreement to a long-term lease on RCA's satellite. Ed Taylor then leased back the earth station from RCA and contracted with WTCG to uplink its signal.

On December 27, 1976, a little more than a year afterward, the FCC finally approved Southern Satellite's application as a common carrier. Anticipating demand among cable operators, the FCC also halved the required size of satellite receiving dishes from thirty feet to fifteen feet, effectively cutting their cost by an additional 60 percent or more. Most commercial dishes today run between a thousand dollars and five thousand dollars, but Scientific-Atlanta's Topol still remembers that first price cut in 1976, which dropped the cost of a dish to fifty thousand dollars. It was the beginning of the deluge, and within five years, thanks in no small part to Ted Turner, Topol's small electronics company would be a billion-dollar business.

By the end of 1976, Turner's station, which he now called a "superstation," was being carried by twenty cable systems in different parts of the country. Satellite transponders solved the age-old problem of expensive and time-consuming expansion of terrestrial networking by substituting instant nationwide distribution of a signal. Cable systems would have to buy a receiving antenna. However, once that step was taken, they would be able to provide Turner's and HBO's programs–and other signals promised for the late 1970s– as added incentives for cable subscribers.

Turner ordered up some fancy on-air graphics for the satellite launch and a new logo for the station. That first day on the satellite, however, Turner's new Superstation was actually serving fewer than ten thousand households, in small cities with cable systems whose downlink facilities were capable of pulling in WTCG's satellite signal.

In 1977, Turner bought the Atlanta Braves and the Atlanta basketball team, the Hawks, in order to broadcast them through his new Superstation.

A typical program schedule from late 1976 was:

8:00–10:00 a.m.	Cartoon Cavalcade
10:30 a.m.	*Steve Allen*
11:00 a.m.	*The Little Rascals*
11:30 a.m.	*Lassie*
noon	*The Flintstones*

| 12:30 p.m. | *Mr. Ed* |
| 1:00 p.m. | *The Munsters* |

Movies were saved for the evenings when the Atlanta Braves and Hawks were not scheduled.

Turner gave the Superstation away to cable systems for nothing, hoping to make a profit from advertising once he could document the size of the audience watching the Superstation. Turner launched a promotion to build the Superstation's audience as big as possible. He set aside more than five hundred thousand dollars for advertising and promotion, then leveraged that amount several times over by persuading local cable operators to advertise his Superstation to build their own subscriber bases. It wasn't a difficult sell, since WTCG was about the only channel cable operators could offer viewers that didn't cost them anything. When Turner began to produce ratings, he underpriced his Superstation against the major networks. Looking for ways to expand its advertising reach, Toyota became the first national advertiser on the Superstation. To show his appreciation, Turner drove a little white 1976 Toyota for the next ten years. Soon other advertisers recognized the unique value Turner offered and began flocking to the Superstation. When *Time* magazine tested a new subscription offer, the publisher was so impressed with the results that *Time* increased its planned expenditure on the Superstation by over eightfold.

Six months after going up on the satellite, Turner's Superstation was adding more than 250,000 new households a month to its rapidly escalating audience.

On June 1, 1980, Turner inaugurated CNN, the world's first live, in-depth, round-the-clock news television network. In late 1981 Turner sued all three major broadcast networks with a landmark antitrust suit, claiming they were conspiring to keep Cable News Network out of the White House television press pool. Turner also sued Ronald Reagan, the president of the United States; James Brady, his press secretary; and General Alexander Haig, the Secretary of State. He was also about to press Congress to investigate CBS, NBC, and ABC for "polluting the minds of the American people," when CNN was allowed in. The major networks criticized Turner's CNN as being unprofessional with low production and editorial quality.

A second all-news service, Headline News, began operation on January 1, 1982, offering updated newscasts every half-hour. Launched in September 1985, CNN International serves as the company's global news service and is distributed in more than 210 countries and territories worldwide. That same year, Turner tried unsuccessfully to acquire CBS for five billion dollars.

In March 1986, the newly named Turner Broadcasting System (TBS) acquired the MGM library of film and television properties. This library formed the initial programming cornerstone of Turner Network Television (TNT), which was launched on October 3, 1988. Versions of TNT are customized for Latin America and the Caribbean, with programming available in English, Spanish, or Portuguese.

In 1987, CNN launched the first global newscast, CNN World Report, providing unedited, uncensored news reports from broadcasters in a hundred countries. By 1989, CNN's operating profit had reached a hundred million dollars.

In 1991, the Gulf War began. CNN reported exclusively live from Baghdad on the first night of the air attacks on Iraq. Its pictures were picked up and retransmitted by terrestrial TV channels around the globe. This was probably the single most significant event in CNN's rise to global recognition.

In December 1991, Turner acquired the rights, library, and production facilities of Hanna-Barbera Cartoons. The Cartoon Network, launched on October 1, 1992, showcases the company's vast library of cartoons and original productions. Cartoon Network in Latin America was launched on April 30, 1993, offering viewers in Latin America and the Caribbean twenty-four hours of cartoons in three languages. TNT and Cartoon Network were launched in Europe on September 17, 1993, offering classic films and animation programming in seven languages. TNT and Cartoon Network in Asia Pacific, launched October 6, 1994, provides programming in English, with some programs dubbed or subtitled in Mandarin and Thai.

> *"You can never quit. Winners never quit, and quitters never win."*
>
> Ted Turner

In January 2002, Turner opened the first Ted's Montana Grill in Columbus, Ohio, with his partner, George W. McKerrow, Jr., founder of the Longhorn Steakhouse chain and several other successful restaurants. Ted's Montana Grill offers classic American comfort food, including bison or beef burgers, in an authentic Montana bar and grill atmosphere. Ted's Montana Grill expects to open up to forty more restaurants in the next few years.

Time magazine made Ted Turner its Man of the Year in 1992.

On January 1, 1993, Turner switched on the first advertiser-sponsored Russian-language television station in the Soviet Union, a joint venture between TBS and Moscow Independent Broadcasting Company. By the end of that year, CNN had operating profits of two hundred million dollars. It then set up its Web site, CNN.com, as the only site with a twenty-four-hour full-time staff, providing constantly updated news augmented by video, sound clips, still photographs, maps, and text.

In January 1994, Turner Broadcasting merged with New Line Cinema. Films from New Line and the combined Turner and Warner Brothers library of film classics provide programming for the Turner Classic Movies channel (TCM), a twenty-four-hour commercial-free network launched in April 1994.

Turner Broadcasting continued to expand its news division with the creation of CNN Radio and CNN Airport Network, which provides programming for airline travelers in U.S. airports, and CNN Interactive, the division responsible for multimedia/online news production and distribution. CNN en Español, which was launched on March 17, 1997, offers twenty-four-hour Spanish-language news to viewers throughout the Americas.

Turner became vice chairman of Time Warner in October 1996, with the merger of Time Warner, Inc., and Turner Broadcasting System, Inc., that made him Time Warner's largest shareholder. Turner oversaw Time Warner's Cable Networks division, which included the assets of Turner Broadcasting System, Inc., the CNN Newsgroup, HBO, Cinemax, and the company's interests in Comedy Central and Court TV. He also oversaw New Line Cinema and the company's professional sports teams—the Atlanta Braves, Atlanta Hawks, and Atlanta Thrashers. However, in the merger, he gave up his control of the company and later regretted that.

When Time Warner and AOL decided to merge, Turner backed the decision, but later he came into conflict with the company's senior executives over its strategy.

In 1997, Turner donated a billion dollars to the United Nations. UN secretary general Kofi Annan called him a "world citizen extraordinaire." That same year, CNN received permission from Fidel Castro to set up a bureau in Cuba—the first American news organization to be allowed into the country for thirty years.

> *"War has been good to me from a financial standpoint but I don't want to make money that way. I don't want blood money."*
>
> Ted Turner

In January 2001 Turner became vice chairman of AOL Time Warner, a position he held until May 2003, when he resigned to pursue his "socially responsible business efforts." In his new position, however, Turner lost the day-to-day control over the cable properties and was effectively ousted. Upon his resignation, AOL Time Warner chief executive Richard Parsons said the company had been grateful for his "vision and genius." In subsequent interviews, Turner claimed that the poor performance of AOL Time Warner's share price had cost him seven or eight billion dollars. Turner is bitter over his experience with the media giant and publicly called for the breakup of all large media companies in the article titled "My Beef with Big Media." In 2003, Turner sold sixty million shares of AOL Time Warner, in a sale that amounted to about a third of his net worth, using calculations from *Forbes* magazine.

By the end of Turner's reign, CNN had eleven different networks. Turner stayed on the board of Time Warner until 2006 when he resigned.

PERSONAL LIFE

Turner has had three wives but is now divorced. He was famously married to actress Jane Fonda for six years but after their divorce has remained single.

Turner met his first wife, Judy Nye, while he was in the Coast Guard. She was also a sailing enthusiast, and they married on June 23, 1962. Turner and Judy had two children together, Teddy IV and Laura, before divorcing when Judy was still pregnant with Laura. Two years after his divorce from Judy Nye and little more than a year after Ed Turner's death, Turner and Jane Shirley

Smith, a flight attendant whom he met at a business party, were married in Birmingham on June 2, 1964. They had three children, Beauregard, Rhett, and Sarah Jean (Jennie), but they also raised Teddy IV and Laura. Turner had spirited his two children from his first marriage away from their mother in Chicago when Judy Nye intimated that her new husband might be taking out his frustrations on them. Nye did not see them again until Laura's wedding in 1990.

His children called Turner abusive and irresponsible, also, however. He was often gone from home, even at Christmas, since December usually found him in Australia, competing in the Hobart to Sydney for the Gold Cup of sailing. Jane Smith Turner admitted to dutifully lining up the kids in front of the TV on Sunday mornings, when Turner hosted the "Academy Award Theater," to remind them what their father looked like.

Turner was not a much better spouse than a parent. Over dinner with friends one night as he was walking out, he shouted at Jane Smith Tuner, "I've told you, Janie. Business comes first. My boat comes second. And you come third. See you later!"

Like his father, Turner devoted considerable time and attention to the pursuit of extramarital affairs, maintaining minimum discretion when he was away sailing but attempting to protect his family man's image when he was back in Atlanta. Ed Turner once told his son that he had slept with over three hundred women by the time he was thirty. Turner's marriage to Jane Smith Turner did not last.

On December 21, 1991, Turner and Jane Fonda were married. Their marriage lasted six years and worked largely, she said, because she had given up acting, moved to Atlanta, and adopted as her hobbies hunting, fishing, and ranch hopping. Fonda stayed in Atlanta after the breakup, and she and Turner are still close.

Turner has been characterized by some as having similar characteristics as individuals who have bipolar disorder. He is, by all accounts, gregarious and outspoken, regardless of the consequences. He began taking daily doses of lithium in 1986 and has tried analysis several times. Turner was descended on his father's side from English, Scottish, and French forbears and on his mother's from rather more substantial German, Irish, and Dutch stock, a genealogical legacy responsible for many of the contradictions that would influence the way he came to view the world and the way he would live his life. Turner tried to explain his individualism: "I got my valiance from the Scots, my work ethic from the Germans, and my colorfulness from the French and the British. My judgment and conservatism come from the Dutch, and the Irish—well, the Irish, they're all off their rockers, unbalanced."

> "My son is now an 'entrepreneur.' That's what you're called when you don't have a job."
>
> Ted Turner

Turner has said that he believes in God but does not regularly attend any church. He once remarked that "Christianity is a religion for losers." Ed

Turner deserted his fundamental Methodist religion of birth. Turner turned toward religion when he was young, and although he has not looked at a Bible in more than forty years, he can still cite passages from memory.

Turner often left his business to pursue his greater interest in sailboat racing. He had overcome the odds in 1971 to capture the prestigious World Ocean Racing Cup, a series of eighteen very difficult races stretched out over a three-year period. Few amateurs have ever maintained such an extended schedule at such a high level of competition with such extraordinary success. Turner managed the feat while overseeing his growing communications company and planning to expand into the uncharted waters of cable television. He became consumed with the prospect of competing in the Olympics and worked with Andy Green, a Fort Worth, Texas, boat builder with a high-tech bent, to develop a new boat design. Turner invested a hundred thousand dollars in PlasTrend, Inc., Green's manufacturing company in Fort Worth, and later insisted that his investment entitled him to a controlling interest. Together Turner and Green came up with new designs. The New York Yacht Club had reluctantly allowed Turner into their charmed circle, although he had the predictably impossible task of sailing a radical aluminum-hulled twelve-meter sailboat in his first America's Cup. The press covered his valiant but losing effort aboard his boat, *Mariner,* in 1974 and in the process made him a media celebrity. In 1977, Turner was able to successfully defend the America's Cup aboard his sailboat, *Courageous.*

Turner has made his mark as one of the most influential philanthropists in the United States. He directs most of his philanthropic activities through Turner Foundation, Inc., which was founded in 1991, the United Nations Foundation, which was created in 1997, and the Nuclear Threat Initiative, which was launched in January 2001.

Turner is chairman of the Turner Foundation, Inc. (TFI), which provides support for clean water and toxics reduction, clean air through improved energy efficiency and renewables, wildlife habitat protection, and the development of equitable practices and policies designed to reduce population growth rates.

TFI has made grants to hundreds of organizations including: Advocates for Youth, Alliance for Affordable Energy, American Bird Conservancy, Coosa River Basin Initiative, Global Green USA, Georgia Campaign for Adolescent Pregnancy Prevention, Montana Land Reliance, National Audubon Society, National Public Radio, National Safe Energy Communications Council, Pacific Rivers Council, Planned Parenthood Federation of America, Sierra Club Foundation, Union of Concerned Scientists, Upper Chattahoochee River-keeper, and the World Watch Institute. In addition, the Turner Community Youth Development Initiative provides support for locally designed youth development programs in thirty rural communities near Turner's properties.

The Turner Endangered Species Fund is a core grantee of the Turner Foundation, which works to conserve biodiversity by emphasizing efforts on private land, particularly on the Turner properties. Endangered species that have been reintroduced or restored include black-footed ferrets, condors, desert bighorn sheep, prairie dogs, Mexican wolves, red-cockaded woodpeckers, and West Slope cutthroat trout.

In September 1997 Turner announced his historic pledge of up to a billion dollars to the United Nations Foundation (UNF). To date, the organization has awarded grants in support of the goals and objectives of the United Nations to promote a more peaceful, prosperous, and just world. UNF has identified four core priorities: women and population, children's health, the environment, and peace and security.

In early 2001, Turner launched the Nuclear Threat Initiative (NTI), a foundation he cochairs with former Senator Sam Nunn. NTI is working to close the growing and increasingly dangerous gap between the threat from nuclear, chemical, and biological weapons and the global response.

NTI is a place of common ground where people with different ideological views can work together to make real and significant progress to reduce the risk of use and prevent the spread of weapons of mass destruction. NTI is committed to increasing public awareness, encouraging dialogue, catalyzing action and promoting new thinking about reducing the danger from nuclear, chemical and biological weapons on a global basis.

Through Turner Enterprises, Turner manages the largest commercial bison herd in North America, with approximately forty thousand head of bison spread among thirteen ranches in Colorado, Kansas, Montana, Nebraska, New Mexico, Oklahoma, and South Dakota. In addition, Turner owns property in California, Florida, Georgia, South Carolina, and Argentina. The mission of Turner Enterprises is to manage Turner lands in an economically sustainable and ecologically sensitive manner while promoting the conservation of native species.

In June 2001, Turner announced the creation of two independent film production companies based in Atlanta, Ted Turner Pictures and Ted Turner Documentaries. *Gods and Generals* was Ted Turner Pictures' first theatrical release. Ted Turner Documentaries is currently in production of an eight-hour documentary series about weapons of mass destruction, *Avoiding Armageddon* that aired on PBS stations in April 2003.

Turner originated the Goodwill Games in 1985 as an international, world-class, quadrennial, multisport competition. The inaugural Goodwill Games were held in July 1986 in Moscow and were followed by the 1990 Games in Seattle, Washington; the 1994 Games in St. Petersburg, Russia; the 1998 Games in New York City; the first winter games in Lake Placid, New York in 2000; and in 2001 the last of the Goodwill Games were held in Brisbane, Australia.

LEADERSHIP LESSONS

When the odds are stacked against Turner, he has usually prevailed, not because he is necessarily the bravest, strongest, or smartest, but because he simply will not give up. He has a tenacity that is rarely equaled. Turner likes the fight and will keep fighting until the battle is won. He is interested in finding out what he could accomplish if he really tried and always pushes the boundaries of that. When he was younger, he was very interested in why people did the things they did and what caused some people to rise to glorious heights. Early on, he had a vision of what he wanted to be, and he did not hesitate to share it with anyone who would listen. These included becoming a millionaire, winning the America's Cup, and being elected president.

Dennis Conner, who has sailed against Turner, says Turner's strong point is neither innate ability nor attention to detail and preparation. It is his enthusiastic competitiveness and leadership ability. It is this innate competitive streak, in addition to the strategic steps, that made Turner take huge risks and achieve the success he has. At times, he bet more than the company was worth on his ideas and took enormous losses for several years, pursuing an end result only he saw as truly probable. When he wanted to buy the TV station, his trusted advisors told him that everything would collapse and that the result couldn't possibly be worth the risk. He was the only one who saw his vision, and he trusted it.

Turner also stepped up to the plate immediately after his father's suicide. Although he didn't know the business well and knew little about finance, he dealt with everyone, including the bankers, directly.

Brand the Product

Early on, Turner used his billboards to help brand his radio and TV stations. When CNN came into being, he focused on running branding promotions on its fellow Turner channels. He also put CNN's logo on the screen at all times. In doing this, he incorporated design, music, graphics, and the general on-air look of the channel and hired creative directors that were so skilled at their jobs that viewers barely noticed the branding.

"Every few seconds it changes—up an eighth, down an eighth—it's like playing a slot machine. I lose $20 million, I gain $20 million."
Ted Turner

Act Quickly

"Of course I did," Turner told his reporters when asked if he'd ever had second thoughts about buying the satellite. "I'm not an idiot. I knew the risks. But I had to move fast, without a lot of people knowing what I was up to. I had to buy the Braves, and I also bought the Hawks for basketball. If the leagues realized what I was doing—broadcasting my sports far, far beyond Atlanta, where the franchise supposedly was—they would have stopped me cold."

Turner recognized the potential for satellites as soon as he learned about the risk HBO was going to take. He went into immediate action. As soon as he recognized the need for around the clock news, he did the same thing. In taking these leaps to be the pioneer without any market research or care to ensure his decisions were correct, Turner was able to take advantage of being the only one in lucrative markets for years.

Be Loyal and Fair

Turner's reputation means everything to him. Loyalty is very important to him as well, most people who know him would say. He expects loyalty from anyone he has to deal with, including banks, customers, and employees, but he gives that loyalty back. There are several instances of people, including his stepmother, crossing Turner and never being able to speak to him again.

His sense of loyalty extends to playing the game itself. He wants a fair playing field, by most accounts, even if that means he concedes the advantage. In one instance, he was attempting to acquire a billboard company that was being sold by sealed bid auction and became furious when one of the people involved offered to tell him the bid he had to beat. "He will risk a lot," one of his employees recalled, "but not his reputation."

When Turner resorted once to a telethon to raise money for his Charlotte station, he kept the names of everyone and how much they sent in. When he sold the station eight years later, Turner sent every one of them a check for what they had contributed.

Turner used his gut instinct to hire people based on whether he thought they would be loyal and fair. He made some of his best hires across a back-alley bar, from inside a bathroom toilet stall, and from an adjoining tourist-class seat on one of the thousands of airline flights he took. He hired his neighbor, Will Sanders, to be his accountant after Irwin Mazo left.

Think Globally

Turner says that his worldwide yacht racing activities had given him a global perspective, according to Don Flournoy and Robert Stewart in *CNN: Making the News in the Global Market*. "The thing that made me think internationally was . . . sailboat racing. I went all over the world racing sailboats . . . [and] I realized how parochial most Americans are. We're such a big country and a wealthy country, and we think that the world—like the Romans did at the time of the Roman Empire—somehow circles around us, that we're the centre of the universe."

> *"The United States has got some of the dumbest people in the world. I want you to know that we know that."*
> Ted Turner

Turner had always felt that the world's TV viewers needed an unbiased news report. Interviewed in 1996, he said, "Nobody ever gave the Palestinians or the Arab side a voice. Not here in the United States anyway. They didn't have a voice. The most angry people in the world are those that don't get listened to" (Flournoy and Stewart, *CNN*).

Through his racing, Turner came to want to be more than to be a large billboard company in a small pond. He realized he needed to expand his reach globally, regardless of what others saw. CNN was able to do this, even though it lost money hand over fist for its first few years, with Turner spending as much as seventy million dollars to keep it afloat. However, this did not stop him launching a second channel, CNN Headline News. Turner combined the CNN and Headline News signals and put them on an international satellite, creating CNN International in 1985.

Sell What You Have However You Can

Turner sold what he had. His focus was on acquiring or setting up what he wanted (the radio station, TV station, satellite, CNN, and so on) and then selling that. He did not first determine what others wanted and try to get it. Turner was on the cutting edge in the long term but found a way to survive in the short term.

He focused on owning content for his television stations and bought whatever content he could find that was already available because he could not afford to create new content. He then sold the black-and-white shows (when everyone else was showing color programming) as being a return to good, innocent family values. According to Porter Bibb's *Ted Turner: It Ain't as Easy as It Looks,* to sell advertising during his old-fashioned programming, Turner would tell potential clients, "You want to avoid clutter? You want shock value? You want your message to stand out the way it never could on any other station? Then run your color commercials on WTCG, where all my programs are black and white!" The audience may not be big, Turner would tell advertisers, "but our viewers are way above the average viewer's mentality. It takes a genius to figure out how to tune a UHF set!" (Bibb 1997). Turner had no Nielsen numbers, no acceptable ratings book to offer advertisers, nothing resembling the accurate market and demographic data required by most advertisers, but he sold his station anyway.

He was always known as being a great salesman, and those skills were essential when he took over his father's business. He sold himself to a lot of people—the bankers and the others—who had no idea what to expect from a twenty-four-year-old. "Ted was one of the greatest salesmen in the world," said Irwin Mazo, his father's company accountant who stayed on for several years after Turner took over.

Still is. Just like his father. Those two, they were so much alike they couldn't stay in the same room ten minutes together without starting to scream at each other, arguing over the best way to do this, or to do that. But either one of

> *"We have to do more than keep media giants from growing larger; they're already too big. We need a new set of rules that will break these huge companies to pieces."*
> Ted Turner

> *"There's nothing wrong with being fired."*
> Ted Turner

them could charm a rattlesnake. . . . I watched Ted put his father's business in order. He did that with his eyes closed, with plenty of time on the side for his sailing. He could have retired anytime during those early years and never looked back. But then we started making acquisitions, always trying to use the other guy's money. That was Ted's genius. He could charm the pants off anybody when he wanted to. Usually the fellow we acquired would turn right around and work twice as hard for Ted as he ever had for himself. That was the other part of Turner's genius, to get people as enthusiastic as he was. He could usually get them to believe anything. (Bibb, *Ted Turner*)

"Over a three year period, I gave away half of what I had. To be honest, my hands shook as I signed it away. I knew I was taking myself out of the race to be the richest man in the world."

Ted Turner

Manufacturing a crisis was one way Turner was able to rally his troops. "Ted created a sense of paranoia within the company, a sense that we were the little guys fighting for our lives against some unknown big guys. That made everything seem a lot more important than it probably was," said Mazo. "After all, we were not doing badly. And Turner Advertising was the biggest billboard company in the South. One of the biggest in the country, actually. Ted compounded the sense of danger, though, with all kinds of subterfuge. He even to make people to believe our phones were tapped. Perhaps it would distract them from how well the business was doing" (Bibb, *Ted Turner*).

POLITICAL INFLUENCE

Turner launched the Cable News Network on June 1, 1980. At the launch ceremony, the flag of the United Nations was raised alongside those of the United States and the state of Georgia, hinting at Turner's global ambitions long before his billion-dollar gift to the United Nations.

Early in his career, Turner was still unformed in his own political views, but he felt at ease among conservatives and following in his father's far-right footsteps. Politics was the last thing Ted Turner had on his mind those days. He was already twenty-five years old and had not yet even registered to vote.

Now things are very different. Turner says that he feels that he carries the burden of saving the world on his shoulders. Turner turned his business into a bully pulpit of social conscience. He is quite serious about many issues and about changing the world. Turner scorns the idea of spending hundreds of millions of dollars to develop HDTV or billions to wire the country with fiber optics when two-thirds of the world still goes to bed hungry every night. Instead he invested in what he believes—Native American film projects, Cousteau documentaries, National Geographic specials, and mass educational ventures like the animated series *Captain Planet*, which carry important messages Turner wants the world to hear. Turner turned TBS's purpose toward social responsibility.

CRITICS

Turner has been severely criticized by many people; however, much of the criticism has come from his business rivals. He is outspoken and will tell anyone what he thinks, regardless of the ramifications. That quality has earned him enemies. However, the critics are not very vocal these days.

FUTURE IMPACT

In 2006, Turner is sixty-eight years old. He recently gave up his Time Warner AOL board seat and unloaded much of his stock. His mark with CNN has been made, and his efforts now revolve around political goals, though he has not said that he wants a political career. Much of what has driven him to succeed—namely the angst he felt in the relationship with his father—has subsided. He has not given any indication of what he might do now that the CNN chapter has closed for him. Undoubtedly, although he is a rancher and the largest private landowner in the United States, he will not ride off into the sunset. There is bound to be more from Ted Turner.

TIMELINE

1938	November 19, Born in Cincinnati, Ohio.
1956	Entered Brown University.
1961	Became an account executive at his father's company.
1963	Ed Turner committed suicide because of financial difficulties. Turner took over the billboard business.
1968	Purchased WAPQ, a Chattanooga, Tennessee radio station.
1970	Changed company to Turner Communications Group and acquired Atlanta UHF television station WJRJ, renaming it WTCG.
1976	Began transmitting WTCG via satellite to cable systems.
1976	Purchased Major League Baseball's Atlanta Braves. WTCG became cable television's first Superstation as it is beamed via satellite to homes across the country.
1977	Turner Communications Group purchased the National Basketball Association's Atlanta Hawks. Turner won the America's Cup.
1979	Turner Communications Group became Turner Broadcasting System, Inc. WTCG was renamed WTBS.
1980	The first twenty-four-hour, all-news network, CNN, is launched with 1.7 million subscribers.
1982	Turner Broadcasting launches CNN, the first around-the-clock, all news television station.

1982	Started CNN Headline News, which offered updated newscasts every half-hour.
1985	CNN International launched; Turner made unsuccessful five-billion-dollar bid to acquire CBS.
1986	*Time* acquired Scott Foresman & Company book publishing unit.
1986	Turner Broadcasting bought the MGM library of movies and television shows.
1988	TNT cable network launched.
1991	Acquired the rights to and library of Hanna-Barbera Cartoons. Turner named *Time*'s Man of the Year. Married Jane Fonda.
1992	America Online became a publicly traded company. Turner Broadcasting launched Cartoon Network.
1993	Turner Broadcasting System merged with Castle Rock and New Line.
1994	Turner Classic Movies launched.
1996	Time Warner acquired Turner Broadcasting System for $7.6 billion, making Turner the major shareholder in Time Warner. He became vice chairman, overseeing the company's cable properties. CNNSI, a sports news channel, was launched.
1997	CNN en Espanol launched. Turner pledged a billion dollars to the United Nations.
1999	Turner acquired a National Hockey League expansion franchise. The Atlanta Thrashers began play in 1999.
2000	AOL and Time Warner announced their $183-billion merger. The largest corporate merger in history was finalized in January 2001. The world's largest media and entertainment company changed its name to AOL Time Warner. Turner named vice chairman and senior advisor of AOL Time Warner, losing day-to-day control.
2001	Turner and Fonda divorced.
2002	Turner opens the first of his Ted's Montana Grills.
2003	Turner resigned as vice chairman of AOL Time Warner.
2004	Time Warner sold the Atlanta Hawks, Atlanta Thrashers, and Philips Arena to a local investment group.
2006	Turner gave up his board position at AOL Time Warner.

RESOURCES

(Unless otherwise attributed, quotes are from *Ted Turner: It Ain't as Easy as It Looks: A Biography*.)

Bibb, Porter. *Ted Turner: It Ain't as Easy as It Looks: A Biography*. Boulder, CO: Johnson Books, 1997.

CNN. January 29, 2003. www.money.cnn.com.

Conner, Dennis and John Rousmaniere. *No Excuse to Lose*. London, England: A & C Black, December, 1988.

Flournoy, Don M., and Robert K. Stewart. *CNN—Making News in the Global Market*. Bedfordshire, UK: University of Luton Press.

Maurer, Harry. Second Career of the Week. *Business Week,* March 13, 2006.

Murray, Michael D. *Encyclopedia of Television News*. Westport, CT: Greenwood Publishing Group, 1998, p. 259.

Pandya, Mukul, and Robbie Shell. *Nightly Business Report Presents Lasting Leadership: What You Can Learn from the Top 25 Business People of our Times*. New Jersey: Pearson Education, 2005, pp. 151–157.

Sterling, Christopher H. *Stay Tuned: A Concise History of American Broadcasting*. Mahwah, NJ: Lawrence Erlbaum Associates, 2002, pp. 412, 507.

Ted Turner: The Man Behind 24/7 News. *Business Strategy Review* 16 (2005):29–30.

Tungate, Mark. *Media Monoliths: How Great Media Brands Thrive and Survive*. London: Kogan Page, 2004.

Turner, Ted. My Beef With Big Media: How government protects big media—and shuts out upstarts like me. *Federal Communications Law Journal*, March 2005, pp. 223–234.

COMPANY INFORMATION

Time Warner Inc.
One Time Warner Center
New York, NY 10019
Phone: (212) 484–8000
www.timewarner.com

AOL
22000 AOL Way
Dulles, VA 20166-9302
Phone: (703) 265–1000
www.aol.com

Turner Broadcasting System
1 CNN Center
Atlanta, GA 30303
Phone: (404) 827–1700
www.cnn.com
New York Stock Exchange symbol: TWX

AP Photo/Danny Johnson.

Sam Walton

Sam Walton revolutionized the business of retail. Before Walton started his discounting operation in smaller towns around the United States, almost no one realized how much potential business there was in rural America. Today, Wal-Mart is the largest civilian employer in the world and alone is responsible for more than 1 percent of America's gross domestic product. Wal-Mart is also credited for changing the way American people live.

Walton started life off in the Depression and worked his way through college. His first job out of school was as a manager trainee for J. C. Penney, making seventy-five dollars a week. He built an empire from the ground up after his father-in-law lent him the money to start his first store in a small town in Arkansas.

Walton worked hard, analyzing his competition in detail by walking their stores. He founded Wal-Mart with his brother in 1962 at the age of forty-four after owning other variety stores because he recognized the need to compete with a new type of discount retailer. His first Wal-Mart discount store was located in Rogers, Arkansas and had merchandise spread out on tables throughout the 16,000-square-foot space. He held on to this store for two years before expanding his discount operations with gusto. The company is now international with stores throughout the United States and in Mexico, Canada, Argentina, Brazil, South Korea, China, Germany, and Puerto Rico.

In 1970, Walton and his brother took the business public. Those fortunate enough to have bought stock then did very well. A hundred shares bought in 1970 would have grown to 204,800 shares worth over twelve million dollars today. Walton died in 1992, but if he were alive today, he would be the world's wealthiest person, twice as rich as Bill Gates.

Most of Walton's fortune was tied up in Wal-Mart stock. To his delight, he spent much of his career largely unnoticed by the public or the press until *Forbes* ranked him as the richest man in the United States in 1985 because of his stock options, a title he held until 1988. In 1989 he lost the distinction when the editors began to credit Walton's fortune jointly to him and his four children. The Waltons currently own about forty percent of Wal-Mart's stock.

Walton was honored for his pioneering efforts in retail in March 1992, when he received the Presidential Medal of Freedom from President George H. W. Bush. In 1998, Walton was included in *Time Magazine*'s list of the one hundred most influential people of the twentieth century.

Wal-Mart Stores, Inc. also runs Sam's Club warehouse stores.

When Walton died in 1992, ownership in Wal-Mart rested with his wife and their children: S. Robson "Rob" Walton, John T. Walton, Jim Walton, and Alice Walton. Rob Walton succeeded his father as the chairman of the board of Wal-Mart, and John was a director until his death in a 2005 plane crash. The Walton family held five spots in the top ten richest people in the United States until 2005.

Walton's widow, Helen, is worth about eighteen billion dollars. Rob Walton is currently chairman of the board of Wal-Mart Stores, Inc., a position he has held since 1992. *Forbes* ranked him at number 10 on its 2005 list of richest Americans, with a fortune estimated at $18.3 billion. According to a *Fortune* profile, Jim Walton presides over many of the family-owned businesses, including Walton Enterprises, which holds ninety billion dollars' worth of Wal-Mart stock, as well as a bank holding company, newspapers, and some

"Most everything I've done I've copied from someone else."

Sam Walton

smaller companies. He is listed at number 11 on the *Forbes* list, with an estimated fortune of $18.2 billion. Alice is ranked at number 13 on the list of wealthiest Americans, with a net worth of eighteen billion dollars, and is considered the world's wealthiest woman.

THE EARLY YEARS

Sam Walton was born to Thomas Gibson and Nannia (Nan) Lee Walton near Kingfisher, Oklahoma, on March 29, 1918, where he lived until he was five. His father was a farmer and a farm-loan appraiser, and his mother was a homemaker and set up a family business selling milk.

Walton grew up in the Depression and sometimes traveled with his father when he had to repossess farms. Walton's father was influential in his life, and strongly discouraged taking on debt. He was known for honesty and integrity and his ability to negotiate and trade. The secret to success, Thomas told his children, was "work, work, work." Walton's mother was also a very hard worker and encouraged her children to succeed. Walton credited his mother for instilling his passionate drive. His parents would often argue heatedly, and Walton grew up sure he did not want to live like that forever.

In 1921 Walton's brother, James "Bud" Walton was born. Soon after, the family moved from Oklahoma to Missouri and continued moving from from one small town to another for several years.

Though he didn't remember ever feeling poor or lacking anything during the Depression, from the time Walton was seven or eight, he contributed to the family income. He sold magazine subcriptions and had paper routes from the seventh grade through college. He also raised and sold rabbits and pigeons.

During his youth, Walton was quite competitve and played team sports and was in the Boy Scouts. He made a bet that he would be the first of his group of friends to reach the rank of Eagle Scout. While attending eighth grade in Shelbina, Missouri, Walton became the youngest Eagle Scout in the state's history. When he was fourteen, he saved another child from drowning.

Walton excelled physically in high school, though he was small at 130 pounds, playing football as starting quarterback for Columbia's Hickman High School in 1935, when the team won the state title. Walton never experienced a loss while playing football. He was drafted for the basketball team, although he wasn't very interested. That team also went undefeated and won the state championship. Walton was an honor student, although he doesn't believe he was gifted in any way—he just studied hard. Besides being athletic and smart he was also a political figure at school. While at Hickman, he served as vice president of the student body his junior year and as president his senior year. He was active in many clubs as well.

Walton went to the University of Missouri and majored in economics as a ROTC officer. During this time, he worked various odd jobs, including waiting tables in exchange for meals and life-guarding at the school pool. He was still working a paper route during college, too, and had hired some people to help him. He made about four to five thousand dollars on the paper route, today's equivalent of over forty thousand dollars, which was quite a lot of money at the end of the Depression. He joined the Zeta Phi chapter of the Beta Theta Pi fraternity, even though he still lived at home and did not come from the same economic background of most of the other members. He was well known, however, throughout the state because of his football success, and the fraternity recruited him to join. Walton was quite active during school, serving as rush captain of his fraternity, which involved traveling the state to recruit and interview potential members. He was also president of the Burall Bible Class and attended church every week. He was also tapped by QEBH, the secret society on campus, honoring the top senior men. He ran for every office that came along. He was also a member of the professional business fraternity, Alpha Kappa Psi, was in the National Honor Society, and was the captain and president of Scabbard and Blade, the elite military organization of ROTC. Upon graduating in 1940, he was voted "permanent president" of the class.

One of Walton's high school girlfriends had a father in the insurance business, and after talking extensively with him, Walton thought he, too, would go into that field after graduate school.

After graduating from college, Walton had plans to attend the Wharton School of Business in Pennsylvania, but he realized as college was winding down that he would not have enough money, even if he continued working as hard as he did. Unsure of what to do next but knowing that he could not keep up the pace he had been going for long, he interviewed with the two recruiters who came to the campus. Through those interviews, Walton got a job as a J. C. Penney management trainee in Des Moines, Iowa, starting three days after graduating from college. He received seventy-five dollars a month.

CAREER PATH

As a trainee at J. C. Penney, Walton visited his competitors' stores during his lunch breaks to see what they were doing. He resigned from J. C. Penney after eighteen months in 1942 because he was depressed about being rejected for military service in World War II due to a minor heart irregularity. He headed south toTulsa, intending to go into the oil business, but instead he got a job at a DuPont gunpowder plant.

Soon afterwards, Walton joined the military in the U.S. Army Intelligence Corps, supervising security at aircraft plants and prisoner-of-war camps. During his time in the army, he found he was still interested in retail outlets and decided he wanted to own his own retail store. He eventually reached the rank of Captain before leaving the military in 1945.

Walton originally looked at going in with another partner on a store, but his wife, Helen, discouraged this, having previously witnessed the negative effects of partnerships. With a loan from his father-in-law of twenty thousand dollars, in addition to the five thousand dollars he had saved from his time in the army, Walton purchased a variety store in Newport, Arkansas. The Ben Franklin store was a franchise of the Butler Brothers chain and was what Walton called a "real dog." Walton's legal and negotiating skills weren't finely tuned then, either. The lack of a renewal option, together with the outrageous rent of 5 percent of sales, became early business lessons to Walton. However, he saw the store's potential and set about to make it the best variety store in the state. He received training in store management from the franchise. Walton continued to learn about his competitors by spending a lot of time in their stores.

It was at his first store that Walton also adapted others' ideas that would prove to be crucial to his success. One of the restrictions Walton faced was that all Ben Franklin franchise owners were expected to buy at least 80 percent of their stores' goods from Butler Brothers. These goods didn't come cheap, given the 25-percent markup that Butler charged its franchisees. Walton decided to go directly to Butler Brothers' local and regional manufacturers to buy his goods, but most of them turned him down, fearing Butler Brothers' wrath. So Walton traveled as far as Missouri and Tennessee to buy goods as cheaply as possible. After working at the store, he would often drive down to Cottonwood Point to catch a ferry to Tennessee, where he would visit suppliers in the mill towns that lined the river. "I'd stuff that car and trailer with whatever I could get good deals on," Walton wrote years later in his memoir, *Made in America*. Usually, this was on "softlines" like "ladies panties and nylons, men's shirts—and I'd bring them back, price them low, and just blow that stuff out of the store." After only two and half years, Walton paid his father-in-law back.

Walton was quite active in his community then and heard that his largest competitor in the town was going to expand his store. Instead of allowing that to happen, Walton talked the competitor's landlord into leasing him the space instead. He didn't know what he was going to do with it, but in the end he decided to open up a department store, the Eagle store, which was across the street from his Ben Franklin variety store. Newport had several department stores already, one of which was owned by the variety store's landlord, P. K. Holmes.

At this time, Walton's brother, Bud, who had been a Green Beret pilot in the war, came home and helped Walton run the two stores. Within five years Walton's variety store soon led in sales and profits in the Butler Brothers franchise, not only in the state but in a six-state region.

Walton's success, however, attracted a lot of attention. His landlord, P. K. Holmes, decided not to renew his lease, knowing that he had nowhere to move the store. It was the low point in Walton's career. Holmes wanted to give the store to his son and did, however, offer to buy the franchise at a fair price, and Walton made fifty thousand dollars on the deal. Before the lease was up, Walton had some time to find another store in another town, and he and Bud decided on Bentonville, although the store there was doing just a fraction of the business the Newport store was doing. Walton then sold his department store's lease to Holmes's competition and moved out of town in January 1951.

In Bentonville, Walton set up another Ben Franklin franchise in 1950, although he called it Walton's Five and Dime. In those days variety stores were characterized by high levels of customer service, with clerks helping customers select all types of items. But by the time Walton's Five and Dime was starting, a new self-service retail model was starting in different parts of the country. When Walton got wind of it, he rode a bus all night to Minnesota to see a self-service store for himself. He was immediately won over, and he set out to copy and improve upon this new model.

Walton also immediately started looking for other store opportunities in other towns. In 1952, he opened another store in Fayetteville, Arkansas, about twenty miles from Bentonville. He called this store Walton's Five and Dime, too, although this one was not a franchise store. Walton knew though he needed a qualified manager to run the store so it would be as successful as his other store. So, he said, "I did something I would do for the rest of my run in the retail business without any shame or embarrassment whatsoever: nose around other people's stores searching for good talent." He hired Willard Walker, the manager of a TG&Y variety store in Tulsa, by offering him a percentage of the store's profits. Walton visited the Fayetteville store weekly and examined the store's books and compiled a profit-and-loss statement.

When Walton heard about a new subdivision going into Ruskin Heights, he called his brother and asked him to go in on a Ben Franklin store in a shopping center in the middle of the subdivision. Bud Walton had meanwhile borrowed some money to start a Ben Franklin store of his own in Versailles, Missouri. They went in on the Ruskin Heights store fifty-fifty. The store did exceedingly well, but on May 20, 1957, a tornado leveled it. The Waltons rebuilt it, and Walton kept opening new stores, many of them Ben Franklin franchises. All the stores were organized as separate partnerships between Walton and his brother and other partners, including his dad, Helen's two brothers, and his children (who invested their paper-route money). By 1962 Walton and his brother owned sixteen variety stores in Arkansas, Missouri, and Kansas.

Within fifteen years, they had become the largest independent variety store operators in the United States. Walton figured that their sales were limited, though, despite all of their success, by the amount of volume they were doing—it was too small per store. When a discounter came into the Fayetteville area and started competing with his store there, Walton knew that the discount idea was the future. He tried to get Butler Brothers to back him in a discounting venture, but they weren't interested.

So on July 2, 1962, at the age of forty-four, Walton opened his first Wal-Mart store. He built the store on his own, although it was going to go up against a Ben Franklin franchise in Rogers, Arkansas. Wal-Mart had begun. Walton didn't find many people willing to take the risk on it, though. His brother put in three percent and another manager, Don Whitaker, put in two percent. The remaining 95 percent was put in by Walton and his wife by borrowing on everything they had. That same year, S. S. Kresge launched Kmart, F. W. Woolworth started Woolco, and Dayton Hudson began the Target chain. Discounting had hit America. At that time, Walton was too far off the beaten path to attract the attention of competitors or suppliers, much less Wall Street. The name Wal-Mart was suggested by Bob Bogle, the first manager of Walton's Five and Dime. His reasoning was that Wal-mart has just seven letters, so it could save a lot of money in neon lettering. Walton liked the name because it was similar to a competitor's name, Fed-Mart.

Walton kept the one Wal-Mart in Rogers for two years before putting up stores in Springdale and Harrison. These early stores looked very little like today's Wal-Marts. Instead, they were generally messy, with things piled up on tables with no organization or departments.

Walton opened his eighteenth store in his old town of Newport, Arkansas. Doing so, he drove his former landlord's son out of business.

In 1966, Walton enrolled in an IBM course for retailers. He recognized that Wal-Mart "had to get better organized" and that "quite a few people were beginning to go into computerization." After this course, Walton began to recruit the personnel who would develop Wal-Mart's systems. In 1968, he hired Ron Mayer as vice president of finance and distribution. Mayer would be instrumental in putting up the first computer systems in place.

Walton built the first Wal-Mart distribution center in 1969, more than two decades after opening his first store. By that year, the Waltons were financially overextended. They wanted to open more stores, but the banks would not lend much more money, so they made the decision to go public.

Wal-Mart went public on October 1, 1970, their stock traded over the counter. They offered 20 percent of the company—three hundred thousand shares—at fifteen dollars each, and they sold for $16.50. They had about eight hundred shareholders after the first issue. In August 1972, Wal-Mart was listed on the New York Stock Exchange.

Near the time of the public offering, Walton instituted a profit-sharing plan for managers. A year later, this was opened up to associates, employees working over a thousand hours a year.

Though Walton cared about the stock price, he continued to focus on store growth and traveled frequently to keep tabs on all the stores.

In 1974, he thought he might want to take more time off and he started leaning more on Ron Mayer and Ferold Arend, two executive vice presidents who did not get along well. Soon, in what would become known as a bad period in Wal-Mart history, Walton resigned as CEO and chairman, turning

> *"We're all working to-gether; that's the secret. And we'll lower the cost of living for everyone, not just in America, but we'll give the world an opportunity to see what it's like to save and have a better lifestyle, a better life for all. We're proud of what we've ac-complished; we've just begun."*
>
> Sam Walton

those roles over to Mayer. Arend became president. This divided the company, with the old guard behind Arend and the newer hires behind Mayer. Walton decided he did not really want to be retired and stepped back into his role as CEO. Mayer resigned, as did many others who were behind him. The meeting Walton had with Mayer took place on a Saturday and is known as the "Saturday night massacre" in Wal-Mart lore.

In 1977, Walton acquired sixteen Mohr-Value stores in Michigan and Illinois. In 1979, Wal-Mart hit a billion dol-lars in sales, with 230 stores. By the end of this year, there were 276 stores located in eleven states. Stores were pri-marily situated in towns with populations of five thousand to twenty-five thousand.

The 1980s were a new era of expansion for Wal-Mart. Stores were now situated in twenty-four states, and Walton opened the first Sam's Club warehouse stores. He also con-centrated on technology in the late 1980s by building a 135,000-square-foot building just to house Wal-Mart's sophisticated computer system. By 1992, the company had spent seven hundred million dollars on its information systems, amassing one of the largest such systems in the world, second only to that of the Pentagon.

In 1984, Walton lost a bet that the company could earn a pretax profit of 8 percent, and, as a result, did the hula on the steps of Merrill Lynch on Wall Street. Other hula dancers joined him, and the picture was widely printed.

In 1985, Walton was named America's richest man by *Forbes*. By 1990, Wal-Mart had expanded to thirty-four states and became the nation's largest retailer chain. New store units averaged 100,000 square feet.

In March 1988, feeling depleted again, this time due to the leukemia he was fighting, Walton handed the CEO reins to David Glass.

In 1992, Walton was awarded the Medal of Freedom by President Bush on March 17, just weeks before his death on April 5 of bone cancer at the age of seventy-four.

PERSONAL LIFE

While working and living near Tulsa at the DuPont gunpowder plant, Walton met his future wife, Helen Robson, in April of 1942. Helen was accom-plished, having been the valedictorian of her high school class and achieving a business degree in finance at the University of Oklahoma at Norman.

One night, Walton decided to go to the local bowling alley, where Helen was on a date with another young man. He approached her and they started talking, discovering they had a friend in common—someone Walton used to date in college. Walton called Helen later and asked for the other woman's number, but soon Walton and Helen were dating. The two were married on February 14, 1943, in her hometown of Claremore, Oklahoma.

Soon after they were married, Walton entered the U.S. Army Intelligence Corps in the continental United States, supervising security at aircraft plants and prisoner-of-war camps. He did not see combat due to his slight heart defect. The Waltons spent two years in the army life, their last post being in Salt Lake City, Utah.

In 1944 the Waltons had their first son, Samuel Robson (Rob). In 1945 when Walton went back to civilian life, he knew he wanted to go into retailing, specifically department stores. Helen had grown weary of traveling so much, having moved sixteen times during the previous two years. She famously put her foot down and said she would move anywhere except to a big city. She wanted to live in a city with fewer than ten thousand people.

Helen's father, Leland Stanford (L. S.) Robson, a prosperous banker and rancher, had a profound impact on Walton and his career. Walton admired Robson's success and characteristics greatly. Though Helen's father had wanted Walton to work for him, the couple decided they wanted to make it on their own, away from Helen's hometown. Robson organized his ranch and family businesses as partnerships, and Helen and her brothers were all partners. He encouraged Walton to do the same, which Walton did early on in Wal-Mart history, saving millions in estate taxes for the family later. He also learned from Robson how to create a cohesive family.

Another son, John Thomas, was born in 1946. Their third son, James Carr (Jim), was born in 1948, followed by daughter Alice, born in 1949.

Walton lived for most of his adult life in Bentonville, Arkansas, after he started Wal-Mart. He drove an old pickup truck, wore Wal-Mart baseball caps, and liked to hunt and play tennis. The Waltons' home burned down in 1972 after being struck by lightning, but they built another house on the same spot.

It was a strain on the family when he was ranked the richest man in America by *Forbes* magazine in 1985 because, prior to that, the family had not been in the public eye very much. In Bentonville, the Waltons were involved in numerous civic activities. Walton served as president of the Rotary Club and the Chamber of Commerce. He was also elected to the city council, served on the hospital board, and launched a Little League baseball program in the city in 1954. He did not live lavishly in Bentonville, and family vacations often consisted of traveling by car around the country, stopping in at retail stores along the way.

Walton was known for his hard work, for being ambitious, and for being down to earth. He was very active in the communities where he lived. He was also an avid pilot, flying himself, executives, and potential business partners around to the various stores. He bought his first plane, a two-seater Air Coupe, whose engine once failed just after take-off from Fort Smith, for $1,850.

Walton's nonchalance toward wealth was solidified by his remarks to a reporter after the great stock market crash of October 19, 1987, when Wal-Mart shares fell 23 percent in a day and wiped out $1.7 billion of Walton's net worth. He responded to questions about his reaction to it by saying, "It's paper anyway. It was paper when we started and it's paper afterward."

Walton went to church weekly, and although he has said that he was not particularly religious, he thought belonging to a church was an important aspect of community life. He sometimes asked potential managerial hires if they went to church.

When he was alive, Walton didn't believe in giving very much money away. As it was set up, the bulk of his wealth was in Wal-Mart stock, which belonged to the entire family. The giving was and is largely administered together, through the Walton Family Foundation. At least twice a year, the family would meet to talk about how to spend its money. After he was beseeched with requests for money once he gained notoriety, Walton said he had a hard time giving "any undeserving stranger a free ride." Nor did he believe in being generous with company profits. "We feel very strongly," he said, "that Wal-Mart really is not, and should not be, in the charity business." Money that Wal-Mart donated to charity, he reasoned, would only come out of the pockets of "either our shareholders or our customers."

Walton did support some charitable causes, including those of the Presbyterian Church. The Sam and Helen R. Walton Award was created in 1991, when the Waltons made a gift of six million dollars, which included an endowment in the amount of three million dollars to provide annual awards to new church developments that are working in creative ways to share the Christian faith in local communities. In 1985, he also began a program designed to stem the "tide of communism" in Central America by promoting capitalism and privatization. His efforts included funding scholarship programs to bring Central American students to Christian universities in the United States, hoping that exposure to American capitalism and Protestant values would dissuade them from becoming involved in communist movements.

Since Walton died in 1992, both Wal-Mart and the family have significantly increased their charitable giving. The company donated twenty million dollars in cash and merchandise to the Hurricane Katrina relief effort. Each of the Walton children also has philanthropic projects of his or her own—Alice, for example, built a world-class art museum in northwest Arkansas.

LEADERSHIP LESSONS

Clearly, one of the most important lessons Walton learned early on was to keep prices low. This was not as basic a lesson then as it is now. At that time, it was revolutionary to think that by lowering prices, you could make much more money because of volume sales. Walton was not naturally a good negotiator, but he had to learn the skill. He also had to learn about merchandising, promotion, and how to operate a large company. "For several years," Walton writes, "the company was just me and the managers in the stores." There was no time for "building the company up" because "we were too busy concentrating on day to day operations." Coordination was accomplished by "a bunch of store managers getting together early Saturday morning" when "we would review what we had bought and see how many dollars we had committed to it" (Walton 1992).

Walton pioneered at his first store many concepts that would prove to be crucial to his success. He stocked the shelves with a wide variety of goods at low prices. His store also stayed open later than most other stores, especially during the Christmas season. He tried to find what the consumer wanted and needed and then followed through.

One of the most critical things Walton did for his success was to avidly study other retailers and discounters. He set about being the best, which meant taking the best ideas and improving them. Later, he was one of the first to implement on a large scale a computerized inventory tracking system.

But, perhaps, one of the things Walton did better than any of his competitors was work harder and longer.

Copy, Ask Questions, and Improve

Walton had a great deal of respect for his competitors, saying "Wal-Mart wouldn't be what it is today without a host of fine competition, most especially Harry Cunningham of Kmart, who really designed the first discount store, and who in my opinion, should be remembered as one of the leading retailers of all time" (Walton 1992). He had so much respect, in fact, that he copied much of what Cunningham did.

Walton was always trying to find new ideas to improve business. His wife, Helen, described one of her husband's most important work habits in his memoir, "What really drove Sam was that competition across the street...always. Looking at his prices, looking at his displays, looking at what was going on. He was always looking for a way to do a better job." From his earliest days in business, Walton raced around with a yellow notebook and a tape recorder in hand, learning from competitors and bringing the best ideas into his stores. He was caught taping a conversation with staff in his competitor Sol Price's store by a manager. His tape had information from other places, and he didn't want to lose it. He gave the tape to the manager, though, with a note to Robert Price, the son of Sol Price. In about four days he got the tape back from Robert, untouched. Walton says he was treated "better than I deserved" (Walton 1992).

"Most everything I've done I've copied from someone else....I probably visited more headquarters offices of more discounters than anybody else—ever. . . . I'd ask lots of questions about pricing and distribution, whatever. I learned a lot that way," he wrote. He studied competitors' prices, displays, merchandising techniques, supply lines, and so on, in order to improve his own stores.

Walton was also a pioneer of the belief that those closest to the customers have the most to teach the company—an idea that would not gain currency for many years. Recalls Glass, "He genuinely believed that all of the best ideas came from the bottom up, not from the top down, and particularly that all those people who interfaced with the customer knew more about the business and more about what we needed to do and more about how to improve it than anyone else."

Walton encouraged his managers to do the same snooping around. He told them to look for the things the competitors did right and not wrong. Even the worst store, he reasoned, was doing something right that they were not. Glass, one of Wal-Mart's earliest managers, said, "He was able to spot a diamond in the rough. Most of the best ideas came from our competitor's stores. . . . I have gone through stores with him many times, thousands of times where the competitors' stores . . . would look really bad . . . almost God awful. But he would never say that. He would always find some good idea in there, and everybody, of course, picked up on that" (Ortega 1998).

Walton would not only take competitors' ideas, he would also take their people, as well. Walton said when discussing one of his first personnel acquisitions in his memoir, *Made in America*., "I did something I would do for the rest of my run in the retail business without any shame or embarrassment whatsoever: nose around other people's stores searching for good talent" (Walton 1997).

When Walton took an idea to implement in his stores, he also tried to make it better. He was interested in taking things beyond where they had been and liked to shake up the system.

Motivate

Despite the recent attention paid by the media to Wal-Mart's worker salaries and benefits, Wal-Mart has been the most successful retailer in motivating employees over the years. Many of the competitor discounters that were around when Wal-Mart was beginning went out of business eventually, even though they were better capitalized and larger. Much of the credit for Wal-Mart's success has been attributed to Walton's ability to motivate people. He believed that if the employees were motivated and treated well, they would pass that on to the customers and keep them coming back. He said in his memoir, "In the whole Wal-Mart scheme of things, the most important contact ever made is between the associate in the store and the customer" (Walton 1992).

Because of Walton's views on this, Wal-Mart uses a total-quality concept in managing executives and employees. The approach is unconventional in the retailing industry and has extraordinarily improved performance. Wal-Mart department heads are able to review financial figures such as costs, freight charges, and profit margins, which are typically not seen by their counterparts in other retail organizations. Walton also ensured that his vision was known by just about every Wal-Mart associate throughout the company.

Walton got some of his ideas about employee motivation from visiting the Far East. After being inspired by Korean workers, Walton introduced a Wal-Mart cheer that employees chant, which begins, "Give me a W," includes a "squiggly" where they wiggle their bodies, and ends, "What's that spell? Wal-Mart! Who's number one? The customer!" Walton also traveled to Japan to study supply chains and Japanese-style company-worker relationships. Wal-Mart even has had its own cheerleading team, the "Shrinkettes," a gospel group called "The Singing Truck Drivers," and a management singing group called "Jimmy Walker and the Accountants."

When Walton hired people, he did not emphasize formal education or training. He'd give people six months, and if he thought they showed any real potential to merchandise a store and manage people, he'd give them a chance. Walton would give a percentage of the profits to lure and motivate good managers, which they could use to buy stock in the company.

Each employee at Wal-Mart is called an associate and receives a portion of the profits, although this was not always the case. Initially, Walton writes, "I was so obsessed with turning in a profit margin of 6 percent or higher that I ignored some of the basic needs of our people." Subsequently, after skirmishes with unions led Walton to start "experimenting with this idea of treating our associates as partners, it didn't take long to realize the enormous potential it had for improving our business."

Lower Costs at All Costs

From the time he started his first variety franchise store and made up his mind that the franchiser's prices were too high, Walton was a warrior for getting low prices from suppliers. Even before he was a true discounter, he made sure his shelves were consistently stocked with a wide range of items at low prices. He bought his goods wholesale, when he could, which allowed him to buy goods at lower prices, which he passed on to his customers. This then drove up his sales volume, which allowed him to negotiate even lower purchase prices with the wholesalers.

Once committed to discounting, Walton began a crusade that lasted the rest of his life: to drive costs out of the merchandising system wherever they lay—in the stores, in the manufacturers' profit margins, and with the middleman—all in the service of driving prices down.

Using that formula, which cut his margins to the bone, it was imperative that Wal-Mart grow sales at a relentless pace. Managerial expenses were kept to a minimum, even when on buying trips. His equation for merchandise sourcing trips to New York City in the beginning was that the trip's expense should be less than one percent of purchases made. This meant that at times eight people would sleep in one hotel room.

Walton found that customers would shop anywhere if the prices were lower. David Glass recounts an amusing episode at the time of the opening of the second Wal-Mart store confirmed the wisdom of Walton's new approach. The store was opening in Harrison, Arkansas, not far from the local (and relatively upscale) Sterling store. In those days, store openings were big events. Kids got free donkey rides, and patrons were offered free watermelon in the parking lot. But this particular store opening was a disaster almost from the start. The scorching heat had two unexpected consequences: exploding watermelons and what might euphemistically be called "excitable" donkeys. As a result, the parking lot turned into a slippery, smelly mess, which made its way into the store on customers' shoes. Nevertheless, shoppers came, browsed, and purchased. They bypassed the tonier store up the street, ignored the mess on the floor, and bought. Walton knew then that low prices were the key to his business.

Even though he made many mistakes in those first years, Walton felt that his vision kept the company on the right track: "What we were obsessed with was keeping our prices below everybody else's." Walton's obsession with low prices helped fuel the company's rapid growth. In Wal-Mart's early years the company was very much a David up against many Goliaths. Five years after starting Wal-Mart, for example, Walton had only five stores, each bringing in less than ten million dollars in revenues annually. In sharp contrast, Kmart had 250 stores with total sales of eight hundred million. Walton believed that he could win in the long run because many discounters never fully committed to the discounting model, which calls for low prices across the board. Walton said in his memoir, *Made in America,*

> It's amazing that our competitors didn't catch on to us quicker and try to stop us. . . . What happened was that they really didn't commit to discounting. They held on to their old variety store concepts too long. They were so accustomed to getting their 45 percent markup, they never let go. With our low costs, our low expense structures, and our low prices, we were ending an era in the heartland. We shut the door on variety thinking. Some retailers, such as Sears, failed to acknowledge that.

By 1980, Wal-Mart had more than 275 stores doing over a billion dollars in sales. By 1990, Wal-Mart had over fifteen hundred stores, and sales had topped twenty-six billion dollars.

Even if there was no other discount store within a hundred miles, Walton made sure that every Wal-Mart stayed true to the vision of low costs. Often, they found themselves in price wars with competitors.

Be on the Ground or in the Air Getting There

Walton believed strongly in being out in the field and seeing in person what his stores and his competitors were doing. Even though Wal-Mart is known for best and innovative applications of information technology, Walton reasoned that those applications could not do everything. "A computer can tell you down to the dime what you've sold. But it can never tell you how much you could have sold." The computer, he said, "will never be a substitute for getting out in your stores and learning what's going on."

Walton used his plane to get around and scout out new store locations. "I'd get down low, turn my plane up on its side, and fly right over a town. . . . There's another good reason I don't like jets. You can't get down low enough to really tell what's going on, the way I could in my little planes. Until we had 500 stores, or at least 400 or so, I kept up with every real estate deal we made and got to view most locations before we signed any kind of commitment," he said in *Made in America*.

Besides scouting new locations, Walton also kept strict tabs on his stores. Walton called this style of his "management by walking and flying around."

Walton wrote in his memoir that until he got "really sick" in 1991, he remained fully engaged in the operational details: "If I wasn't in the stores trying to pump up our associates to do an even better job, or in the office looking over the numbers to see where the next trouble spot was going to pop up, or leading cheers at a Saturday morning meeting, I was probably at the stick of my airplane . . . checking out the number of cars in those Kmart parking lots."

Promote and Merchandise

"In Retail, you are either operations driven—where your main thrust is towards reducing expenses and improving efficiency—or you are merchandise driven. The ones that are truly merchandise driven can always work on improving operations. But the ones that are operations driven tend to level off and begin to deteriorate," he wrote in *Made in America*. What he meant was that a retailer has to know how to merchandise. They have to have good product to sell, and they have to know how to place it and promote it in order for it to sell.

Wal-Mart stores don't stock many brands. They feature only a few brands, ones on which they get good volume discounts. What makes them work is the breadth—every category is represented—not depth within a category. Wal-Mart's merchandising strategy was formed early on and changed little over the years. Walton loved to buy an incredible amount of one item and place it on a table in front of the registers or otherwise make it visible in his stores. Walton felt that his competitors failed when they lost their merchandising instincts. Walton also encouraged his managers to try their hand at merchandising, as well. One of his managers, Phil Green, once made the world's largest laundry detergent display at one of the oldest Wal-Mart stores, which scared Walton at first because of the amount of detergent ordered, but it was wildly successful.

Walton was also a master at promotion. In fact, his first bank loan, taken after a lifetime of hearing from his father about how bad debt was, was for promotion. He bought an eighteen-hunded-dollar icecream machine as a prop for the first Newport store.

Manage Product and Information

Wal-Mart's logistics strategy has long been one of the key case studies for business students. Distribution centers were one of the primary reasons the company could expand as it did. Walton placed each store within a day's drive of a distribution center. Wal-Mart could replenish store inventories, Walton estimated in 1992, more than twice as fast and at about a 3,540 percent lower cost than its competitors.

The strategy was born out of necessity. The company started building its first distribution center in 1968, according to Walton, because distributors weren't trying as hard to service them as they were Walton's larger competitors. His only alternative, he concluded, was to build his own warehouses in order to buy in volume at better prices.

Investments in computer and communications systems have been another important critical element of the retailer's strategy. It would have been impossible for Walton to have built a retailing empire the size of what he built, the way he built it, without the computer.

For many years, however, Walton relied on rudimentary, labor-intensive systems. From the start, Walton understood that automating the management of inventory was a great way to save money. In 1966, Walton enrolled in an IBM course on using punch cards to track information. What he learned was how to track his merchandise to ensure that the right goods arrived at the right store in the right quantity at the right time. This meant fewer missed sales due to empty shelves, less handling of products in the warehouse and in the store, less need to check inventory physically, and fewer returns to the warehouse or the manufacturers. Over time, he learned that his stock-tracking system also gave him power over his employees and over many of the manufacturers that sold to his company.

Walton said that the faster people got information, the faster they would use it. Useful applications emerged almost immediately. The company has implemented cross-stocking. More than 75 percent of incoming merchandise is received by one of seventeen distribution centers within one day of the order, serving from 100 to 150 stores. The balance of merchandise is received by the individual store direct from the vendor within seven days of the initial order.

Wal-Mart uses its information to better its alliances with suppliers. A very sophisticated satellite communications system links Wal-Mart with suppliers. This allows Wal-Mart's management to track the sales of every item in every store daily and report to the supplier how much to order to make up for what was sold.

According to David Glass, Wal-Mart was the first company to transform the supplier relationship from an adversarial one to something more akin to a partnership. As Glass puts it,

> We used to go through a spiel that we'd say to the supplier, we're not really your customer. The consumer is your customer. We're only a conduit to get your merchandise to them. So if you believe that, then the right thing to do is say, all right, let's look at the whole thing from the time you manufacture the goods until the consumer carries them out of the store, and what's the most efficient way to do it. And what we found was that they could eliminate a lot of costs that they built into their business to protect their interests against us, and we could eliminate costs and do things more efficiently.... If you form this partnership and it works, then you can really revolutionize the business. (Ortega 1998)

Outwork the Competition

Walton was always known for his hard work. He visited stores often and was always analyzing what they could do better. David Glass remarked that "It's often been said that he spent more time in competitors' stores than they did. In a lot of cases, that's true" (Ortega 1998).

Walton also demanded hard work from his managers in Bentonville. Every Saturday morning, they would meet to go over company goals and strategies. Choosing Saturday mornings to meet with his managers to discuss how to incorporate what they had learned into the business was one of Walton's best competitive moves. Walton said that it was in those meetings that the company first decided to try things that seemed unattainable. Those meetings were pivotal, because they were the vehicles Walton used to make his "corrections." He had two days before the competition had a chance to catch up.

POLITICAL INFLUENCE

Although Walton was quite active in school politics in high school and college, he generally avoided them during the remainder of his life. Although he was a Republican and lobbied for some things, including estate tax cuts, and gave money to some campaigns, including that of President George H. W. Bush, he was not very publicly active in that arena.

His family is quite active now, however, significantly changing their past behavior. Led by Alice, the family spent $3.2 million on lobbying, conservative causes, and candidates for the 2004 federal elections. They are trying to repeal the estate tax, primarily.

Wal-Mart's political action committee (PAC), now the third-largest corporate PAC and the second-largest corporate donor to the GOP, gave away $2.1 million in 2004, compared with just a hundred thousand dollars in 1994. The Walton family, too, has greatly increased its political giving; in 2004, for example, Alice donated $2.6 million to the influential Republican PAC Progress for America, which supported the Swift Boat Veterans for Truth and gave President George W. Bush a critical push in the election's final months.

In addition to spending on Republican candidates, since their father's death, the Walton children have lavished funds on right-wing ideological institutions. Since 1998 they have contributed over $25,000 to the Heritage Foundation, $15,000 to the Cato Institute, $125,000 to the Hudson Institute, $155,000 to the Goldwater Institute, $70,000 to the National Right to Work Legal Defense Foundation, $300,000 to the Mackinac Center for Public Policy, $185,000 to the Pacific Research Institute for Public Policy, and $350,000 to the Evergreen Freedom Foundation.

CRITICS

Since Walton died, Wal-Mart has come under intense criticism for how it treats its workers, for its political lobbying, and even for its newfound philanthropy. Some critics say the Waltons are giving now to stem the tide of criticism over their previous worker policies. Many wonder, however, whether Wal-Mart's current culture and policies would be in place if Walton were still alive and active in the company.

Today, Wal-Mart's critics say the store is in too many places and is replacing the mom-and-pop local retailers, putting them out of business. When Walton was alive, and Wal-Mart was just taking off as the largest national retailer, his critics were not as focused on the urban sprawl the name of the company now seems to conjure. Although as Wal-Mart's influence was growing and once it passed that of competitors Kmart and Sears, Walton did begin to be harshly criticized by some, especially the beleaguered small-town merchants. Walton was blamed for the loss of their businesses, although he responded that if he hadn't done it, someone else would have in response to the customer. He believed that many of the smaller businesses were not running their stores correctly, often overcharging customers and wasting money. He said, "There is only one boss. The customer. And he can fire everybody in the company from the chairman on down, simply by spending his money somewhere else" (Walton 1992).

Walton also was hit with the charge that much of his garment production took place out of the country, using child labor. By 1985, many of Wal-Mart's products were manufactured in Central American maquilas that pay low wages, in countries where workers lack the same rights available in industrialized countries. To alleviate this situation there, Walton began a scholarship program to bring Central American students to Christian universities in the United States.

TIMELINE

1918	Born on March 29 near Kingfisher, Oklahoma.
1921	Bud Walton born.
1931	Became youngest-ever Eagle Scout in Missouri.
1936	Graduated from high school in Columbia, Missouri.
1940	Graduated from the University of Missouri at Columbia with a BA in economics.
	Took a job as a management trainee at J. C. Penney.
1942	Resigned from J. C. Penney and worked at a Tulsa DuPont gunpowder plant.
	Called up for active duty in the army.
1942 to 1945	Served as a captain in the U.S. Army Intelligence Corps.
1943	February 14, Married Helen Robson.
1944	Samuel Robson (Rob) Walton born.
1946	Bought franchised Ben Franklin store in Newport, Arkansas.
1946	John Thomas Walton born.
1948	James (Jim) Carr Walton born.
1949	Alice S. Robson Walton born.
1950	Discovered that his Newport lease would not be renewed and found space in Bentonville, Arkansas for another store.
1951	Opened the Walton Five & Dime in Bentonville, a Ben Franklin franchise.
1952	Opened another Walton Five & Dime in Fayetteville; this store was not a franchise.
	Continued to look for other store opportunities. Opened another franchise store in Ruskin Heights with his brother Bud as 50–50 partner.
1957	May 20, Ruskin Heights store leveled by a tornado.
1962	July 2, Opened the first Wal-Mart in nearby Rogers, Arkansas.

	Walton and his brother had sixteen variety stores in Arkansas, Kansas, and Missouri.
1964	Second Wal-Mart opened.
1966	Enrolled in IBM computer course.
1968	Hired Ron Mayer as vice president of finance and distribution.
1969	First distribution center built.
1970	October 1, Wal-Mart stock first traded over the counter as publicly held company.
1971	First 100 percent stock split. Stock valued at forty-seven dollars per share.
1972	Wal-Mart listed on the New York Stock Exchange.
1974	Took time off and handed over CEO reins to Ron Mayer.
1976	Took CEO title back from Mayer.
1977	Acquired Mohr-Value stores in Michigan and Illinois.
1979	Wal-Mart hit a billion dollars in sales with 230 stores.
1980	Started building the 135,000-square-foot building to house the sophisticated computer system.
1983	The first Sam's Club was opened in April in Midwest City, Oklahoma.
1983	The "People Greeter" program is introduced in all stores.
1984	Did the hula on Wall Street after posting 8 percent profits in 1983.
1985	*Forbes* named Sam Walton the richest man in America.
1988	First Supercenter opened in Washington, Missouri.
1990	Wal-Mart positioned as the nation's number-one retailer.
1991	Opened first international store with Club Aurrera in Mexico City.
1992	Died on April 5.

RESOURCES

Bhide, Amar V. *Origin and Evolution of New Businesses.* New York: Oxford University Press, 2003, pp. 16, 220, 239–241, 270–278.

Krames, Jeffrey A. *What the Best CEOs Know: 7 Exceptional Leaders and Their Lessons for Transforming Any Business.* New York: McGraw-Hill Companies, 2003, pp.11–12, 22–24, 33, 51, 198–218.

Lynn, Barry C. *End of the Line: The Rise and Coming Fall of the Global Corporation.* New York: Doubleday Publishing, 2005, pp. 8, 104–108, 118, 126.

Michman, Ronald D. *Retailing Triumphs and Blunders: Victims of Competition in the New Age of Marketing Management.* Westport, CT: Greenwood Publishing Group, 1995, pp. 6, 97–119, 140–160, 197, 206.

Ortega, Bob. *In Sam We Trust: The Untold Story of Sam Walton and How Wal-Mart is Devouring America.* New York: Random House, 1998.

Walton, Sam, with John Huey. *Made in America.* New York: Doubleday, 1992.

COMPANY INFORMATION

Wal-Mart Stores, Inc.
702 S.W. 8th Street
Bentonville, AR 72716
Phone: 1–800–Walmart
www.walmart.com
New York Stock Exchange symbol: WMT

AP Photo/Hans Punz.

Jack Welch

Jack Francis Welch, Jr., was the CEO of General Electric (GE), one of the world's largest companies, for twenty years, and, as a result of his leadership, GE grew their profits by a staggering amount. In his first year in charge, GE was America's eleventh-largest company, worth twelve billion dollars, and when he left, it was number one, worth an estimated four hundred billion dollars. No other CEO has created as much shareholder value as Welch did. For four years in succession, between 1998 and 2001, the *Financial Times* ranked him as the "world's most respected business leader."

Although Welch retired in 2001, many of the principles he used to recreate GE have been implemented in companies throughout the world. Although he has retired, he is still actively giving business advice to many companies and is a highly requested speaker. His advice and programs are cornerstones of graduate business education today, and many business professionals who want to succeed in their careers analyze his career in detail.

Why he is still a management superstar all these years after retiring has a lot to do with not only his success as chairman and CEO, but also with his tough-talking, working-class Irish American persona. He used a common-sense approach to business and workforce management that worked. Although he was called Neutron Jack, cut 10 percent of his staff every year, and was voted the one-time "Toughest Boss in America" (*Fortune*, 1984), he managed almost everyone with fairness and encouragement so that they became productive and successful. Indeed, three of his former top lieutenants now head Fortune 500 companies (Robert Nardelli at Home Depot, Jeffrey Immelt at GE, and James McNerney at 3M and then at Boeing).

His leadership style has been contentious at times, but it is also the attribute to which most people credit his success. Welch was a no-nonsense manager who gave free reign to his most deserving (that is, successful) employees. He was hard driving yet was the type of manager who also wanted to befriend his employees. He knew the names and responsibilities of the top thousand people in the organization. He was an acknowledged workaholic and expected those who worked for him to also give their jobs their all as well.

Welch was able to navigate GE to success using a combination of business practices and techniques, including the Six Sigma quality initiative and the controversial 20–70–10 employee assessment plan. Welch credits the 20–70–10 plan (known by its critics as "rank and yank"), which involved giving the top 20 percent of the workforce each year a very large raise, and firing the bottom 10 percent, with transforming companies from mediocre to outstanding.

Jack Welch has been widely scrutinized by the media. There have been hundreds of publications written and several interviews with Welch over the past forty years. His career has been full of controversy. He went from "prince to pig," as he says, in the media at least four times.

> *"People always overestimate how complex business is. This isn't rocket science."*
> Jack Welch

Welch managed the company through many changes, including over six hundred acquisitions. Some went smoothly, while others did not. He was able to celebrate many successes along the way, including the acquisition of NBC, and learn from the costly mistakes, including the acquisition of Kidder Peabody.

At the end of his reign, GE was a company that had changed dramatically. Welch improved not only the value of the company but also the way the company was managed. He had streamlined it, running the company with far fewer people, and introduced and perfected management and quality programs that other companies are still implementing today.

- Jack Welch became the youngest CEO of GE at age forty-five and remained in his position for twenty years.
- In 1999, *Fortune* named Jack Welch "Manager of the Century."
- Jack Welch turned GE into a several-hundred-billion-dollar company from a twelve-billion-dollar company.

THE EARLY YEARS

John Francis Welch, Jr., known to the world as Jack, was born on November 19, 1935. His parents, John and Grace Welch, were part of a working-class family. His father worked as a railroad conductor, and his mother was a full-time housewife. Welch was born in Peabody, Massachusetts, and raised in Salem, Massachusetts, as an only child in a Catholic home.

Welch now believes that because he was the only child of relatively older parents by the standards of that day, his mother poured all of her attention, love, and discipline into him. He credits her with building his confidence and demonstrating what would later become his leadership style—getting the most out of people by being tough, aggressive, warm, and generous. Confidence, according to Welch, leads people to courage, to the willingness to reach further. Because of his mother's encouragement and cheerleading (which included calling the local paper whenever he achieved something), Welch developed a great deal of confidence. He would later look for that quality in others and try to build it in his employees in much the same way as his mother had done with him. Without his mother's vigorous help, his self-esteem most certainly would have suffered. Welch grew up with a speech impediment, a stutter that continued through college. For years, he says, he believed his mother's excuse that his stuttering was a result of his brain working so fast his mouth couldn't keep up.

Welch's father also seemed to look at things in the best light. His father would tell him how lucky they were to live across the street from a factory because no one was around on the weekends and they were always quiet. Although Welch did not receive much nurturing from his father mainly because his father was not often at home, Welch did learn the value of hard work. His father's job as a railroad conductor took him away from the house early in the morning until past 7:00 p.m. each evening. When he returned, he would bring a bundle of newspapers passengers left on the train, and Welch developed a lifelong habit of reading the news every day.

His father also got him started playing golf, a habit that would last most of his life until back problems after retirement forced him to quit. Because the businessmen on the train would often talk about their golf games, Welch's father believed this would be an important game for his son to learn. With his father's encouragement, Welch became a caddy at the age of nine and kept

"The ability to energize is the ingredient that counts."
Jack Welch

that job, along with others, until the age of seventeen. He became quite good at golf, which was lucky, because although he was a good athlete as a younger boy, he peaked early and by high school could no longer keep up with the other boys. Golf was something at which he would continue to excel. As a caddy, Welch became familiar with people who had achieved a measure of success. Some of those people, he found, were great people, while others were mean-spirited, and their personalities shone through on the golf course. The end of his caddying career came when he was confronted by one of the stingiest members of the country club. The man topped his ball right into the muddy pond. He asked Welch to get it. Welch refused, and when he insisted, Welch threw the man's clubs into the water and stormed off the course.

Jack Welch was the first person in his immediate family to go to college.

Although Grace Welch had a lot of support to give her son, she also delivered discipline. She would not stand for her son giving up or competing poorly. Words that would come back to Welch throughout his career were hers. When he thought that a business deal could miraculously improve, he would hear her saying, "There are no shortcuts. Don't kid yourself." Then he would get back to work. He remembers an effective lesson he received from her in sportsmanship. At the end of an unfortunate loss at a final hockey game of the season, Welch threw his stick across the ice. He skated to get it and then went to the locker room. His mother stormed in a short time later, grabbed him by the top of his uniform while his teammates watched in stunned silence, and announced that if he didn't know how to lose, he would never know how to win, and he should not be playing. Surprisingly, Grace did not discipline Welch for his caddying behavior on his final day of work. However disappointed she may have been because he lost his job, she seemed to understand.

Welch was an excellent student in both high school and college, after an initial struggle his freshman year. Although he had not been accepted for a naval scholarship that he could have used to attend a great school, he was accepted by the University of Massachusetts. There, he pledged to the Phi Sigma Kappa fraternity in his sophomore year, and the hard partying he found there helped alleviate the homesickness he had experienced earlier. Welch did much better in school after joining the fraternity, as well. He found a mentor in the chemical engineering department who liked him and pushed him through the program. In 1957, he was one of the university's two best students, graduating with a degree in chemical engineering. He was courted by several companies after graduation, but turned down the offers in order to go to graduate school at the University of Illinois at Champaign, where he received a scholarship. There he found he was not the smartest, and he had to study and focus much more than he had previously done. With the strong support of yet another professor, Welch received a PhD in three years. He maintains that his degree in chemical engineering was one of the best backgrounds for his business career, mainly because the subject teaches one important lesson: there are no finite answers to many questions and what counts is the thought process you use. This is true for most business problems as well, and if you wait for the perfect answer, Welch believes, the world will pass you by.

CAREER PATH

Welch and his first wife, Carolyn, spent their honeymoon traveling across the United States and Canada, where Welch interviewed for jobs. He had several offers but decided on the one that paid the best. He went to work for the chemical development operation for GE in Pittsfield, Massachusetts. He had opted to use his new degree not in education as a professor and researcher but in business because, as he recalls, when he took inventory of his skills his people skills, in his opinion, far surpassed his scientific and laboratory skills. His desire upon graduation was to apply his skills in bridging the gap between the research and people.

General Electric hired Jack Welch as a chemical engineer in its plastics division after his completion of school in 1960. They wanted his help in designing a new plastic—PPO. His starting salary was $10,500, and although he had been aggressively wooed by the company before accepting employment, he was given no favors after his first day of work. Although his ideal was somewhat tarnished because of this immediate and drastically different way of treatment, he did enjoy a few things the first year. He was able to design and build a new pilot plant, and he had a group of people he worked with who gave him the sense of being part of a team in a small company. It was during this time that Welch for the first time in his professional career, tried out his persuasion abilities. He had to convince other researchers and scientists to help on his project versus spending time on other people's projects.

> *"Differentiation is all about being extreme, rewarding the best and weeding out the ineffective. Rigorous differentiation delivers real stars—and stars build great businesses."*
> Jack Welch

During his first year, Welch worked extremely hard to differentiate himself from the pack. When he was asked for answers to questions, he would submit a detailed analytical report and try to look at the reasoning behind the question and address that. He would always give his bosses more than was expected.

Welch quickly grew tired of the penny-pinching behavior GE used with his group. He and his peers had to share a cramped office, a telephone, and hotel rooms on business trips. At the end of his first year of employment at GE,

Welch, along with everyone on his team, received a thousand-dollar bonus. This threw him over the edge, and he decided he was qualified for more. He made the decision to quit GE and take a job offer at International Minerals and Chemicals back in Illinois.

"When people make mistakes, the last thing they need is discipline. It's time for encouragement and confidence-building."

Jack Welch

Welch never took that job, however. Instead, Rueben Gutoff, an executive for GE, decided that Jack Welch had a lot more potential than some might have seen. Gutoff knew Welch was worth fighting for and was able to convince him to stay with GE by putting more money on the table, enough to match his new job offer, and making a deal that he would work hard to eliminate most of the bureaucracy that currently was taking place in GE. With Gutoff's recognition, Welch accepted that differentiation is key to motivating and managing employees. Even though everyone may contribute to the team, their contributions will not necessarily be equal, and their rewards do not have to be equal. This would become a key ingredient in Welch's leadership tactics.

I believe in giving people "runway assignments" –the capacity to grow. . . . Stretch them early in their careers."

Jack Welch

One of Welch's early career moves was to blow up one of the GE factories. The roof of the new pilot plant he was helping to design was blown off because a chemical process he was supervising had gone awry. Although no one was injured, he still had a lot of explaining to do. He made the drive to the corporate headquarters going over his explanation of the accident and how he would fix it. When he arrived to the office of his boss's boss, Charlie Reed, he was unprepared for how comfortable he was made to feel. Reed encouraged Welch to examine the accident but was not emotional. He asked his opinions on whether to continue with the project. Reed's reaction made a powerful impact on Welch. When people make mistakes, Welch realized, the last thing they need is discipline. It's time for encouragement and confidence building.

In 1964, the general manager's position of the polymer products operation became open. Welch lobbied hard for the position, and although he had no marketing experience, he won the job. It was trial by fire. Just as he began his new position, it became clear that the product he was in charge of was seriously flawed. It took six months of frantic work before it was fixed.

With sales of the new product growing quickly, Welch received his next big break. He was promoted to general manager of the plastics division. This made him, at thirty-two, the company's youngest general manager. To advertise the industrial plastics, Welch and his team turned to marketing techniques used by mainstream retail products: billboards, comedy, radio ads, gimmicks in the company parking lot, and television ads featuring a bull in a china shop full of plastic china that did not break. This new approach paid off

---

In one of Jack Welch's early annual reviews, he included that "his long term goal is to become CEO of GE."

---

and Welch was able to double the profits of the plastics business in less than three years.

By Welch's own admission, he was not classic GE material. He could be blunt, emotional, candid, or rude, as some would suggest throughout the years. He loved constructive conflict and would get so involved in an argument that he would make what some would consider outrageous comments, such as "My six-year-old kid could do better than that!" or "Don't Walter Cronkite me," which was understood to mean don't mention what needs to be fixed without showing how it can be fixed. He would fire people who could not work within the informal environment or who were arrogant. In the way of his mother, Grace Welch, though, he would tell it like he saw it but would also be the first to reward good performers.

Despite a negative evaluation citing his emotional involvement and arrogance, Welch was promoted to vice president of the Chemical and Metallurgical Division in 1971. He approached this new job by first taking a critical look at his team. He impulsively removed people who were not impressive to him, and he quickly promoted people who were.

When Reginald Jones announced his imminent departure as CEO of GE, Welch's name had actually been excluded from an early list of successor candidates. He was too young, too impatient, too reckless. He stammered. But when Reg Jones and Ted LeVino instituted a very rigorous and challenging succession process, inviting six key candidates and putting them in jobs for which they were not experienced, Welch was there. Welch got the job, and the other candidates left the company. Jones did not say exactly why he chose Welch, though it was by all accounts a risky move. Welch was quite unlike past GE CEOs. But Jones saw a danger for the company on the horizon. As a director at Bethlehem Steel, he'd seen what happens when foreign competition hits a slumbering bureaucracy, and he feared what it might do to GE. He liked that Welch saw similar dangers and knew he needed to pick a different type of leader than GE had had previously.

PERSONAL LIFE

Welch grew up with devout Catholic parents and was an altar boy when he was young. He continued going to mass during college, and it was there where he first saw Carolyn Osburn doing the Stations of the Cross during Lent. Five months after their first date, she became his first wife. They had four children and remained together for twenty-eight years before amicably divorcing six years after Welch was made CEO. Welch admits that he never

Reg Jones

Jack Welch's predecessor and mentor, Reginald H. Jones, was the most admired CEO of his era, the inflation-wracked 1970s. Reg Jones made the wise decision to name Welch as his successor despite the fact that the younger manager was considered too inexperienced, too impatient, and too reckless for the job. Though they were opposites in many ways, each was perfectly attuned to his era.

An accountant by training, the dignified and even-tempered Jones ran GE during the 1970s—a time of simultaneous recession and inflation, when he nonetheless managed to sustain strong growth in both revenue and profits. He was well suited to an environment where rational planning and prudent investments were the order of the day. It was also a time of heavy regulation, and Jones's statesmanlike demeanor made him particularly effective in negotiations with government regulators. Jones personified the traditional ideal of the CEO as statesman and guided GE to twenty-six successive quarters of rising earnings through two recessions. At a time of befuddling turbulence, Reg Jones and GE embodied the stability the nation had known previously.

Jones, like Welch, was a self-made man from working-class roots who worked and fought hard for what he achieved. He grew up in a row house, and his dad worked as a foreman in a steel mill. The family had arrived in the United States in Trenton, New Jersey, when Jones was eight. Jones was fond of saying "I'm English. I'm too damn poor to be British." He excelled in school, working his way through Wharton Business School by tutoring other students and stacking books. He went straight to GE and climbed the corporate ladder through the company's powerful finance function. He did an eight-year tour on the audit staff that took him to nearly every plant in the company business. He was an operating manager in several businesses before being named chief financial officer in 1968. In 1972 he became president, then chairman and CEO. There he brought fresh vitality and new strategic direction to one of the most diversified enterprises in the world. Most of that diversification came from strong internal growth fostered by research and development, strategic planning and the introduction of the sector structure, which "prepared the organization and the people to meet General Electric's long-range growth opportunities in the decade ahead." Under Jones's administration, the company's sales more than doubled (from ten billion dollars to twenty-two billion) and earnings grew even faster (from $572 million to $1.4 billion). A major thrust was made into international markets. As chairman of the President's Export Council, Reg Jones became an eloquent voice for the expansion of world trade and the restoration of U.S. competitiveness.

tried to have a work-life balance. His work was his main enjoyment, while Carolyn did the majority of raising the family. After their divorce, Carolyn went on to law school and to marry her undergraduate sweetheart.

Welch soon married Jane Beasley, a mergers-and-acquisitions lawyer at Shearman & Sterling, after meeting her on a blind date arranged by one of his GE directors. Jane quit her position as an associate to make Welch her full-time occupation and frequently traveled with him. She adapted to his passions, skiing and golf, while encouraging him to learn about hers. Welch also helped teach Jane golf, and though she had never played before meeting him, she learned quickly. She won two club championships in a row on Nantucket and became a great golf partner for Welch. They were married for thirteen years, but their divorce was the source of one of the greatest scandals in his life.

In 2001 Welch was interviewed by Suzy Wetlaufer in her capacity as editor of the *Harvard Business Review*. Before long they were having an affair. Jane discovered this when she picked up his BlackBerry and read several messages from Suzy. The ensuing divorce negotiations exposed Welch's private life and financial picture, including retirement perks from GE, which allowed him to keep using a company apartment and airplanes. He was later compelled to return the perks after intense media scrutiny. The Welches were worth a billion dollars at the time of the divorce, and the prenuptial agreement they had signed expired on their tenth anniversary in 1999.

The divorce proceeding showed that Welch at the time spent $8,982 a month on food and beverages, including wine, $1,903 a month on his wardrobe, and $1,482 a month on vacations. His six homes were worth more than thirty million dollars combined. Monthly "shelter expenses" were listed as $51,531. He gave $614 a month to charity, though his foundation donated $3.1 million in 1998.

In 2004, Welch married Suzy, and they have since written a book together, *Winning*. They are together almost all of the time, traveling the world to his speaking engagements.

The private Welch is a sports fanatic, a movie buff, and a gossip junkie. After a vigorous forty-five-minute workout in his home at 5:30 a.m., he begins every weekday by scanning the "What's News" column of the *Wall Street Journal*. Immediately afterward, he reads his favorite newspaper, the *New York Post*. He used to spend a great deal of time playing golf, but since his retirement, back injuries have prevented him from playing the game.

LEADERSHIP LESSONS

When Welch took over as CEO, he was concerned about what he perceived to be an uncertain future. Welch feared that GE's rivals would get stronger at GE's expense and foreign competition would take a serious toll on the

> *"If you pick the right people and give them the opportunity to spread their wings and put compensation as a carrier behind it you almost don't have to manage them."*
>
> Jack Welch

business. He wanted to make the company more competitive, and to achieve that goal Welch felt he needed a sleek and aggressive company. This meant a smaller GE—a much smaller GE. At the time Welch began his tenure as CEO, the company had 412,000 employees. There were an astounding twenty-five thousand employees who bore the title of manager, about five hundred senior managers, and 130 at vice president level or higher. Welch believed that GE's bloated ranks had become a failed strategy, costing GE inordinate amounts of money. One of his main strategies involved cutting the workforce by a significant amount, and cultivating the best employees he kept. The nickname "Neutron Jack" first appeared in *Newsweek* in 1982, an allusion to the neutron bomb that removes the people but leaves the buildings standing.

Welch took pride in not implementing too many corporate-wide initiatives, and the ones he did champion were very successful. He oversaw numerous acquisitions and was not afraid to mess with a stable, established GE.

Managing People

One of Welch's driving philosophies is that leaders have to inspire their people with clear visions of how things can be done better. There should be constant improvements.

Welch set precise performance targets and monitored them throughout the year. And every one of Welch's direct reports—from his three vice chairmen to each of the operating heads of GE's twelve businesses—also received a handwritten, two-page evaluation of his performance at the end of every year. "I do the evaluations on Sunday nights in my library at home," said Welch. "It gives me a chance to reflect on each business." Attached to the detailed notes were his jottings from a year earlier, with new comments written in red pencil in the margins: "Nice job." "Still needs work" (Welch 2001).

There were no form letters from Welch, not to employees, managers, executives, or even directors in the GE boardroom. Every salary increase or decrease, every bonus, and every stock-option grant to Welch's twenty or so direct reports came with a candid talk about expectations and performance.

Welch knew by sight the names and responsibilities of at least the top thousand people at GE.

Four Es.   To evaluate managers and potential leaders, Welch used the Four Es. This process assesses four essential traits of leadership. He believes that, first, successful leaders have tons of positive energy. They love action and relish change. Two, they have the ability to energize others—they love people and can inspire them to move mountains when they have to. Three, they have edge, the courage to make tough yes-or-no decisions—no maybes. And finally, they can execute. They get the job done.

Company Values. Welch also looks at managers in terms of their values and whether they match those of the company. If managers' values don't match up, they should be let go immediately, no matter what their performance is like. If managers' values do match but their performance is suffering, they should be mentored or moved around and given additional chances.

All GE employees had wallet-sized value cards that they carried around with them.

20–70–10 Plan. Welch strongly believes in differentiation—treating people differently based on their performance. He asked his managers to separate everyone into the top 20 percent, the middle 70 percent, and the bottom 10 percent, and then act on that. He suggests that most of the effort and rewards should go into the top 20 percent performers while not neglecting the middle 70 percent. This middle group is the majority and is very much needed. Managing this group is about training, positive feedback, and thoughtful goal setting.

The bottom 10 percent should be fired immediately. Welch believes these people can go on to successful careers at other companies, but in a top company, you need top performers. Welch is relentless about this. Pay highest wages, but have lowest wage costs—pay for good people; dump the ones you don't need. This process, although painful, was made easier at GE, which could afford to pay very good severance packages.

Session C reviews are intensive reviews that force those running the business units to identify their future leaders, make bets on early-career "stretch" assignments, develop succession plans for all key jobs, and decide which high-potential executives should be sent to Crotonville, the leadership training site GE operates. These took place every year. With three of his senior executives, Welch traveled into the field to each of his twelve businesses to review the progress of the company's top three thousand executives. He kept closest tabs on the upper five hundred.

Managing Corporate Communication

Welch inherited a very strong company. It has always had a strong manpower and selection system. It was and is a "womb to tomb" company, in that it hires from the college graduate market and develops its own talent. What the talent was not doing, however, before Welch took over, was sharing knowledge. He instilled systems that not only encouraged but demanded knowledge sharing. He wanted to make his organization "boundaryless," and he provided the forum for this to happen.

GE Values Card

GE Leaders...Always with Unyielding Integrity:

- Have a Passion for Excellence and Hate Bureaucracy
- Are Open to Ideas from Anywhere...and Committed to Work-Out
- Live Quality...and Drive Cost and Speed for Competitive Advantage
- Have the Self-Confidence to Involve Everyone and Behave in a Boundaryless Fashion
- Create a Clear, Simple, Reality-Based Vision...and Communicate It to All Constituencies
- Have Enormous Energy and The Ability to Energize Others
- Stretch...Set Aggressive Goals...Reward Progress...Yet Understand Accountability and Commitment
- See Change as Opportunity...Not Threat
- Have Global Brains...and Build Diverse and Global Teams

Boundaryless Organization. Welch took the opportunity as CEO to rid GE of some of its bureaucracy and become somewhat more boundaryless. He felt that bureaucracy was a formality that slowed the process of progress down throughout the company, and information needed to be shared quickly throughout the organization. Welch wanted to give his management team the freedom and trust to make faster decisions in order to become more effective in the company. As a result he deleted layers from the organizational chart of the company.

> *"Hiring good people is hard. Hiring great people is brutally hard. Yet nothing matters more in winning than getting the right people on the field, then guiding them on the right way to succeed and get ahead."*
>
> Jack Welch

In addition, he forged an operating system that relied on a boundaryless sharing of ideas, an intense focus on people, and an informal, give-and-take style that makes bureaucracy the enemy. The formal divisions of the company were divided by functional objectives, which Welch believes keeps the organization from becoming world class. He has said that world-class organizations have three major focus areas: being customer focused, process focused, and employee focused. Eliminating the function boundaries meant making the company "informal" and violating the chain of command, communicating across layers, and paying people as if they worked not for a big company but for a demanding entrepreneur where nearly everyone knows the boss.

Bureaucracy had always seemed like the enemy to Welch. When he was hired to develop new businesses in GE's chemical development operation, he and his superiors were appalled at the vast bureaucracy they encountered around the company, especially at headquarters. "We had a Green Beret, almost SWAT team, mentality," recalled Reuben Gutoff, Welch's boss for twelve years. "The enemies were not just outside competitors but the GE bureaucracy as well. We talked a lot about that—the bureaucracy speak, the bureaucracy-babble. We had met the enemy, and it was us."

Before Welch started his revolution, the basic task of GE managers was to monitor their subordinates' performance. But that sort of command-and-control management style did not permit managers to spot trouble soon enough. Senior managers all around GE were merely firing memos at one another. They prevented the CEO from talking directly with junior managers and rank-and-file workers. In order to create a more boundaryless organization, Welch had to remove the levels of bureaucracy, a process he called delayering. He then had to create a forum where ideas could be shared and taught throughout the company.

Crotonville. The GE training center at Croton-on-Hudson, known as Crotonville, had been established long before Welch took over as CEO. It was invented to help GE implement decentralization and was the first corporate training locale equivalent to Harvard and other key business schools. It was used to introduce and get commitment to strategic planning, which was one of the keys to enabling GE to create the strong business portfolio that Welch inherited. Welch himself had never attended any training sessions there as a student, however. After becoming CEO, Welch made Crotonville a mandatory stop for promising managers and created an environment where "best practices" would get transferred among GE's differing businesses. He made the place a central part of his mission to transform GE into an informal learning organization, and he did what no other CEO had done to advance his cause. He became a strong participant, committed to sharing, challenging, and teaching personally. The courses taught there were directly linked to the strategic priorities of the company, and executives went there to work on issues that perplexed them back at the office. Welch would address the audience often in the Pit there, a bright, multitiered lecture hall.

Work-Out. When attending training at Crotonville, managers would be required to recount how they used new ideas to squeeze out more profit. They had to explain how quality efforts cut costs and mistakes, enhanced productivity, led to greater market share, or eliminated the need for investment in new plant and equipment.

Welch would be at the training and sharing session often, and he would seldom disappear early. In his address to the audience, he would encourage even more performance.

Welch also recommended to all of the employees to think of ways to improve the company. He called this the "Work-Out" program.

Managing Innovation

Welch believes that people should be encouraged to take "big swings." This means that people who miss, no matter what the cost to the company, should not be reprimanded. They should be rewarded even if the goal was not achieved because they reached for it. This encourages more people to exercise their creativity and drive.

"Change before you have to."

Jack Welch

There are a number of other procedures that Welch practiced throughout his career as CEO that include globalization and e-business. Welch also believed being innovative and "on top of the game" by going global and entering the e-business world.

Managing Business Units

"You've got to balance freedom with some control, but you've got to have more freedom than you ever dreamed of."

Jack Welch

Much of what Welch learned in his career was how to make GE a successful, well-run company that was profitable each year—by a large amount. During his time at GE, Welch came up with many strategies, many of which continue as part GE's business environment, and some others have been adapted.

Number 1 or Number 2 or Fix, Close, or Sell It. From 1981 to 1995, Welch's chosen mission for GE was to be the most competitive enterprise in the world by being number one or number two in every market. If a business unit was not performing to its top ability, the managers of that section had a chance to either fix it or sell it. If there was not a chance for survival for the business, it was then sold. If Welch saw potential for the business to become either number one or number two in its category, the business was given an opportunity to prove it could be the best. One of GE's greatest fix it stories is the one of NBC. The early 1990s were not going well for NBC until Welch hired the right people to come in and fix it. Today NBC is a leading network in many categories.

"Numbers aren't the vision; numbers are the product. I never talk about numbers."

Jack Welch

Welch developed this philosophy after reading two of Peter Drucker's questions: "If you weren't already in the business, would you enter it today?" and "If no, what are you going to do about it?"

This philosophy, even initially, had some limits. It would not work with commodities, such as toasters, because even having a leadership positions would not give you competitive advantage or pricing power. It would not work with some businesses, like financial services, which have a strong niche, so they succeed even they're not number one or number 2.

Expand Market Definition. This philosophy was later modified because the business units within GE would define themselves in terms of very narrow markets to ensure their number one or two position. This limited the growth and expansion the company could achieve. In 1995, GE had the business units expand the idea of their markets so that no division had more than 10 percent of the market. This opened up an examination of the mission of each business, and a new mandate was issued to pursue a larger part of the newly defined market.

Managing Quality—The Six Sigma Initiative

Six Sigma is a popular management philosophy that companies around the world are now using. Its goal is to make an organization more effective and efficient. Although many people credit Jack Welch for the Six Sigma initiative, it was actually borrowed from Motorola, where it originated in 1980, and AlliedSignal, Inc., where it was used in the early 1990s. In fact, for years, Welch had been skeptical of the quality programs that were the rage in the 1980s. He felt that they were too heavy on slogans and too light on results. When he starting talking with former GE vice chairman Lawrence A. Bossidy, a longtime friend, about the benefits Bossidy was reaping from Six Sigma at Al-

"Use the brains of every worker."

Jack Welch

liedSignal where he was CEO, Welch decided to look into it more. In the mid-1990s, GE adopted Six Sigma as its premier management philosophy, and as successful as Motorola and AlliedSignal were in their implementation of Six Sigma, GE is the organization that used Six Sigma most impressively to drive improvement and realize tremendous cost savings.

Six Sigma is a quality of measure to bring defects to almost zero and reduce costs at the same time. Its applications are now widely used for manufactured products, but the techniques can be applied to any type of organization. The process is a complex statistical analysis based on errors per million units, which basically focuses on consistency. It uses the statistical element of variance instead of that of average to measure this.

In his autobiography, *Straight from the Gut,* Welch described multiple successes that were generated through the application of Six Sigma. GE Plastics had wanted to obtain Sony's business for Lexan polycarbonates in the making of CD-ROMs and CDs. However, purity standards were very high, and GE couldn't meet them. After applying Six Sigma improvement methods, they improved the quality significantly and earned Sony's business. At GE Power Systems, rotors were cracking due to high vibration. A third of the thirty-seven operating units had to have rotors replaced due to the high level of poor performance. Through application of Six Sigma methods, vibrations were reduced by 300 percent and at the time of publication of Jack Welch's book, there had been no replacements necessary. At GE Capital, customer response time dramatically improved in the mortgage business. At one point

Six Sigma Primer

The Six Sigma process is designed to improve the effectiveness and efficiency of the company by increasing customer satisfaction. Many times customers will not complain to the company when a product doesn't meet their requirements, so the company has to determine every part of the business transaction that goes into making a customer satisfied.

Six Sigma involves all of the company's management. The basics of the process include identifying the key processes that affect the strategic business objectives of the organization, measuring current effectiveness and efficiency, and then targeting the processes for improvement.

Implementing Six Sigma starts with identifying the processes involved in a customer experience. Key managers get together in the same room and begin identifying these processes, at the same time recognizing that there must be a better way to manage the business.

Once management identifies its key processes, it is important to assign process ownership. The process owner has the responsibility to acquire the key measures of performance for the process. In some cases, process owners will be current management. In other cases, a process owner might be taken from nonmanagement. A process owner might be one of the following:

- A subject matter expert.
- Someone who experiences the gain if the process is working well and the pain if the process is working poorly.
- Someone who has respect among employees in preceding and subsequent processes.
- Someone with an aptitude for process thinking and improvement.

Process owners have to first determine what the measures of effectiveness and efficiency are for the process. The first activity is usually to find out who the customer is.

Each process owner, in the first months of creating the Six Sigma strategy, validates the measures of effectiveness and efficiency for the process. Once the process owner knows what the more important measures are for their processes, they are expected to start collecting data on those measures.

They then calculate the baseline sigma performance of the process, which is the acceptable range of performance. They then create a graph, or frequency distribution, to visually see how many times they fall out of the acceptable range. This window of allowable performance helps to define what is unacceptable to the customer. Anything that is unacceptable to the customer in terms of a product or service is considered a defect. Determining the number of defects is a critical part of calculating sigma performance. The easiest way to calculate sigma performance is defects per unit. The process owner takes the number of defects and divides it by the total number of units of whatever is being measured to get a percentage of defects. This percentage is then converted to a sigma number using a conversion chart. For instance, a 42.1 percent defect percentage would be a sigma of approximately 1.3. A yield of 41 percent would be 1.29. Most businesses in the United States operate between two- and three-sigma performance. Operating at between two and three sigma in the eyes of the external customer will likely eventually lead to an organization's failure.

Management gets together again after the current sigma is calculated to see where the company is and what it needs to do to begin fixing the process.

---

getting a customer representative by phone averaged only 75 percent. After applying Six Sigma methods, this improved to over 99 percent.

POLITICAL INFLUENCE

Welch is a stolid Republican, and in his final year as CEO, GE donated $1.1 million to campaigns, according to the Center for Responsive Politics. He was actively involved in GOP causes and met with the White House and industry leaders in order to give advice on policy. In 2000, he advised President Bush on tax cut policies, along with about twenty other industry executives who gathered at the White House for a private luncheon. Others at the luncheon were President Bush's longtime financial backer, Kenneth Lay, the previous chairman and CEO of Enron Corporation, which donated $1.8 million to Republicans and an additional three hundred thousand to Bush's inaugural; Maurice "Hank" Greenberg, chairman and CEO of American International Group, which donated $801,951 to Republicans; and Leslie Warner, chairman and CEO of Limited, Inc., which donated $983,769.

Welch spoke out in favor of Bush in the elections and said about him, "I happen to think he's got all the right stuff, including the right character, and the right economic and national security policies." He wrote an article in which he evaluated Democratic political candidates according to his Four Es standard, in which no candidate fared well on all four.

Welch also strongly supported Ronald Reagan, believing him to be a man of conviction who stuck to what he believed was right for the country, regardless of the popularity of the decision. Welch believes that leaders of the country must have Reagan's "optimism, courage and conviction" if they want to be great.

CRITICS

There were many critics of Jack Welch and the way he ran GE early in his CEO career, although the numbers significantly declined as his tenure

---

Leadership Lessons in a Nutshell

"Act like a leader, not a manager."

In the book *The GE Way*, Robert Slater describes what Jack Welch believes it takes to be a successful leader. Jack Welch further expands on leadership in his two books *Jack, Straight From the Gut* and *Winning*. One lesson that Welch has always led by is "Act like a leader, not a manager."

Managers need to lead their employees to be successful by giving them the freedom, vision, and financial ability to do so. Some managers may tend to overmanage when they should be leading and inspiring their employees.

Welch believes in macromanaging his employees. A leader should work with employees by talking to them individually and giving them the opportunity to grow and succeed by creating new and improved ideas for bettering the company. Each individual should have the opportunity to succeed.

In his books and talks, Welch promotes several main leadership practices:

1. Leaders relentlessly upgrade their teams, using every encounter as an opportunity to evaluate, coach, and build self-confidence.
2. Leaders make sure people not only see the vision, they live and breathe it. They constantly promote a simple and consistent message.
3. Leaders get into everyone's skin, exuding positive energy and optimism.
4. Leaders establish trust with candor, transparence, and credit.
5. Leaders have the courage to make unpopular decisions and gut calls.
6. Leaders probe and push with curiosity that borders on skepticism, making sure their questions are answered with action.
7. Leaders inspire risk taking and learning by setting the example.
8. Leaders celebrate.
9. Leaders use the brains of every worker. They involve everyone in planning.
10. Leaders tear down the boundaries that stifle communication.
11. Leaders create a learning culture.
12. Leaders make quality the job of every employee.

---

progressed. At first, many were critical of Welch's age and management style and did not think he fit they typical image of the stoic GE CEO. Welch was forty-five years old when he assumed the role, the youngest CEO in GE history. Many people felt Welch did not have the experience or knowledge to run a twelve-billion-dollar company.

Once Welch took over as CEO, he began immediate restructuring of the company, and massive layoffs and downsizing were conducted. Welch oversaw the loss of more than a hundred thousand employees and was not well received early in his career.

Political critics abounded and were especially critical during the 2000 presidential election. Representative Henry A. Waxman, a Democrat from California, released an eight-page letter detailing alleged efforts by Welch to intervene in NBC's election-night decision making. According to Waxman's sources, Welch spent much of the election night at NBC's decision desk, where election returns were projected. Waxman said that Welch and other visitors "distracted" NBC News Director of Elections Sheldon R. Gawiser with repeated questions about how his projection decisions were made. Welch had access to raw election data that weren't available to news anchors, writers, producers or other on-air reporters. After instruction about reading the data, Welch later concluded that Bush had won Florida, and shared his analysis with Gawiser. Welch denied any involvement with calling the election before the results were in.

Critics were also vocal about some of the characteristics that contributed to Welch's success. Some believed that Welch emphasized winning too much and would do anything to achieve it. The argued with his belief that employers should not care about their employee's work–life balance issues. Welch had said that managers should make an employee's "job so exciting that personal life becomes a less compelling draw." He has said that managers view children as competition and most executives think of home and family as something to be dealt with like a physical or emotional handicap. According to Welch, the typical boss is willing to accommodate work–life balance challenges if an employee has earned it with performance.

The big scandal in his personal life earned him many critics, as well. When he had an affair with Suzy, who is now his third wife, Welch was criticized severely. The relationship cost Suzy her job and Welch his second marriage. During Welch's divorce negotiations, Jane's lawyers leaked details of his lavish GE retirement contract, which allowed him unfettered use of a corporate jet, a company-owned apartment overlooking Central Park, a limousine, a cook, and free flowers, tickets to sporting events such as Wimbledon, and free laundry services, among other items.

These revelations created a second wave of scandal. Welch's response to this was that the perks were justified because he did not take all of the money GE had offered him upon retirement in order not to advise any other competitor. He didn't need the money, but he wanted to live the same lifestyle, so he opted for the perks. The scandal hit in the middle of the Enron scandal and, because of this, Welch believed it received much more attention than it would have otherwise. However, in the end, Welch returned the perks in order to stop the damage he thought was being done to the GE company.

POSSIBLE FUTURE IMPACT

Currently Welch is an author and business consultant. Welch and wife Suzy Welch cowrote *Winning*, which was published in May 2005. It is Welch's third book.

> *"I've learned that mistakes can often be as good a teacher as success."*
>
> Jack Welch

Welch also conducts business leadership seminars for CEOs, businesspeople, and students, which pay him an average of $150,000 a seminar. His leadership and management skills are still emulated around the world. There is a large demand for Welch and his ideas in the business world. People want to hear what he has to say and learn from his great successes and failures as former CEO of GE.

With Jack Welch's publication of *Winning* and continuing seminars, his experiences and knowledge will continue to be sought after. Welch's success with GE and his no-nonsense style of management will continue to impact the future of many businesses around the word.

TIMELINE

1935	Born in Peabody, Massachusetts.
1957	Graduated with a bachelor's degree in chemical engineering from the University of Massachusetts.
1959	Married Carolyn Osburn, with whom he later had four children.
1960	Obtained his PhD and MS at the University of Illinois.
	Began his career with General Electric as a chemical engineer.
1964	Became the general manager of the polymer products operation.
1965	Grace Welch died at age sixty-six.
1966	John Welch, Sr., dies.
1968	Was pronounced GE's youngest general manager of a major division.
1971	Named vice president of Chemical and Metallurgical Division.
1977	Became senior vice president.
1979	Became vice chairman.
1980	Jack Welch became known as "Neutron Jack."
1981	Became youngest CEO and president of GE at age forty-five.
1982	Began streamlining GE and letting employees go.
1984	GE sold its housewares unit and entered medical equipment industry.
1985	GE purchased Kidder-Peabody, an investment firm, for six hundred million dollars. It proved to be one of Welch's worst decisions.

By the end of 1985, GE employed 299,000 employees, down from 411,000 in early 1980, a difference of 112,000 people. NBC acquisition completed.

1987   April, Welch and Carolyn divorce after twenty-eight years of marriage.

1989   Welch married Jane Beasley in April.

1995   Welch introduced Six Sigma to GE.
May, Welch had open-heart surgery; recovered by September. GE's revenue at seventy billion dollars.

1999   Welch named "Manager of the Century" by *Fortune*.

2000   GE's revenue at $130 billion.

2001   Welch retired as CEO of GE.
September, Published *Jack, Straight from the Gut*.

2002   A messy divorce between Welch and his wife Jane. Many questions were raised regarding Welch's retirement perks from GE. Jane is believed to have settled for $180 million.

2004   Welch married Suzy Wetlaufer.

2005   Welch and Suzy's cowritten book, *Winning*, published.

RESOURCES

Eckes, George. *Six Sigma for Everyone*. Hoboken, New Jersey: John Wiley & Sons, 2003.

General Electric, www.ge.com.

Murray, Matt, Rachel Emma Silverman, Carol Hymowitz, Alessandra Galloni. GE's *Jack Welch* Meets His Match In Divorce Court. (cover story). November 11, 2002.

Slater, Robert. *Jack Welch & the GE Way: Management Insights & Leadership Secrets of the Legendary CEO*. New York: McGraw-Hill Professional Book Group, 1998.

Smart, Tim. How Jack Welch Brought GE To Life. *Business Week*, October 26, 1992, pp. 13–14.

Welch, Jack. Five Questions to Ask. *Wall Street Journal*. October 28, 2004, p. A-14.

Welch, Jack, and John Byrne. *Jack, Straight from the Gut*. New York: Warner Books. 2001.

Welch, Jack, and Suzy Welch. *Winning*. New York: Harper Collins, 2005.

COMPANY INFORMATION

General Electric Company
3135 Easton Turnpike
Fairfield, CT 06828–0001
Phone: (203) 373–2211
Fax: (203) 373–3131
New York Stock Exchange symbol: GE

Courtesy of Photofest.

Oprah Winfrey

Oprah Winfrey, the first woman African-American billionaire in U.S. history, rose from poverty in rural Mississippi to become host of her own talk show, the head of a huge media company, and the most powerful woman in entertainment. As one of the richest people in the world, worth about $1.4 billion, she heads an entertainment kingdom composed of publishing, television, and film production. The Oprah Winfrey Show has been the number one talk show for the last 18 years, airs in almost every domestic market, reaching some 30 million viewers per week in the U.S., and is distributed in 111 countries. She built her company, Harpo, (Oprah spelled backwards) into a powerhouse, with almost $300 million in annual sales. Winfrey is Chairman, and owns

90% of the company that includes Harpo Video; Harpo Productions, Inc., which produces the talk show; Harpo Print L.L.C.; and Harpo Films, the maker of big-screen films such as *Beloved* and made-for-TV movies through a long-term deal with ABC. Winfrey launched O, the magazine, in 2000 in conjunction with Hearst, and, with 2.7 million subscribers, it has more paid circulation than *Redbook, Martha Stewart Living* or *Glamour*. It boasts 13 million readers, netted $207 million in revenues last year, and is widely proclaimed to be the most successful magazine in history.

Winfrey's Harpo Studios launched the lucrative "Dr. Phil" spinoff, now the second-highest-rated talk strip, and produces top rated telepics, including the recent "Their Eyes Were Watching God," for which Halle Berry won an Emmy nomination. Winfrey is also the cofounder of Oxygen Media, a 24-hour cable TV network with 54 million viewers across the country, launched in 1998. The network airs Oprah After the Show, an informal, unscripted conversation with Winfrey's studio audience and guests. Five million people visit her web site, oprah.com, each month. Winfrey also became an accomplished screen actress and earned an Academy Award nomination for her role in the Steven Spielberg produced, *The Color Purple.*

Time magazine named her one of the 20th century's 100 most influential people, and in 1998, she received a Lifetime Achievement Award from the National Academy of Television Arts and Sciences. She has received numerous daytime Emmy awards, and in 1993 she won the Horatio Alger Award given to those who overcome adversity to become leaders in their fields. She was inducted into the Television Hall of Fame in 1994 and received the George Foster Peabody Individual Achievement Award, one of broadcasting's most coveted awards, following the 1995–1996 season.

Her Oprah Book Club titles turn authors into literary stars. Since her book club's 1996 launch, all of the books she has recommended have made the New York Times best-seller list. In 1999 she was presented with the National Book Foundation's 50th anniversary gold medal for her service to books and authors. Her influence extends to other industries, including music, as well. Dick Parsons, CEO of Time Warner, says that when Winfrey makes an endorsement of a product or has a musical act appear on her show, sales increase tenfold.

> *"What I've learned is that when I don't know what to do, do nothing. Sit still and listen for that small voice that will always lead you and guide you. If you're quiet and listen, you will hear it."*
>
> Oprah Winfrey

Winfrey has received numerous awards for her leadership in social causes and philanthropy. Her Oprah's Angel Network charity has raised more than $27 million since its inception in 1998.

She has most recently produced "The Color Purple," a new musical based on the Pulitzer Prize-winning novel by Alice Walker on Broadway, and, her name appears on the title on the show's marquee.

THE EARLY YEARS

Oprah Gail Winfrey was born on January 29, 1954 in Kosciusko, Mississippi to nineteen-year old Vernita Lee. She was the result of what she refers to as a "one-day fling under an oak tree." Neither of her parents were around for most of her early childhood. Vernita left Oprah, as a baby, in the care of maternal grandparents, Hattie May and Earless Lee. Her father, Vernon Winfrey, left town shortly after impregnating Vernita, and found out about Oprah's birth when he received a birth announcement with a note asking for baby clothes.

Oprah felt a lot of love from Hattie May, and although the house had no indoor plumbing, and Oprah had to share a bed with her grandmother, she remembers feeling quite happy there overall. There were a couple of incidents with her grandfather who was ill-tempered and frightening.

A strict disciplinarian, Hattie May taught Oprah to read and write by the time she was three. Together, they studied the bible, a habit Oprah continues today. Much of their life revolved around the Baptist church, where Oprah recited Bible verses at the Sunday school performances. She was quite well-received by the congregation, demonstrating her rapport with an audience early on. In one of her first recitations before the entire congregation, three-year-old Oprah told the story of Jesus' resurrection on Easter. She impressed the adults who both praised Oprah and her grandmother. On one occasion Oprah was paid $500, a huge amount of money at the time, especially for a child, for giving a speech to a church group.

> *For everyone of us that succeeds, it's because there's somebody there to show you the way out. The light doesn't always necessarily have to be in your family; for me it was teachers and school.*
>
> Oprah Winfrey

When Oprah was five her mother, Vernita, sent for her, and she had to leave her grandmother and rural Mississippi for inner-city Milwaukee. Vernita enrolled her in kindergarten, but she was in class for only a couple of weeks before she wrote her kindergarten teacher a note saying that she didn't think she belonged in the class. Impressed, her teacher moved Oprah up a grade. A year later, she told the same thing to her second grade teacher and was moved up another grade.

Her early school years went quite well, but her home life did not. By the time Oprah was eight, Vernita had had two other children, Patricia and Jeffrey Lee, and was struggling as a single mother. She sent Oprah to live with her father, Vernon, who was married and living in Nashville. She was returned to her mother's house when she turned 9. Her family disagrees with her now about how badly things were at that time. While Oprah recalls significant poverty, her family downplays that. What no one disputes, however, is that at the age of nine, Oprah was sexually abused by a 19-year-old cousin. The abuse would continue by another cousin's boyfriend and by a favorite uncle until she was 14.

When Oprah was 12, she was so far ahead of the rest of her class, one of her teachers, Eugene Abrams, enrolled her in an "Upward Bound" program to help her get the skills needed for college. He arranged for her to get a scholarship to enter a better high school in Milwaukee, which was also nearly all-white. She excelled in her studies there, too, although her younger sister, Patricia Lee, recalls that she did not have many friends. No other children praised her because she was smart and did a lot of reading. She remembers being teased because she was always sitting in a corner, reading.

As so happens with many incest victims, Oprah became promiscuous, and at the age of 13, invited men over during the day while her mother was working. In addition, Oprah was also stealing from her mother and telling lies to cover that. She ran away from home and was gone a week until she showed up at her pastor's house. Oprah's bad behavior continued for another year. Not knowing what to do with her, Vernita took her to a detention home for girls. Fortunately for Oprah, the Milwaukee system was overburdened and she would have to wait at least two weeks to be admitted. Vernita couldn't wait that long and called Vernon, who agreed to take Oprah with him. Oprah credits her father with changing her life.

Not long after arriving in Nashville, Oprah gave birth to a stillborn baby boy. Vernita had not known she was pregnant, but rushed to Nashville to take care of her daughter. This was a very painful time for Oprah, and she did not mention it for many years. In fact, she claimed in at least one instance that the one pitfall of the streets that she had avoided was pregnancy. In October 1993, in *Ebony* magazine, however, she finally discussed what she regarded as "my greatest shame."

In Nashville, Oprah turned her life around with the help of her father, a barber and a city councilman, who was a strict disciplinarian. Her father and stepmother insisted that she get good grades in school and read good books. Oprah and her stepmother visited the public library regularly, and Oprah was required to read at least five books every two weeks. Vernon insisted that his daughter memorize twenty new vocabulary words a week and give him weekly book reports. She also began keeping a journal, which she still does today. She became an honors student, joined the drama club, student council, and was chosen as one of two students in the state to go to the *White House Conference on Youth*. Oprah was still an excellent student, and, in high school in Nashville, had many friends and a steady boyfriend. She was voted "Most Popular" in 1971, the year of her graduation. She won a $1,000 college scholarship after delivering a short speech entitled "The Negro, the Constitution, and the United States" to 10,000 Elks Club members in Philadelphia.

> *It's very difficult for me to even see myself as successful because I still see myself as in the process of becoming successful. To me, "successful" is getting to the point where you are absolutely comfortable with yourself. And it does not matter how many things you have acquired.*
>
> Oprah Winfrey

During her senior year, she was offered a part-time job at a radio station, beginning her career in media. As a participant in the March of Dimes Walk-a-Thon, Winfrey requested a donation from a disc jockey at WVOL. Agreeing to do so, the disc jockey requested that Winfrey make a voice tape, which was later submitted to the WVOL manager. Winfrey was hired as a weekend newscaster.

CAREER PATH

Winfrey's accomplishments in high school won her a four-year scholarship to the all-black Tennessee State University. While there she distinguished herself with dramatic readings and by acting in university plays. Earlier she had been first black woman to win Nashville's Miss Fire Prevention title. In 1972 she entered another beauty contest and became Miss Black Nashville. She later went on to win Miss Black Tennessee. As a result of her win and this exposure, she was asked to be an on-air reporter at WTVF-TV, a local CBS affiliate. At 19, she was the youngest and the first African-American woman anchor the station had hired. In her senior year, in 1976, she was offered a job in Baltimore as a co-anchor on the 6 p.m. news on WJZ-TV. Her father did not want her to take the job, preferring that she finish her education, but she took it anyway.

Her first job paid her $10,000 a year. At that time her goal was to make her age times $1000. When she was 22, she was making $22,000, and she remembers being in the bathroom at the television station in Baltimore with her friend, Gayle. They were jumping up and down and Gayle said, "Oh, my God, can you imagine if you're 40 and you're making $40,000?"

Winfrey had trouble at her job as co-anchor, however. She did not have the objectivity expected of news journalists and found herself empathizing too much with the people whose stories she covered. She was criticized by some people for straying from the script, letting viewers see that she was not comfortable with her co-anchor, and for her appearance. The station ordered a makeover, including new clothes and a perm that made her hair fall out. Her head proved too big for wigs, so she wore scarves while she was on the air, until her hair grew back. Her bosses wanted her to have plastic surgery to move her eyes closer together and to narrow her nose, but she refused. Nine months after beginning her anchor job, she was removed from the position.

In 1977, a new manager came to the station, however, and offered her the position of co-anchor of a new morning talk show that they were starting. The show, *People Are Talking*, with co-host Richard Sher, was a success. The style that made Winfrey unsuccessful as a news anchor made her highly popular with audiences in this new format. She looked, as she continues to do, for the personal aspects of people's stories.

After seven years in Baltimore, Winfrey was hired by Dennis Swanson, the general manager of WLS-TV, ABC's Chicago affiliate, after he saw Winfrey in an audition tape sent in by her former producer, Debra DiMaio, who had taken a job at WLS-TV. She was offered the job as anchor of the morning talk show, *A.M. Chicago*. Winfrey was afraid that a heavyset black woman would be unwelcome on television in Chicago, which had a reputation for racial conflict, but Swanson insisted. She accepted the job, and WJZ-TV let her out of her contract. Winfrey did a complete overhaul of the show, changing its focus to current and controversial topics. The effect was immediate: one month later the show, which had previously been last in the market, was ranked even with the popular Phil Donahue's program. Three months later it had inched ahead. In September 1985 it was renamed *The Oprah Winfrey Show* and was expanded to one hour.

To get some help with her contract for the new job, she visited a Chicago lawyer, Jeff Jacobs. After three years of doing work mainly for Winfrey, he came in house in 1987 and became her lifelong adviser and business manager. He now owns 10% of Harpo, Inc.

The tremendous popularity of her program soon gave Winfrey other opportunities. When Quincy Jones saw her show in 1985, he immediately thought of casting her in a movie he was co-producing with director Stephen Spielberg, a screen adaptation of Alice Walker's novel, *The Color Purple*. She was on her way to becoming an accomplished screen actress. She was especially taken with her role of Sofia, a very strong woman who was abused by her husband and by prison guards, but never lost her dignity. Critics praised her performance, and she was nominated for an Academy Award as best supporting actress. Though Winfrey had never had any formal acting lessons and little exposure to the theater, she enjoyed acting and went on to take other significant parts.

While negotiating Winfrey's appearance in *The Color Purple,* Jacobs pushed for more money against Winfrey's desires and set up the relational dynamic they continue to have. Jacobs focuses on the bottom line and Winfrey avoids looking at it. Jacobs was fierce in his financial protection of his client, and this protection set Winfrey up to gain control of her empire. Her Chicago station would not approve an extra week off during the production of the movie, and Winfrey was not happy. She wanted more control over her schedule and her content. In 1986, she incorporated Harpo, Inc. and set up Harpo Productions. Jacobs was the one to realize that she needed to control the talk show. He immediately looked for a syndication contract and soon made a deal with King World, who was distributing other syndicated shows, such as *Jeopardy* and *Wheel of Fortune*. WLS-TV was prohibited from distributing a syndicated Oprah show because it was owned by ABC-TV, and the FCC did not allow a network to syndicated its own programs. The first contract guaranteed Winfrey approximately 25% of net revenues. Winfrey gained more control of the company in 1988, incorporated Harpo Productions and became the first black woman to own a production studio. The studio, 100,000 square feet, occupies almost one city block.

In October, 1988, Harpo Productions, Inc. acquired ownership and all production responsibilities for "The Oprah Winfrey Show" from Capitol Cities/ABC, making Winfrey the first woman in history to own and produce her own talk show. One of the first productions scheduled was *The Woman of Brewster Place* in 1990, with Oprah Winfrey as star and Executive Producer, and it was the highest rated miniseries of the 1988–89 season. Harpo has since produced several television programs based on stories written by black authors, including *The Wedding* and *Before Women Had Wings*. Winfrey purchased the movie and television rights to several books, including Toni Morrison's *Paradise*, and has an exclusive agreement to produce feature films for the Walt Disney Motion Pictures Group. The first film under the agreement was the 1998 release of Toni Morrison's best-selling novel *Beloved*. In addition to serving as producer, Winfrey also starred in the film, and its commercial failure wounded Winfrey deeply.

Winfrey has also used her influence beyond video and print. Although shunning all attempts to license her name for products, she did expand into a partnership to create *The Eccentric,* a Chicago restaurant, in 1989.

In 1991, motivated in part by her own memories of childhood abuse, she initiated a campaign to establish a national database of convicted child abusers, and testified before a U.S. Senate Judiciary Committee on behalf of a National Child Protection Act. President Clinton signed the "Oprah Bill" into law in 1993, establishing the national database she had sought, which is now available to law enforcement agencies and concerned parties across the country.

In 1995, Winfrey entered the online world, with a partnership with America Online. She subsequently started her own web site, oprah.com.

One of the most influential projects she has tackled is literacy. The reading club she started in September 1996, "Oprah's Book Club," reenergized the publishing business, where the choice for Oprah's Book Club is a writer's ticket to the bestseller list. This is all the more impressive because her choices are often literary novels that would not normally attract a mass audience.

She established Oprah's Angel Network, a non-profit organization for the needy, in 1997. In its inaugural year, Oprah's Angel Network raised over $3.5 million to fund college scholarships for students with financial needs. Beginning in April 2000, the Angel Network has been handing out "Use Your Life" awards on Winfrey's television show. The awards of $100,000 each are given to people who use their lives to better the lives of others.

In late 1998 Winfrey became involved with the formation of Oxygen Media, which includes a cable television station aimed at women. Since its initial debut, the Oxygen Network has stumbled in the ratings, and Winfrey has become less involved in the project. In addition to her media projects, in 1999 Winfrey joined the faculty of Northwestern University's Kellogg Graduate School of Management to teach the course "Dynamics of Leadership." Winfrey's partner, Stedman Graham, was the co-teacher. Needing to lighten her daily schedule, Winfrey stepped down from her teaching position in 2001.

In April 2000 Winfrey took her television show's self-help message and transferred it to print when she started *O*, a lifestyle magazine for women, in a partnership with Hearst. As one of the most successful startups in the industry, *O* inspires some 13 million readers and has a subscription base of 2.5 million readers.

Her most recent project is the production of the Broadway musical version of *The Color Purple*. She has also launched "Oprah & Friends" on satellite radio.

PERSONAL LIFE

Although many aspects of Winfrey's life are talked about openly on her show, she keeps most of her life surprisingly private. Harpo employees are barred from talking or writing about her personal or business affairs and those of her company for the rest of their lives. Only once did a former employee, Elizabeth Coady, challenge it in court. Coady lost and none of Winfrey's employees or former employees have shared any personal information about her on the record.

> *"Real marriage is the sacrificing of your ego, not for the other person, but for the relationship. That's how you become one, because the relationship becomes the number-one priority. I am really not in that place."*
>
> Oprah Winfrey

Her companion since 1986, Stedman Graham, is a prominent management and marketing consultant with two best-selling books to his name. Over the years, they have been engaged and wedding preparations made, but Winfrey subsequently announced that she would never get married. She never had children. Before meeting Graham, Winfrey was involved in several bad relationships, including one with a married man, which Winfrey says made her contemplate suicide.

Although she was not close to her mother, she took care of her, financially. She did the same for her half-sister, Patricia Lee, until Patricia started becoming self-destructive. Then, Winfrey rescinded the support, although she kept it up for Patricia's two daughters. Winfrey's half-brother, Jeffrey Lee, died of AIDS, and, although the two were estranged, it has been reported that they had a reconciliation on his deathbed.

She met her lifelong best friend, Gayle King, in 1976 while she was an anchor at WJZ-TV in Baltimore. King was a production assistant who one night stayed at Winfrey's house during a major snowstorm. King helps to run *O* magazine.

Winfrey has made generous contributions to charitable organizations and institutions such as Morehouse College, the Harold Washington Library, the United Negro College Fund, and Tennessee State University. She is actively involved in many philanthropic activities. She donated over $50 million in 2003 to the Oprah Winfrey Foundation, which provides educational and other programs that help women and children. Winfrey has entered a partnership with Habitat for Humanity, which builds houses for impoverished Americans throughout the country, and she is helping minority students get a better education through her involvement with A Better Chance, a Boston-based privately funded program that provides inner-city youth with the opportunity to attend college preparatory schools. She gives proceeds from her inspirational video "Oprah: Make the Connection" to A Better Chance. She has traveled to South Africa repeatedly to bestow gifts on 50,000 orphans and bolster awareness of the AIDS epidemic. The Oprah South African Leadership Project was started in 2004 to provide ethical leadership training and community service in both Atlanta and South Africa. It was made possible through a $1 million gift from Winfrey and centers on the services provided by the non-governmental organization (NGO) eTaseni in Cape Town. The Leadership Academy for Girls in South Africa is currently under way. Winfrey revealed that she had her DNA tested and found out that she is a member of the Zulu tribe of Africa. Winfrey donated over $10 million for relief efforts for Hurricane Katrina.

"We must break down the notion of our children versus African children or Bosnian children or Afghan children. The truth is: Our children live in every country and come from every culture. By keeping children illiterate, enslavement of some kind is inevitable."

Oprah Winfrey

Winfrey has recently partnered with the FBI to take on child predators. Broadcasting details about fugitives and offering a $100,000 reward for information leading to their capture, Winfrey contributed to the arrest of three convicted sexual abusers within one month.

Winfrey has cultivated a reputation for championing causes in her programs and ventures that other leading media ignore.

LEADERSHIP LESSONS

Winfrey says she's never thought of herself as a businesswoman, and, indeed, she has had no formal business training. She has only given one interview in her life to a business journal, *Fortune,* and says that she will not talk about business or making money again. She does not believe her goals have ever been about increasing the value of her business, financially. She doesn't like for her employees to know the financial status of the company,

"If you don't know what your passion is, realize that one reason for your existence on earth is to find it. Real success means creating a life of meaning through service that fulfills your reason for being here."

Oprah Winfrey

believing it will stifle their creativity and coverage of issues that are more important than money. Despite this belief, however, Winfrey has steadfast principles she follows in doing business, which came about as a result of several early mistakes.

Early on, Winfrey tried to run Harpo like it was a family and did not understand that the business was a system that needed a structure. She said she made what she now knows are classic business mistakes. She learned that people handle power differently and communicate differently. The business was soon set up with the typical departments: Finance, Human Resources, Marketing, etc. Winfrey has also had to learn how to be confrontational.

Listen to Your Intuition

Winfrey's primary leadership lesson is to listen to her inner voice when it comes to making decisions. Her style is coined as management by instinct by some, and indeed, she does use intuition to make almost all of her decisions. Intuitive decision making can be defined as a subconscious process of making decisions on the basis of experience and accumulated judgement. Comparing how a good decision feels right immediately to how a good shoe fits, Winfrey relies on her own instinct and mostly disregards others' opinions and factual data. She chalks up the times when she has made bad decisions to ignoring her instinct. If she feels doubt about something, she does nothing and waits to see what she feels later.

> *"What I've learned is that when I don't know what to do, do nothing. Sit still and listen for that small voice that will always lead you and guide you. If you're quiet and listen, you will hear it."*
>
> Oprah Winfrey

She is very spiritual and believes that what she does is the result of a higher power guiding her. She prays every morning for the power in the universe to use her life as a vessel for its work. Winfrey told *Redbook*. "I feel positive about the future, but I do believe that we are in a time where there are forces of good and evil in TV making themselves known." She commented in *Good Housekeeping*. "I'm always trying to figure out how to take the power I have and use it."

Winfrey's intuition does not, however, extend to generating big ideas. She can intuit if an idea is right, but she needs others to come up with the ideas in the first place.

Control

Harpo Inc. started in 1984, when entertainment lawyer, Jeff Jacobs talked Oprah into starting up her own company rather than being like most celebrities, just a "talent for hire." Winfrey holds 90% stock of Harpo Inc and Jeff Jacobs holds the remaining 10%. They have no board members and no other complications.

Winfrey negotiated a lucrative deal with KingWorld, her show's distributor, and walked away with the rights to co-produce and host the Oprah Winfrey

Show. Winfrey runs a tight ship. Despite having various media interests, she keeps close control over all of them. This control has been most evident in her TV show. Although she avoids looking at financial figures and lets Jacobs control that end of the company, she signs every check in order to always have a handle on where the money goes.

Build the Brand

Winfrey is in the business of building equity in the Oprah brand. She is a personification of a brand that has been built holistically. Every aspect of a brand affects its image and reputation, not just what it looks like on the outside. Consistency and being true to the brand promise is key to building a powerful brand, and Winfrey has recognized that. She has said that she knows that everything she does in her personal life is a reflection of her brand and she has to be very careful with that.

Winfrey has not licensed her name, as other name-brand business moguls have done, to retail products, although there has been a lot of pressure for her to do so. There would also be a lot of monetary gain, but Winfrey is not interested. She prefers to use her name, when she does, to promote social causes and education.

Clearly committed to using her name to provide global education for her philanthropic activities, Winfrey also sees education as the basis of her brand. After her show in Chicago became successful, she understood that she had a power base that could be a force for something good. Much of that good revolves around education. "Education is freedom. It is the only way out ..." You can overcome poverty and despair in your life with an education. I am living proof of that." Her main message is that people are responsible for their own lives and everyone shares a common denominator—they all want to be heard. Winfrey believes that her show and company have been successful because she's always aiming for the truth and everything branded Oprah represents that. People turn to her show and magazine to save them. Stephen Spielberg once said that every day on her TV show Oprah tried to save the entire world.

Be Real

Winfrey can talk about anything to anybody with a sense of respect and integrity and an agenda of educating others. Her effective managerial style comes into play in all of her media ventures, especially her TV show. From pop-culture icons to unknown activists from half a world away, from survivors of childhood abuse to spouse abusers, Winfrey talks to them all as equals, seeing herself as a human being first, trying to make a connection with others.

POLITICAL INFLUENCE

Winfrey has not contributed any money to political campaign contributions since 1999. Before that, she gave the largest percentage to Democratic candidates, donating $16,000 in 1997, versus $1000 to Republican candidates in the same year.

CRITICS

A number of distinct criticisms have been thrown at Winfrey. Though her influence is largely seen as good for industry, increasing sales of books and products seen on her show, it can also be used to harm industry. Her overwhelming reach once brought the cattle industry to its knees, for instance. Ranchers claimed a $12 million loss after Winfrey swore off hamburgers on her show for fear of mad cow disease. She broadcast an episode of her show in 1996 about the problems surrounding the outbreak of mad cow disease in Great Britain. The episode, which was labeled "dangerous food," included a guest who suggested that unless the U.S. banned certain practices, a mad cow disease epidemic in the U.S. would "make AIDS look like the common cold." Texas had enacted food- and business-disparagement laws that allow victims of false statements about their perishable food or business to sue for damages. Beginning the day of the broadcast, the price of beef dropped drastically and remained low for two weeks. The Texas Beef Group filed a civil lawsuit against Winfrey, her company, and the guest alleging that comments made on the program had violated Texas's disparagement laws. Though she won the suit, the trial showed the remarkable influence Winfrey has.

Winfrey is often criticized for her refusal to be negative, a frequent definition of objectivity, and some analysts claim she aided the 2000 election of George W. Bush by not asking him any tough questions.

More often, than not, the criticism aimed at Winfrey is mainly about talk shows themselves. U.S. Senator Joseph Lieberman (D-CT) and U.S. Department of Health and Human Services Secretary Donna Shalala refer to talk shows as "trash TV." One such criticism is that talk shows give viewers a warped sense of reality in which dysfunctional relationships and bizarre problems seem typical of life in the United States. As the viewers' perceptions of society change, those people become more tolerant of deviant behaviors and possibly more willing to try such behaviors themselves. A second criticism is that viewers who watch talk shows on a regular basis become desensitized to the graphic discussions and emotional outbursts of the participants and subsequently develop a callous attitude toward misfortune even outside the realm of talk shows. A third criticism is that talk shows, by using personal exemplars and by offering simplistic advice such as "love conquers all" or "race shouldn't matter" as solutions to problems, cause viewers to trivialize complex social issues. Finally, talk shows have been charged by authors such as Elaine Showalter (1997) and Jeanne Heaton and Nona Wilson (1998) with contributing to hysteria and misinformation on issues such as repressed memory, satanic ritual abuse, and alien abduction. Winfrey, herself, is criticized for sympathizing with perpetrators of crime, and critics charge that this increases overall sympathy. John Hill and Dolf Zillmann (1999) found that undergraduate students who watched segments of *Oprah Winfrey* with mitigating information present gave lighter prison sentences to criminals depicted in the segments than did those who saw the segments without the mitigating information.

Winfrey was also criticized for her choice of authors in her book club, which focused on the classics for two and a half years. She has now opened it up to contemporary authors, again, as the result of a public relations campaign by current authors. One hundred authors signed a letter this spring urging her to resume making a book club selection featuring new American novels. The letter from members of Word of Mouth, an online association of female writers, cited a three-year slump in sales of new fiction.

One of the first contemporary novels chosen, after she decided to open up the book club beyond classics, was James Frey's *A Million Little Pieces*. A minor scandal ensued after Frey appeared on her show and the book, already a strong seller, was boosted into the seven-figure realm. Frey's story was investigated by *The Smoking Gun* for inconsistencies, and it was shown to have several. Winfrey, however, backed Frey initially, saying that the embellishments did not affect the fundamental truth of his addiction story. However, she received much criticism for her support of Frey and subsequently denounced his actions on her show.

> *"Every person in the world has a purpose for being here — a calling. The work of your life is to discover that purpose, and get on with the business of living it out. The only courage you need is the courage to find and follow your passion."*
>
> Oprah Winfrey

Winfrey has chosen over fifty books for the book club, each reaching bestseller status. However, almost all of the books belong to the top seven trade houses (with annual revenues of more than $125 million.) She has been criticized by some of the smaller houses for not choosing their books, focusing instead on the major publishers.

POSSIBLE FUTURE IMPACT

Winfrey is in her 22nd season of The Oprah Show and will likely continue that for several more years. She also plans continued production of television movies through Harpo's longterm contract with ABC.

Her Leadership Academy for girls is scheduled to pen in Scheduled to open in South Africa in 2007.

TIMELINE

1954	Born in Kosciusko, MS, on January 29.
1970	Moved to her father's house in Nashville, Tennessee.
1971	Hired by Nashville radio station, WVOL, to read on-air news. Named Miss Fire Prevention.
	Enrolled at Tennessee State University.
1973	Became first African-American TV news anchor for WTVF-TV.
1976	Moved to Baltimore to become news anchor of WJZ-TV.
1978	Began job as anchor for Baltimore's WJZ-TV's *People Are Talking*.
1984	Relocated to Chicago to host *A.M. Chicago*, which becomes number one talk show in the market.
	Meets Jeff Jacobs.
1985	*A.M. Chicago* is renamed *The Oprah Winfrey Show*.
	Cast in Steven Spielberg's *The Color Purple*.
1986	Established Harpo, Inc.
	Syndicates *The Oprah Winfrey Show* with King World Productions.
1988	Established Harpo Productions.
1990	Opened Harpo Studios in Chicago.
	Establishes Harpo Films.
1991	Initiated the National Child Protection Act and testifies before U.S. Senate Judiciary Committee.
1993	The Oprah Bill is signed into law, creating a national database of child abusers.
1995	Debuted Oprah Online on AOL.
1996	Received the George Foster Peabody Individual Achievement Award.
	Launched Oprah's Book Club.
1998	Established Oprah's Angel Network.
	Won six-week libel trial in Amarilla, Texas over comments made in 1996 related to Mad Cow Disease.
	Names one of *Time* magazine's 100 Most Influential People of the 20th Century.
1999	Taught *Dynamics of Leadership* at the Kellogg Graduate School with Stedman Graham.
2000	Launched *O, The Oprah Magazine*, with Hearst Magazines.
2002	Established the Oprah Winfrey Leadership Academy for Girls in South Africa.
2004	Received the United Nations Association of the United States of America's Global Humanitarian Action Award.

2005   Launched Oprah's Child Predator Watch List.
        The Color Purple, produced by Oprah Winfrey, opens on
        Broadway.

RESOURCES

Adler, Bill, ed. The Uncommon Wisdom of Oprah Winfrey: A Portrait in Her Own Words. Secaucus, N. J.: Birch Lane Press Book, 1997.

Bayles, Martha. "Bookends: Imus, Oprah, and the Literary Elite." *New York Times Book Review*, 29 August 1999.

Bly, Nellie. Oprah! *Up Close and Down Home*. New York: Zebra Books, 1993.

Clemetson, Lynette; Joan Raymond, Bret Begun, Ana Figueroa, Julie Halpert. "Oprah on Oprah." *Newsweek*, 8 January 200, pp. 38–47.

Davis, Stacy, and Mares, Marie-Louise. (1998). "Effects of Talk Show Viewing on Adolescents." *Journal of Communication* 48(3):69–86.

Dedman, Bill. "Personal Business: Professor Oprah, Preaching What She Practices." *New York Times*, 10 October 1999, p. 39.

Donahue, Deirdre. " 'Oprah's Book Club' is a boon" *USA Today*, December 12, 1996, p. D4.

Economist Staff. "Dumbing Up." *The Economist*, 17 October 1998, p. 76.

Farley, Christopher John. "Queen of All Media." *Time*, 5 October 1998, pp. 82–85.

Gamson, Joshua. (1998). *Freaks Talk Back: Tabloid Talk Shows and Sexual Nonconformity*. Chicago: University of Chicago Press.

Greenberg, Bradley S.; Sherry, John L.; Busselle, Rick W.; Hnilo, Lynn; and Smith, Sandi W. (1997). "Day-time Television Talk Shows: Guests, Content and Interactions." *Journal of Broadcasting and Electronic Media* 41(3):412–426.

Haig, Matt. *Brand Royalty*. London, GBR: Kogan Page, Limited, 2004, p. 148.

Heaton, Jeanne, A., and Wilson, Nona, L. (1998). "Memory, Media, and the Creation of Mass Confusion." In *Truth in Memory*, eds. Steven Lynn and Kevin McConkey. New York: Guilford Press.

Hill, John R., and Zillmann, Dolf. (1999). "The Oprahization of America: Sympathetic Crime Talk and Leniency." *Journal of Broadcasting and Electronic Media* 43(1):67–82.

King, Norman. *Everybody Loves Oprah! Her Remarkable Life Story: An Unauthorized Biography*. New York: William Morrow, 1987.

Krohn, Katherine E. Oprah Winfrey (Just the Facts Biographies) Minneapolis, MN: Lerner Publications Company 2005.

Lisotta, Christopher " 'Oprah' Tops Strips as Daytime Surges," *Television Week*, 6/6/2005, Vol. 24, Issue 23.

Lowe, Janet. *Oprah Winfrey Speaks: Insight from the World's Most Influential Voice*. New York: John Wiley & Sons: 1998.

Mair, George. *Oprah Winfrey! The Real Story*. Secaucus, N. J.: Carol Publishing Co., 1996.

McCrossan, John Anthony. *Books & Reading in the Lives of Notable Americans: A Biographical Sourcebook*. Westport, CT, USA: Greenwood Publishing Group, Incorporated, 2000, pp. 255–260.

Mullman, Jeremy "Oprah Winfrey." Crain's Chicago Business, 7 June 2004, p. W84.

Nicholson, Lois P. *Oprah Winfrey*. New York: Chelsea House, 1994.

Oprah Winfrey Fact Sheet. Available at http://www.oprah.com.

Oprah Winfrey. *Time*, 18 April 2005, Vol. 165 Issue 16, pp. 88–89.

Poitier, Sidney "OPRAH WINFREY: Talk-Show Inspiration." *Time* Canada; 26 April 2004, p. 123.

Priest, Patricia. (1996). "Gilt by Association: Talk Show Participants' Televisually Enhanced Status and Self-Esteem." In *Constructing the Self in a Mediated World*, eds. Debra Grodin and Thomas R. Lindlof. Thousand Oaks, CA: Sage Publications.

Priest, Patricia, and Dominick, Joseph R. (1994). "Pulp Pulpits: Self-Disclosure on 'Donahue.'" *Journal of Communication* 44(4):74–97.

Showalter, Elaine. (1997). *Hystories: Hysterical Epidemics and Modern Culture*. New York: Columbia University Press.

U.S. News & World Report Staff. AMERICA'S BEST LEADERS 2005, *U.S. News & World Report*, 31 October 2005, pp. 18–19.

Waldron, Robert. *Oprah*. New York: St. Martin's Press, 1987.

Walker, Juliet E. K.(Editor). *Encyclopedia of African American Business History*. Westport, CT, USA: Greenwood Publishing Group, Incorporated, 1999, pp. 452, 483, 595–597, 608, 629.

Winfrey, Oprah and Bill Adler. *The Uncommon Wisdom of Oprah Winfrey: A Portrait in Her Own Words*. Secaucus, NJ: Birch Lane January, 1997.

Wooten, Sara McIntosh. *Oprah Winfrey: Talk Show Legend Berkeley*. Heights, NJ : Enslow Publishers, 1999.

COMPANY INFORMATION

Harpo Productions, Inc.
110 North Carpenter Street
Chicago, IL 60607(312) 633–0808
www.oprah.com

AP Photo/Keystone, Martial Trezzini.

Muhammad Yunus

Muhammad Yunus, winner of the 2006 Nobel Peace Prize, is a former economics professor who has had phenomenal success helping people lift themselves out of poverty in rural Bangladesh by providing them with minuscule amounts of credit. His revolutionary microcredit system has been implemented throughout the developing world and according to many experts is the single-most important development in the Third World in the last century. Targeting the rural poor in Bangladesh, Yunus tapped into a market that no one had even defined, much less approached.

Grameen Bank reversed conventional banking wisdom by focusing on female borrowers, dispensing with the requirement of collateral, and extending loans only to the very poorest borrowers. In fact, to qualify for a loan from the Grameen Bank, a villager must demonstrate that her family owns *less* than one half-acre of land. The system is largely based on mutual trust, and the enterprise and accountability of millions of female villagers. With small loans, women start small enterprises that can include weaving, running roadside vegetable stands, or processing rice.

Yunus reasoned that if financial resources can be made available to the poor on terms and conditions that are appropriate and reasonable, millions of

"Poverty is like a bonsai tree. You get only this little base to grow from. You are a stunted little thing. Maybe you could be a giant thing, but you never find out. That's poverty."
Muhammad Yunus

people with their millions of small pursuits can add up to create an extremely large economic impact. His reasoning proved to be right. Grameen Bank has inspired people and institutions throughout the world with its success in alleviating poverty. Today, more than 250 institutions in nearly a hundred countries operate microcredit programs based on the Grameen Bank model, while thousands of other microcredit programs have emulated, adapted, or been inspired and funded by the Grameen Bank. The bank has provided $4.7 billion to 4.4 million families in rural Bangladesh. With 1,417 branches, Grameen provides services in fifty-one thousand villages, covering three quarters of all the villages in Bangladesh.

Employing sound financial principles, the bank has helped poor families build their assets by developing small businesses. At the same time, the bank has been rewarded with a loan repayment rate of nearly 100 percent.

Yunus started his microcredit venture by striving to ensure that half of his borrowers were women, which was a difficult feat. In implementing this weapon in the fight against poverty, Yunus had to overcome deep religious taboos and the permeating belief that women were no good and brought only misery to their families. His microcredit lending program whose female borrowers, who now comprise 96 percent of the 5.58 million borrowers, offers initial loans of roughly twenty-five dollars. Through this, Yunus has transformed Bangladesh's society into one in which women have more self-esteem. The rate of domestic violence against women has dramatically decreased and the system of dowry, where women's families pay husband's families, is being eliminated. Women are now also active in local politics and by voting as a block have become a powerful political force. They have access to money and can now plan for and dream of their futures. Their children are in school and many of them are going into higher education. The economy as a whole has changed as well because people are creating their own jobs and are not waiting for someone else to hire them.

Yunus' program began with a single village and a lending program administered by one of the country's major national banks. By 1980, the Grameen Bank was ready to go off on its own, and by 1990, it had branches in a quarter of Bangladesh's villages, eight hundred thousand borrowers, and an average of $5.6 million a month in new loans. Borrowers are also shareholders, owning 94 percent of the bank's stock. The government of Bangladesh owns the remaining 6 percent, down from its initial ownership of 60 percent.

Since its inception, the total amount of loans disbursed by Grameen Bank is $5.23 billion. Out of this, $4.64 billion has since been repaid. In 2005, Grameen Bank disbursed $611.74 million. Requiring no collateral for loans, Grameen's loan recovery rate is 99.01 percent, well ahead of every other traditional bank.

Grameen Bank now finances 100 percent of its outstanding loan from its deposits. Most of its deposits come from bank's own borrowers. Since Grameen Bank came into being, it has made a profit every year save three (1983, 1991, and 1992). It has published its balance sheet every year, audited by two internationally reputed audit firms. Total revenue generated by Grameen Bank in 2004 was seventy-nine million dollars and profits were $7.16 million. The profit is transferred to a Rehabilitation Fund created to cope with disaster situations and to help start schools, build clinics, and improve the infrastructure of the villages.

This is done in fulfillment of a condition imposed by the government for exempting Grameen Bank from paying corporate income tax.

Grameen has different interest rates for loans: 20 percent for income-generating loans, 8 percent for housing loans, 5 percent for student loans, and a recently implemented Struggling Members program for beggars, which gives out zero-interest loans. About sixty-three thousand beggars have already joined the program, which has given out loans of $930,000—of which over half a million dollars has already been paid off. The bank offers between 8.5 percent and 12 percent for deposits, which by the end of 2005 totaled $481.22 million, and every year gives about nine thousand scholarships at various levels of education. Grameen also gives life insurance benefits at no cost to borrowers as well as a pension fund.

> *"Just like food, credit is a human right."*
> Muhammad Yunus

Yunus's ultimate vision is to build a world that is free of poverty. "We have created a slavery-free world, a smallpox-free world, an apartheid-free world," he wrote in his autobiography, *Banker to the Poor*. "Creating a poverty-free world would be greater than all these accomplishments while at the same time reinforcing them. This would be a world that we could all be proud to live in." His stated goal is to drastically reduce the number of poor people by his target date of 2015.

THE EARLY YEARS

Yunus was born on June 29, 1940, in the village of Bathua in Bangladesh, seven miles from the largest port, Chittagong, to his softhearted father, Dula Mia, and a strong mother, Sofia Khatun. Yunus was the third of fourteen children; the eldest was his sister Momtaz. Five years after her came Salam, Yunus, Ibrahim, Tunu, Ayub, Azam, Jahangir, and Moinu.

His family moved to the jeweler's section of Chittagong, Sonapotti, at Number 20 Boxihart Road. His father worked downstairs where he made and showed jewelry. The family occupied the upstairs rooms, consisting of his mother's room, the radio room, the big room, and a kitchen. Yunus played on the flat roof and in 1943 watched as the Japanese dropped leaflets over the city.

His older brother, Salam, was his playmate. The boys attended the Lamar Bazar Free Primary School, which was not coed. They read as much and as often as they could, often resorting to borrowing and stealing reading material. Yunus won a scholarship in high school, which provided him some pocket money that he spent on movies, eating out, and a camera. He often painted and drew, apprenticing with a commercial artist and hiding his interest from his father who, as a devout Muslim, did not believe in reproducing the human figure.

His father made three pilgrimages to Mecca and dressed in all white while Yunus was growing up.

His mother often put away money for the poor and helped Yunus discover his interest in social reform. Sofia came from a family of traders and merchants. However, when Yunus was nine years old, his mother's behavior became increasingly abnormal. Although she would return to being the same sweet mother the children had known, the recovery was always temporary. Though Dula Mia tried everything he could to find a cure, none were successful, and he cared for her until her death, after fifty-two years of marriage, in 1982.

Yunus joined Chittagong Collegiate School, the most highly respected school in the subcontinent, attended by sons of government officials. The school hosted a Boy Scout program in which Yunus excelled. He was offered the opportunity to travel abroad for the first time through this program, and he made trips to Canada, Japan, and the Philippines. After graduating from Chittagong College, he was offered a job there as a teacher of economics. It was during this time that he started his own packaging and printing business. He applied for a loan that was immediately approved and eventually made the business a success, turning a profit every year and hiring a hundred people. His father acted as the chairman of the board and encouraged Yunus to pay off the debt as quickly as possible. The company's products included cigarette packages, boxes, cartons, cosmetics boxes, cards, calendars, and books. The success of the business convinced Yunus and his family that he could excel in business.

Yunus was offered a Fulbright Scholarship in 1965 to get a PhD in the United States. He started out by spending a summer in Boulder at the University of Colorado, where he experienced a great deal of culture shock before adapting and having a lot of fun. After the summer, he moved to Vanderbilt University in Tennessee, where he had a different experience. The school was in turmoil because it had just recently been desegregated. In addition, he found his classes boring, and the winter cold. He fortunately connected with a famous Romanian professor, Nicholas Georgescu-Roegen, who was an important influence. Yunus got his PhD in economics from Vanderbilt University in 1969.

CAREER PATH

After receiving his PhD from Vanderbilt, Yunus took a job in Murfreesboro, south of Nashville, teaching at Middle Tennessee State University.

Grameen II has instituted a "five star" system of staff incentives based on branch and staff performance. For each performance area where targets are met, a colored star is awarded, which can be worn by staff. Stars can also be earned by individual staff member performance. Performance stars are awarded for a mixture of outreach, impact and financial/operational objectives: 100 percent repayment record, profitability, savings deposits, school attendance and completion of primary school, borrowers crossing the poverty line.

Daley-Harris, Sam. *Pathways Out of Poverty: Innovations in Microfinance for the Poorest Families.* Bloomfield, CT: Kumarian Press, 2002.

In 1971, when Yunus was comfortably settled into his new job, he found out that his home country was in a crisis. Pakistan had moved in to crush the Bengalis. Bangladesh at that time was within Pakistan and had no formal government of its own. He organized the five other Bengalis in Nashville to find as much information as they could and to bring attention to what was happening in their country. They each donated a thousand dollars to create a fund, and they organized to meet with reporters of local TV stations and editors of the local newspapers. They also decided to give 10 percent of their monthly salary to the fund until Bangladesh became independent. Yunus then went to meet with other Bengalis in Washington, DC. He met with ambassadors of as many countries as he could, explaining their cause and asking them to recognize Bangladesh as an independent state. Realizing that Bangladesh would have to have its own government, Yunus and his Bengali friends set up a radio station to broadcast to the people inside Bangladesh what was happening. Yunus bought a transmitter with the money from the fund in order to mount it to a vehicle that could come in and out of Bangladesh from India, returning to India whenever it was chased by the Pakistani army.

At the Indian embassy, Yunus was treated as a diplomat and was able to convince officials there to open India's border to refugees, provide free access to Calcutta for expatriate Bangladeshis and relax rules surrounding Indian visas for Bengalis with Pakistani passports. They tried to stop military aid to Pakistan from the United States and Canada and concentrated their efforts on getting Bangladesh recognized as a country. On December 16, 1971, after three million Bengalis had been killed and ten million had left for India, this finally happened. The Bangladesh economy was shattered, and Yunus knew he had to return home to participate in the rebuilding of his country.

Returning to Bangladesh in 1972, Yunus took a job on the government's Planning Commission though he soon resigned to take a job as the head of the Economics Department at Chittagong University. At the time, universities were required to be located outside of city centers, so Yunus, who was living in the city with his family, borrowed his father's car and commuted to the university by driving through the neighboring village of Jobra. Yunus grew curious about the village and the fields that were not being cultivated, so he launched a university project to study the village.

Yunus first got into the business of fighting poverty during a 1974 famine in Bangladesh, one of the poorest countries in the world. Many starving people came into the cities, and Yunus started to dread lecturing to students about economics when poverty and starvation were rampant. "We tried to ignore it," he says in his autobiography, *Banker to the Poor.* "But then skeleton-like people began showing up in the capital, Dhaka. Soon the trickle became a flood. Hungry people were everywhere. Often they sat so still that one could not be sure whether they were alive or dead. They all looked alike: men, women, children. Old people looked like children, and children looked like old people." The thrill he had once experienced studying economics and teaching his students elegant economic theories that could supposedly cure societal problems soon left him entirely. As the famine worsened he began to dread his own lectures. "Nothing in the economic theories I taught reflected the life around me. How could I go on telling my students make believe stories in the name of economics? I needed to run away from these theories and from my textbooks and discover the real-life economics of a poor person's existence."

His economic theories did not mesh with reality, and he set about studying Jobra more intensely. Yunus focused the new nation on the issue of famine and experimented in Jobra on a microlevel by helping the villagers grow more food. He called the project the Chittagong University Rural Development Project. In 1975, the project centered on solving the problem of irrigation to raise an extra winter crop. During the monsoon season every bit of land was used, but during the winter some land remained unused. Yunus discovered that the problem lay with the villagers, who were fighting over who was going to pay for the water. Investing his own money, Yunus convinced them to tend the fields. The project was a success for the farmers, but Yunus lost money because some of the farmers paid him back less than promised.

As he continued to study poverty in Jobra, Yunus differentiated the poor into three categories. P1 signified the bottom 20 percent of the population who were "hard-core," absolutely poor. P2 were the bottom 35 percent, and P3 were the bottom 50 percent. Within each of these categories, he also created subclassifications on the basis of region, occupation, ethnic background, sex, and age. The poor that Yunus studied included weavers, rice farmers, and others who earned so little that they had to beg. There was no way for them to get out of the cycle of poverty. Yunus decided to focus his attention on the landless poor. In his experience in Jobra, he saw that many poverty programs attempted to alleviate the suffering of the poor but often benefited the nonpoor as well. When this happened, the nonpoor in effect edged the poor out of the program and took most of the benefits.

In 1976, Yunus began visiting the poorest people in Jobra to see how he could help them directly. One of the first women he met told him that she earned two cents per day, working all day long plaiting bamboo stools. She told Yunus that she borrowed the money for the bamboo from the money-lender who charged 10 percent interest per week. She would make the stools, sell them to the trader, and pay the moneylender back, earning barely enough for food for her children. She could not break the poverty cycle because she didn't have the money for the bamboo, and the trader paid her very little over the cost of the materials for her efforts. Angry after this conversation, especially at his field of economics that did not begin to address the situation of poverty, Yunus realized that if this woman did not have to pay the money-lender immediately she could start to earn more and break out of the survival cycle she was in. Yunus asked a student to collect data on other people who were dependent on traders, and the student came back with a list of forty-two people who had borrowed less than twenty-seven dollars. When he realized how little money it would take to help so many families get out of their dire situations, Yunus decided he could do something about it. He immediately gave the student the twenty-seven dollars and told her to lend it to the villagers to be repaid whenever they could with no interest. Yunus decided to take the next step of institutionalizing the concept of microloans. He talked to the government bank, Janata Bank, about the idea of making small loans to poor people without the need for collateral. His argument was that the bank should make the loan because the poor have more incentive to pay back the loan than anyone. If they don't, then they would not be able to borrow more and continue to make the money needed for their very survival.

After arguing his case for six months, he finally succeeded in taking out a loan for the villagers on the condition that he was the guarantor. He agreed to this in order to satisfy their bureaucratic rules, but he also clearly told the bank that he would not pay if the villagers defaulted and would call the bank on their bluff to sue him for it. The bank would not sue, they said, because it would bring negative publicity to them, however they would still require him to sign for every loan. The bureaucracy took its toll on Yunus, who had to sign every application. When he was traveling, his signature had to be faxed from wherever he was around the world. As Yunus summed it up in *Banker to the Poor*,

> The villagers got very excited that I gave them the ($27). To them, it was like a miracle. Seeing this, a question came to my mind. If you can make so many people so happy with such a small amount of money, why shouldn't you do more of it? Why shouldn't you reach out to many more people? I could do this by linking these people with a bank that could lend them the money. So I went to the bank and proposed that they lend money to the poor people. The bankers almost fell over. They couldn't believe what had been proposed to them. They explained to me that the bank cannot lend money to poor people because these people are not creditworthy. So a long series of debates began with me and the banking system. Finally, I resolved it after about six months by offering myself as a guarantor.... The banks had been saying that I would never get the money back and would ultimately have to pay it back myself. I said, "I don't know anything. Let me try it out." And I tried it, and it worked.

Lump sum payments are made at the end of a traditional loan, but Yunus reasoned that they would have a negative impact on his borrowers, so he initially set daily loan payments that were so small that borrowers would barely miss the money. Another early principle of the Grameen Bank was to encourage borrowers to form groups to support each other. Yunus left it to the villagers to form their own groups, which was not easy initially. Many women faced pressure from their families, and it took a large amount of courage for them to take the loans and convince others to do so as well. Today, all borrowers have to belong to a group of five, who all have to take a test together in order to gain the certification required by Grameen. Yunus believes that the group membership is one of the biggest reasons Grameen has succeeded. Another caveat Yunus made early on was that half of the borrowers had to be women. He decided this because he thought it unfair that the banks would only lend to women if their husbands were supportive. After a little while, Yunus recognized that significant changes were being made as a result of the loans to women. Women were more concerned with the household and took the loan repayment more seriously. However, initially getting women to take the loans proved difficult. Poor women could not read advertisements. Men were not allowed to talk to women as a result of the Muslim tradition, so Yunus found that he could only communicate with them by standing in the middle of a group of huts and shouting out. He attempted to navigate around this problem during his pilot project by hiring female bank workers to help, but their families were not happy about the work, which required them to travel without a male companion.

In October 1977 Yunus had a chance meeting with the director of one of the largest national banks, Bangladesh Krisi (Agriculture) Bank (BKB). As Yunus details in his autobiography, A. M. Anisuzzaman approached Yunus and launched into a blistering attack:

> You academics are failing us. You are failing in your social duties.... No one is accountable to anyone for anything. Certainly not you lily-white-handed academics with your cushy jobs and your jaunts abroad. You are useless all of you. Utterly useless! I am absolutely disgusted by what I see in this society. No one thinks of the poor. (Yunus 1999)

After Yunus's response ("Well, sir, I am happy to hear you say all this because I just happen to have a proposal that may interest you") the two put together plans for Yunus to run his own bank branch, which they named the "Experimental Grameen Branch of the Agriculture Bank." Yunus remained a professor but oversaw the branch, which he staffed with former students. When Yunus gave a presentation about his experiment at a USAID conference, the deputy governor of the Central Bank of Bangladesh was in the audience. He indicated that he wanted to help Yunus expand the experiment throughout the country. Yunus agreed, taking a two-year leave of absence from his academic job. On June 6, 1979, Yunus began the Grameen Bank Project in the District of Tangail.

By November 1982 Grameen Bank membership was at twenty-eight thousand, of which fewer than half were women. After the success of the Tangail project, Yunus outlined a five-year expansion plan. He organized the money, which mainly came from the Ford Foundation who gave him eight hundred thousand dollars as a guarantee fund. With this, he was able to negotiate a loan of $3.4 million from the International Fund for Agricultural Development, based in Rome. The Central Bank matched this fund, and they launched the expansion program across the country. By the end of 1981, cumulative loan disbursements totaled $13.4 million. In 1982, they were able to increase this amount by an additional $10.5 million. By September 1990 there were 754 banks in over 18,500 villages.

Grameen Bank introduced housing loans in 1984. Though they first submitted the application for the Central Bank to offer the program, it was rejected because the Central Bank felt the loans were too small to support real houses. Grameen resubmitted the application as shelter loans, but this was rejected also. Then Grameen submitted the application for factory loans because the majority of the borrowers were women who worked from home. This eventually passed, and the program was very successful. Five years later Grameen was awarded the Aga Khan International Award for Architecture. The houses are designed by the villagers.

While in the United States during the Pakistani crackdown on Bengalis, Yunus met the economic counselor to the Pakistan Embassy in Washington, DC, A. M. A. Muhith, who helped Yunus create public support for Bangladesh. They met again at a conference where Yunus was scheduled to talk. However, during the conference, there was a coup d'etat in the country, and they were not permitted to leave the building or hold the conference. Passing the time, Muhith and Yunus talked about Grameen and the Central Bank's bureaucracy. In the following days, Muhith was unexpectedly named the new finance minister and managed to make Grameen Bank its own financial institution, with the government owning 60 percent of it, on October 2, 1983. Yunus had wanted Grameen to be owned entirely by the borrowers, but he is still waiting for this. In the meantime, Grameen grew at over a hundred branches a year, and Grameen outperformed all other banks in the country. In 1985, Grameen's ownership changed quietly to be only 25 percent government owned. Yunus was still a government-appointed managing director, however, and was at the mercy of a changing government. He hired an attorney to create an amendment to the Grameen legislation that removed the ability of the government to dismiss him without the approval of the board of directors.

In 1995, Grameen Bank decided not to receive any more donor funds. The bank was able to sell $163 million in bonds to regular commercial banks in Bangladesh and thereby cut free from dependence on the donor agencies that

"Anywhere anybody is rejected by the banking system, you have room for a Grameen-type program."

Muhammad Yunus

helped Yunus get started. Since then, it has not requested any fresh funds from donors for Bangladesh. The last installment of donor funds was received in 1998. The growing amount of deposits has been more than enough to run and expand Grameen's credit program and repay its existing loans.

Yunus has taken his program out of Bangladesh and around the world by setting up the Grameen Trust, which was able to get funding from the Rockefeller Foundations, the World Bank, the U.S. government, the UN Capital Development Fund, and the German government, which granted over eighty-eight million dollars. By the end of 2005, the trust had set up 89 replication projects in almost thirty countries. The list of nongovernmental organizations that were quick to recognize the value of microcredit to help women start microenterprises is impressive, and in a vote of confidence, the World Bank has set aside two hundred million dollars for microcredit programs.

Then Governor Bill Clinton of Arkansas brought the microcredit program to that state in 1985, after he learned of the program through one of Grameen's employees, Jan Piercy, who had been one of Hillary Rodham Clinton's best friends at Wellesley College. Clinton arranged to meet Yunus for breakfast in Washington one morning, and Yunus explained how the microcredit program worked. Yunus and Clinton then set up the Southern Development Bank Corporation in Arkadelphia. The Development Finance Authority put up some of the initial money, but most of it came from corporations that Bill and Hillary Clinton asked to invest in it. When he became president, Bill Clinton secured congressional approval for a national loan program modeled on the Grameen Bank. The U.S. Agency for International Development also funded two million microcredit loans a year in poor villages in Africa, Latin America, and East Asia. After the success in Arkansas and Hillary Clinton's visit to the Grameen Bank in April 1995, the program has spread throughout the United States.

Professor Muhammad Yunus, founder of the Grameen Bank, has related that his "Sixteen Decisions" were formulated and promulgated in response to early demand from the female clients of the bank. In fact, client representatives soon requested more than sixteen "decisions," but Professor Yunus saw that the social change agenda of the bank could not be allowed to expand further without eventually interfering with the primary work of staff to provide microcredit loans and recover them.

There are now more than two dozen organizations within the Grameen family of enterprises. These include the replication and research activities of Grameen Trust; handloom enterprises of Grameen Uddog; fisheries pond management by Grameen Motsho or the Fisheries Foundation; the cellular phone company, Grameen Telecom; Grameen Cybernet, a for-profit Internet service provider; and Grameen Textile Mills. Grameen Telecom is now the largest cellular phone operator in Bangladesh. In addition to these, Grameen set up special housing loans. In September 1990, 85,500 houses had been constructed with loans of $22.7 million.

PERSONAL LIFE

Although Yunus had no intention of finding an American wife when he came to the United States on a Fulbright scholarship, he did just that. In 1967, he met Vera Forostenko in the Vanderbilt library. Two years after meeting, Vera moved back to her hometown of Trenton, New Jersey, and Yunus made plans to return to Bangladesh. Vera told him that she wanted to move with him to Bangladesh one day. Though Yunus knew that she would have a difficult time with the culture when that day came, the couple was married in 1970 and moved to Murfreesboro, south of Nashville where he was teaching at Middle Tennessee State University.

When Yunus returned to Bangladesh after the Pakistan conflict, Vera soon joined him. In March 1977, Yunus and Vera had a daughter they named Monica. Shorter after the birth, however, Vera decided that she had had enough of Bangladesh and did not want to raise a daughter there. Though the couple still loved each other, Yunus could not leave his country just as his experiment with microcredit was proving to make a big difference in the lives of the poor, so the couple decided to divorce in December.

Yunus was introduced to Afrozi Begum, a Bangladeshi researcher in advanced physics at the University of Manchester. After their wedding in March 1980, Afrozi remained in England to finish her research while Yunus stayed in Tangail. When Afrozi moved to Bangladesh, the two lived above Yunus's office. Their daughter, Deena Afroz Yunus, was born on January 24, 1986.

LEADERSHIP LESSONS

Yunus's genius has been in recognizing a need and providing an economically feasible way to sustain a solution. He has done this primarily by motivating his bank workers to find and work with the poor. The Grameen Bank is an extraordinary example of grassroots mobilization through inspired and innovative efforts. The bank demands so much of field officers that overwork, exhaustion, and burnout are common. Yunus has had to communicate his vision and link that vision to the everyday efforts of the people within the organizations.

Yunus differentiated the poor among several criteria and decided to focus on one sector: the landless poor. His premise was to take what traditional bankers did and do almost exactly the opposite. He focused on a market that was completely ignored because it did not have collateral to obtain credit. Yunus approached the members of this class, treated them with dignity, and encouraged them to support each other. As the bank grew and became its own entity, Yunus kept the principles simple. He was not intimidated by banking procedures he didn't understand, and he trained his workers in the way he wanted them to be, which was entirely different from how other bank workers operated.

Treat People with Dignity

Yunus recognized that poor people are enterprising. They don't need charitable handouts or government aids, he determined. They just need a system within which they can use their own ingenuity. Yunus's microcredit program does not provide any training at all for borrowers unless they specifically ask for it because Yunus recognized that poor people have skills already.

> A poor person is just as good a human being as anyone else in the world, but she is a victim of circumstances; the way in which she lives is only a reflection of the way in which society has rejected her. Instead of looking at her like a different kind of human being, we should be treating her as an equal and extend to her the kinds of services that others enjoy. Once we do that, we will get out of the charitable mode of thinking. We will get out of the welfare system mode. (Yunus 1999)

One of Grameen's basic assumptions is that people are honest and highly motivated to pay back their loans. They don't require collateral and will not use any lawyers or outsiders to settle outstanding debts. The remarkably high rate of repayment is not unrelated to the way borrowers have responded to their treatment by Grameen. "Poor people are not the authors of their poverty," states Yunus in his autobiography. "Poverty is a creation of a complex system of conceptions, rules and attitudes we have thought up ourselves. Therefore, if you want to eradicate poverty you have to go back to the drawing board, discover where we have planted the seeds of poverty and make changes there."

Yunus reasons that

> the microcredit we give to the women is a tool to explore one's self, how much capacity that is stored up inside: 'I never knew that I had the capacity. That creativity. That ingenuity. To make money to express myself. So that money gives, for the first time, an occasion for me to find out how much I can do.' When you were successful in the first round, when you took tiny amounts— $30, $35—and went into business and paid back the loan, you are now much more equipped to do better. Bigger. So you ask for a $50 loan, a $60 loan, because you think you can do bigger business and more challenging business than when you first took out an easy loan. (Yunus 1999)

Yunus has described poor people as bonsai trees,

> that little tree that grows in a flower pot. I said you pick the best seed of the tallest tree in the forest, and plant it in a flower pot, and it will grow into a tiny

tree. Is there anything wrong with the seed? Nothing is wrong with the seed. It's the best seed. Then why is it tiny? Because you planted it in a flower pot. You didn't allow it to grow in the real soil. The poor people are the bonsai people. Society has not allowed them the real soil. If you allow them the real soil, real opportunities, they will grow as tall as everybody else. (Yunus 1999)

There's no training for Grameen borrowers because those programs are less effective in reducing poverty than those that unleash the creativity and energy of the poor, according to Yunus. By giving people credit, he reasoned, the poor can immediately put into practice the skills they already know.

Grameen Bank does, however, provide extensive training to its staff, which runs the village-based lending program, in how to treat the borrowers with the same dignity and respect corporate clients from larger banks.

Keep it Simple

Professor Nicholas Georgescu-Roegen from Vanderbilt, one of the influential figures in Yunus's life, not only taught Yunus the economic basis to help him build up Grameen but more importantly showed him that things were not as complicated as they seemed. Through him, Yunus realized there was little need for memorizing economic formulas. Georgescu-Roegen impressed upon Yunus that "it is only our arrogance that prompts us to find unnecessarily complicated answers to simple problems." When Yunus was confronted with the bureaucracy and complications of the banking and finance industries, he was not intimidated. He knew that the bankers were making the system far more complicated than it need be, so he whittled away until he came up with a system that could be used for a microcredit system, and in doing so, created a new industry.

Yunus has intentionally made everything from the repayment of loans to the application process within Grameen as simple and straightforward as possible.

Encourage Support Groups

Yunus recognized early on how important support groups were to people, and this was soon made a requirement for Grameen borrowers. The women form small groups of five with an agreement of mutual liability, and the group pays from its profits if one individual member defaults. The peer pressure and support have helped all the group members succeed. The group builds up savings it can use by depositing 5 percent of their loan to a group fund. Any borrower can take an interest-free loan from the group fund if all members approve.

Loans can be arranged in minutes and sometimes are paid back the same day. A woman can borrow enough money in the morning, for instance, to buy merchandise to sell at a roadside stand. In the evening she would return what she borrowed, keep the profit to feed her family, and repeat the process the next day.

By 1979 Yunus could report that his clients had a repayment rate of 99%.

Hire New Workers and Train Them

One of the biggest reasons for Grameen's success is dedication of the workers. The bank employees are critical to the bank's success, and the hiring and training process are very rigorous. Grameen hires anyone younger than twenty-eight with a master's degree and at least a B average. It screens many candidates through interviews and hires only a limited number of people, who then will watch another manager for six months, sharply critique the experienced manager, and then start their own new bank branch. Most of the branch managers are from rural settings who have never even visited the capital of Bangladesh. Grameen does not give its new workers any formal introduction to the new area where the branch will be. They do not get an office or a place to stay, and their first assignment is to document everything about the area. Yunus does this so his staff appears to be as different from other banking officials as possible. Other officials stay with the wealthiest family in the village, have a big office, and are intimidating to most of the villagers. For Yunus to attract his borrowers, the bank workers take a different approach. Yunus tells his staff that anyone who asks for a loan is a "fake poor person. The person you are looking for will never come to you. When you find her, she will say, 'Oh, I don't need the money.' When you hear that, you have found your person" (Yunus 1999).

Grameen emphasizes employee autonomy at each level of the organization. Each employee's territory is his or her own province and the ability of other people to interfere in this area is extremely limited. Even Yunus himself can only visit the centers at the invitation of the staff member in charge.

Portrait of a Grameen Borrower

"At first Murshida borrowed 1,000 Taka ($17) to purchase a goat and she paid off the loan in six months with the profits from selling the milk. She was left with a goat, a kid, and no debt. Encouraged, she borrowed 2,000 Taka, bought raw cotton and a spinning wheel, and began manufacturing ladies' scarves. She now sells her scarves wholesale for 100 Taka with tassels and 50 Taka without. Murshida's business has grown so much that during peak periods she employs as many as twenty-five women in her village to manufacture scarves. In addition, she has bought an acre of farmland with her profits, built a house with a Grameen Bank housing loan, and set up her brothers in businesses that include sari trading and raw cotton trading."

POLITICAL INFLUENCE

Yunus was very politically active in his younger life, even helping to form his own sovereign country of Bangladesh. He lobbied actively throughout Washington, DC, to get the country recognized and to stop military aid to its aggressor. In more recent years, Yunus used the political system to create his bank as a formal financial institution. He encourages his borrowers to form voting blocks so their votes can make a real difference in local, regional, and national politics. His political lobbying these days centers on creating systems within countries in which poverty can be alleviated.

Yunus was against the U.S. invasion of Iraq because of the impact it had on poverty. "And then," he says, "came '9/11.'"

> That day plunged the entire world into confusion. It gave the U.S. president an excuse to send the world in a different direction, which created a global divide. Now everyone has become distrustful, anyone could be a terrorist. It will take a long time to get the world back on the track of optimism and on the track of a battle that I consider more important than that of exacting democracy in all corners of the world: the battle to grant very ordinary rights to people who are shut out and, as a result, live in inhuman poverty. (Yunus 1999)

CRITICS

Yunus has had fairly vocal critics since he came up with the idea of microcredit. "Things were always difficult for us, but I knew they would be because I was trying to do something that no one else believed in" (Yunus 1999). Early on, everyone told him that the idea would not work because the poor would not pay back the loans. Bankers did not want to become involved. When the idea did work in certain areas, critics told him he could not replicate the program on a larger scale.

Some critics now say that Yunus focuses only on the top tier of the poor. The poorest of the poor, they argue, have no need for credit—they need water and food that can only be provided by credit. Yunus is absolutely against a system of charity, believing that it undermines the poor, keeps them in a cycle of poverty and dependent on changing government mandates. Yunus is vocal against government aid to developing nations, as well.

Some economists have said microcredit does not foster true economic growth, and Yunus argues that economic growth, then, is not being measured properly. When it focuses on gross national product and does not look at the poverty situation, the measurement of economic growth, Yunus reasons, is faulty and needs to be updated.

Religious leaders within the developing countries in which he operates have opposed Yunus because the bank gives loans to women, disrupting a male-dominant society. Yunus has had to overcome Muslim critics who charge that the Quran states clearly that it is immoral to charge interest. Yunus counters this by saying that because the borrowers are also owners, it is not immoral. He has received resistance within villages from the local religious leader, although most of the time, the pressure from the villagers to have Grameen present wins out.

And although 98 percent of loans are repaid, the Grameen Bank has come under criticism by development activists and the rural poor, who question the ethics of putting eight million Bangladeshi families into debt.

POSSIBLE FUTURE IMPACT

Yunus's vision for the future focuses on two things: to make credit a human right so that each individual human being will have the opportunity to take loans and implement his or her ideas and to create a world where nobody has to suffer from poverty—a world completely free from poverty. "Not a single human being will suffer from the misery and indignity of poverty. Poverty is unnecessary," says Yunus. He will likely explore different ways of eradicating poverty as well: "Credit is one of the barriers we must eliminate so that the poor can clamber out of poverty. But it is not enough" (Yunus 1999). He announced, for instance, that the bank is working with the government to replace the nationalized health care system with a system for poor people on a cost-recovery basis.

Yunus has said that the poor must have access to information technology because knowledge is power. For centuries, the supply of news has been dominated by journalists who decided which information was appropriate to pass on and which was not. But with the Internet, a whole range of news sources has emerged, which is liberating to the poor because it will not be as easy to cheat them if they know what is going on. With mobile telephone technology using solar power, for instance, farmers in Bangladesh can negotiate directly with their customers about the price. Via the Internet, farmers can find out the actual market value of their goods, enabling them to strengthen their negotiating position. With technology, poor farmers are no longer limited to the village economy or reliant on not-altogether-honest middlemen. Grameen Telecom is setting up cyber kiosks in rural villages, complete with Internet, faxing, and worldwide networking.

Yunus also wants to revamp the field of economics. "Our textbooks," he says,

> have greatly simplified the world economy: it's an open market, it's a free world. But just try and launch a medicine on the Japanese market; they'll tell you all about the rules. In the real world, the market is only open to other parties insofar as it has been made accessible by those who write the laws and the supervisory authorities....Take the corner grocer on your street where

you've been shopping for years. A big supermarket is being built nearby that is much cheaper and offers freebies. Before you know it, you're standing in that supermarket with your cart and that nice grocer has lost all his customers. Where are the regulations protecting the grocer? Where are the regulations governing the supermarket? Aha! So it's only a free market when you're big and have a lot of money. The economics textbooks are ripe for revision. Then we can also rectify the misconception that a company is not always just a way to make money and a businessperson is not always someone who wants to maximize profits. (Yunus 1999)

Yunus wants to see companies serve a greater societal purpose whose first priority is striving toward a good aim. "We need businesspeople who are not driven by money but by their desire to contribute to society." He doesn't believe that corporate social responsibility and profit maximization ideals can mix, though he sees a new company who wants to make a profit while also contributing to the community as a whole. He believes that the people interested in social development go into different fields other than business, but business is an effective way to create a better world. Yunus wants to create the incentives for new socially conscious companies to form. "Sometimes I dream of an international stock exchange where 'social companies' are listed," Yunus stated.

If you want to help poor women in Latin America, you can invest in a Bolivian Internet company that sells clothing made by local women. If you have more affinity with new technology, you can invest in a Vietnamese company that brings computers with speech technology to villages. Universities should set up business schools for young social entrepreneurs who don't learn how to make as much money as possible but the best way to realize a social goal. And there should be a *Wall Street Journal* that reports on this new group of companies. A whole new counterbalance should be created that will greatly enrich society. (Yunus 1999)

TIMELINE

1940	June 29, Born in Bangladesh.
	Received a Fulbright Scholarship and went to Boulder, Colorado, for the summer.
	Went to Vanderbilt University in Nashville, Tennessee to study economics.
1969	Received his PhD in economics from Vanderbilt.
1970	Married Vera Forostenko and moved to Murfreesboro to teach at Middle Tennessee State University.
1971	Helped Bangladesh gain its independence from Pakistan.
	Flood added to the widespread destruction and poverty of Bangladesh.

	Made a personal loan to villagers in Jobra and develops the idea for institutionalizing microcredit.
1976	Set up a new credit program.
	March, Monica Yunus born.
	December, Vera and Yunus divorce. Vera moves back to the United States with Monica.
	Took a two-year leave of absence from the university to start the Grameen Bank Project in Tangail.
1980	March, married Afrozi Begum.
1981	Ford Foundation gave eight hundred thousand dollars to use as a guarantee.
1983	Grameen received approval from the government to establish itself as its own bank.
1984	Applied for help introducing housing program to borrowers.
1985	Pilot project launched in Arkansas championed by Governor Bill Clinton.
1986	January 24, Deena Afroz Yunus born.
1990	Grameen and Yunus featured on CBS's *60 Minutes*.
1995	Grameen made enough profit for the first time to operate on a fully commercial basis and phased out grants.
1996	Grameen extended its one-billionth dollar in loans.
1998	Grameen extended its two-billionth dollar in loans.
2003	Grameen started the Struggling Members Program for beggars.
2006	Was awarded the Nobel Peace Prize for implementing microcredit and alleviating poverty in many areas of the developing world.

RESOURCES

Bloom, David E. *The Demographic Dividend: A New Perspective on the Economic Consequences of Population Change.* Santa Monica, CA: Rand Corporation, 2003, p. 76.

Clinton, Bill. *My Life.* New York: Knopf Publishing Group, 2005, p. 329.

Daley-Harris, Sam. *Pathways Out of Poverty: Innovations in Microfinance for the Poorest Families.* Bloomfield, CT: Kumarian Press, 2002, pp. 110n5, 235.

Daniels, Mark R. (Editor). *Creating Sustainable Community Programs: Examples of Collaborative Public Administration.* Westport, CT: Greenwood Publishing Group, 2001, p. 96.

Ehrenfeld, David. *Swimming Lessons: Keeping Afloat in the Age of Technology.* New York: Oxford University Press, 2002, pp. 189–190.

Friedman, Marilyn (Editor). *Women and Citizenship.* New York: Oxford University Press, 2005, p. 101.

Gup, Benton E. (Editor). *Future of Banking.* Westport, CT: Greenwood Publishing Group, 2002, pp. 319–320, 324, 331.

Hauss, Charles. *Beyond Confrontation: Transforming the New World Order.* Westport, CT: Greenwood Publishing Group, 1996, p. 182.

Kramarae, Cheris (Editor). *Routledge International Encyclopedia of Women: Global Women's Issues and Knowledge.* New York: Routledge, 2000, p. 439.

Lenssen, Gilbert (Editor). *Responding to Societal Expectations: A Special Issue from the European Academy of Business in Society and Vlerick Leuven Gent Management School.* Bradford, UK: Emerald Group Publishing, 2005, p. 100.

McEachern, Doug. *Environment & Politics.* New York: Routledge, 2001, p. 95.

Narayan, Deepa (Editor). *Empowerment and Poverty Reduction: A Sourcebook.* Washington, DC: World Bank, 2002, p. 111.

Oster, Sharon M. *Strategic Management for Nonprofit Organizations: Theory and Cases.* New York: Oxford University Press, 1995, p. 250.

Pandya, Mukul, and Robbie Shell. Nightly business report presents Lasting Leadership, Wharton School Publishing. Upper Saddle River, NJ: Pearson Education, 2005, pp. 93–101.

Paratian, Rajendra. *Bangladesh.* Geneva 22, CHE: International Labour Office Bureau International du Travail, 2001, p. 69.

Rank, Mark R. *One Nation, Underprivileged: Why American Poverty Affects Us All.* New York: Oxford University Press, 2004, pp. 300–310.

Robinson, Marguerite. *Microfinance Revolution: Sustainable Finance for the Poor.* Washington, DC: World Bank, 2001.

Segal, Sheldon J. *Under the Banyan Tree: A Population Scientist's Odyssey.* Cary, NC: Oxford University Press, 2003, pp. 27–28.

Sen, Amartya. *Development as Freedom.* New York: Alfred A. Knopf, 1999, p. 218.

Walden Publishing, Ltd. *Bangladesh Business Intelligence Report (2001/July).* Cambridge: World of Information, 2001, p. 23.

Wolbarst, Anthony B. (Editor). *Solutions for an Environment in Peril.* Baltimore, MD: Johns Hopkins University Press, 2001, p. 193.

Yunus, Muhammed. *Banker to the Poor.* New York: Public Affairs. 1999.

COMPANY INFORMATION

Grameen Bank Bhavan
Mirpur–1, Dhaka–1216
Bangladesh
Phone: 88 02 9005257–69
www.grameen.com

Selected Bibliography

BUSINESS BIOGRAPHIES, AUTOBIOGRAPHIES, AND PROFILES

The list below represents a variety of books by and about the business icons profiled in this set, as well as other business pioneers (historical and contemporary) and iconic businesses. This list is not intended to be comprehensive, but to showcase the breadth of resources available on the subject of business biography and history.

Adams, Ruseell B., Jr. *King C. Gillette: The Man and His Wonderful Shaving Device*. Boston: Little, Brown, 1978.

Allen, Lloyd. *Being Martha: The Inside Story of Martha Stewart and Her Amazing Life*. Hoboken, NJ: Wiley, 2006.

Angel, Karen. *Inside Yahoo! Reinvention and the Road Ahead*. Hoboken, NJ: Wiley, 2002.

Auletta, Ken. *Media Man: Ted Turner's Improbable Empire*. New York: W.W. Norton, 2005 (paperback reprint).

Battelle, John. *The Search: How Google and Its Rivals Rewrote the Rules of Business and Transformed Our Culture*. New York: Portfolio, 2005.

Bibb, Porter. *Ted Turner: It Ain't As Easy as It Looks: A Biography*. Boulder, CO: Johnson Books, 1997.

Brands, H.W. *Masters of Enterprise: Giants of American Business from John Jacob Astor and J.P. Morgan to Bill Gates and Oprah Winfrey*. New York: Free Press, 1999.

Branson, Richard. *Losing My Virginity: How I've Survived, Had Fun, and Made a Fortune Doing Business My Way*. New York: Three Rivers, 1999 (paperback reprint).

Brayer, Elizabeth. *George Eastman: A Biography*. Baltimore: Johns Hopkins University Press, 1996.

Buffett, Warren E. *The Essays of Warren Buffett: Lessons for Corporate America*. The Cunningham Group, 2001.

Burrows, Peter. *Backfire: Carly Fiorina's High-Stakes Battle for the Soul of Hewlett-Packard*. Hoboken, NJ: Wiley, 2003.

Byron, Christopher M. *Martha Inc.: The Incredible Story of Martha Stewart Living Omnimedia*. Hoboken, NJ: Wiley, 2003 (paperback reprint).

Carlzon, Jan. *Moments of Truth*. New York: Collins, 1989 (paperback reprint).

Carnegie, Andrew. *The Autobiography of Andrew Carnegie*. Reprinted by Filiquarian Publishing, 2006.

Carnegie, Andrew. *The Empire of Business*. New York: Doubleday, Doran & Co., 1902. (Reprinted by Kessinger Publishing, 2004).

Casson, Herber N. *Cyrus Hall McCormick: His Life and Work*. Beard Books, 2001 (paperback reprint).

Chernow, Ron. *The House of Morgan: An American Banking Dynasty and the Rise of Modern Finance*. Grove Press, 2001 (paperback reprint).

Chernow, Ron. *Titan: The Life of John D. Rockefeller, Sr.* New York: Vintage, 2004 (paperback reprint).

Cohen, Adam. *The Perfect Store: Inside eBay*. New York: Little, Brown, 2002.

Cohen, Ben and Jerry Greenfield. *Ben & Jerry's Double Dip: How to Run a Values Led Business and Make Money Too*. New York: Simon & Schuster, 1998 (paperback reprint).

D'Antonio, Michael. *Hershey: Milton S. Hershey's Extraordinary Life of Wealth, Empire, and Utopian Dreams*. New York: Simon and Schuster, 2006.

Dell, Michael with Catherine Fredman. *Direct from Dell: Strategies that Revolutionized an Industry*. New York: Collins, 2000 (paperback reprint).

Deutschman, Alan. *The Second Coming of Steve Jobs*. New York: Broadway, 2001 (paperback reprint).

Forbes Magazine Staff. *Forbes Greatest Business Stories of All Time*. Hoboken, NJ: Wiley, 1997.

Ford, Henry and Samual Crowther. *My Life and Work*. New York: Doubleday, Page & Co., 1923 (reprinted by Kessinger Publishing, 2003).

Frieberg, Kevin and Jackie Freiberg. *Nuts! Southwest Airlines' Crazy Recipe for Business and Personal Success*. New York: Broadway, 1998 (paperback reprint).

Gabler, Neal. *Walt Disney: The Triumph of the American Imagination*. New York: Knopf, 2006.

Garr, Doug. *IBM Redux: Lou Gerstner and the Business Turnaround of the Decade*. New York: Collins, 2000 (paperback reprint).

Garson, Helen S. *Oprah Winfrey: A Biography*. Westport, CT: Greenwood Press, 2004.

Gates, Bill. *Business @ the Speed of Thought: Succeeding in the Digital Economy*. New York: Warner, 2000 (paperback reprint).

Gittell, Jody Hoffer. *The Southwest Airlines Way: Using the Power of Relationships to Achieve High Performance*. New York: McGraw-Hill, 2002.

Gerstner, Louis V., Jr. *Who Says Elephants Can't Dance? Inside IBM's Historic Turnaround*. New York: Collins, 2002.

Goldman, Robert and Stephen Papson. *Nike Culture: The Sign of the Swoosh*. Thousand Oaks, CA: Sage Publications, 1999.

Grove, Andrew S. *Only the Paranoid Survive: How to Achieve a Success That's Just a Disaster Away*. New York: Currency, 1999 (paperback reprint).

Hagstrom, Robert G. *The Warren Buffett Way*, Second Edition. Hoboken, NJ: Wiley, 2004.

Hertzfeld, Andy. *Revolution in the Valley*. Sebastopol, CA: O'Reilly Media, 2004.

Iacocca, Lee with William Novak. *Iacocca: An Autobiography*. New York: Bantam, 1984.

Iacocca, Lee. *Talking Straight*. New York: Bantam, 1988.

Israel, Paul. *Edison: A Life of Invention*. New York: Wiley, 2000 (paperback reprint).

Jackson, Tim. *Inside Intel: Andy Grove and the Rise of the World's Most Powerful Chip Company*. New York: Plume, 1998 (paperback reprint).

Kamprad, Ingvar and Bertil Torekull. *Leading by Design: The IKEA Story*. New York: Collins, 1999.

Kaufman, Michael T., *Soros: The Life and Times of a Messianic Billionaire*. New York: Alfred A. Knopf, 2002.

Klein, Alec. *Stealing Time: Steve Case, Jerry Levin, and the Collapse of AOL Time Warner*. New York: Simon & Schuster, 2004 (paperback reprint).

Koehn, Nancy F. Brand New: *How Entrepreneurs Earned Consumers' Trust from Wedgwood to Dell*. Boston: Harvard Business School Press, 2001.

Krass, Peter. *Carnegie*. Hoboken, NJ: Wiley, 2002.

Kroc, Ray, with Robert Anderson. *Grinding It Out: The Making of McDonald's*. New York: St. Martin's, 1990 (paperback reprint).

Lager, Fred. *Ben & Jerry's: The Inside Scoop: How Two Real Guys Built a Business with a Social Conscience and a Sense of Humor*. New York: Three Rivers Press, 1995, (paperback reprint).

Levy, Steven. *Insanely Great: The Life and Times of Macintosh, the Computer That Changed Everything*. New York: Penguin, 2000 (paperback reprint).

Lowenstein, Roger. *Buffett: The Making of an American Capitalist*. Main Street Books, 1996 (paperback reprint).

Love, John F. *McDonald's: Behind The Arches*. New York: Bantam, 1995 (paperback reprint).

McLean, Bethany and Peter Elkind. *The Smartest Guys in the Room: The Amazing Rise and Scandalous Fall of Enron*. New York: Portfolio, 2003.

Manes, Stephen and Paul Andrews. *Gates: How Microsoft's Mogul reinvented an Industry—and Made Himself the Richest Man in America*. New York: Touchstone, 2003 (paperback reprint).

Martin, Justin. *Greenspan: The Man Behind Money*. Cambridge, MA: Perseus Publishing 2000.

Masters, Kim. *Keys to the Kingdom: The Rise of Michael Eisner and the Fall of Everybody Else*. New York: Collins, 2001 (paperback reprint).

Mayo, Anthony J., Nitin Nohria, and Laura G. Singleton. *Paths to Power: How Insiders and Outsiders Shaped American Business Leadership*. Boston: Harvard Business School Press, 2006.

Moore, Kenny. *Bowerman and the Men of Oregon: The Story of Oregon's Legendary Coach and Nike's Cofounder*. Emmaus, PA: Rodale, 2006.

Morris, Charles R. *The Tycoons: How Andrew Carnegie, John D. Rockefeller, Jay Gould, and J. P. Morgan Invented the American Supereconomy*. New York: Times Books, 2005.

Movers and Shakers: The 100 Most Influential Figures in Modern Business. New York: Basic Books, 2003.

Munk, Nina. *Fools Rush In: Steve Case, Jerry Levin, and the Unmaking of AOL Time Warner*. New York: Collins, 2004.

Neff, Thomas J. and James Citrin. *Lessons from the Top: The 50 Most Successful Business Leaders in America—and What You Can Learn From Them*. New York: Currency, 2001.

O'Neil, William J. *Business Leaders and Success: 55 Top Business Leaders and How They Achieved Greatness*. New York: McGraw-Hill 2003.

Packard, David. *The HP Way: How Bill Hewlett and I Built Our Company*. New York: Collins, 1996 (paperback reprint).

Pendergrast, Mark. *For God, Country and Coca-Cola: The Unauthorized History of the Great American Soft Drink and the Company That Makes It*, Second Edition. New York: Basic Books, 2000.

Perseus Publishing Staff. *Business: The Ultimate Resource*. Cambridge, MA: Perseus Publishing, 2002.

Roddick, Anita. *Business As Unusual: My Entrepreneurial Journey, Profits With Principles*. Anita Roddick Press, 2005 (paperback reprint).

Roddick, Anita. *Take It Personally: How to Make Conscious Choices to Change the World*. San Francisco: Red Wheel/Weiser, 2001.

Rothman, Howard. *Companies That Changed the World: Incisive Profiles of the 50 Organizations—Large & Small—That Have Shaped the Course of Modern Business*. Franklin Lakes, NJ: Career Press, 2001.

Saunders, Rebecca. *Business the Amazon.com Way: Secrets of the Worlds Most Astonishing Web Business*. Oxford: Capstone, 2002.

Schultz, Howard. *Pour Your Heart into It: How Starbucks Built a Company One Cup at a Time*. New York: Hyperion, 1999 (paperback reprint).

Shawcross, William. *Murdoch: The Making of a Media Empire*. New York: Simon & Schuster, 1997 (paperback reprint, revised and updated).

Slater, Robert. *The Eye of the Storm: How John Chambers Steered Cisco Through the Technology Collapse*. New York: Collins, 2003.

Slater, Robert. *Jack Welch & the GE Way: Management Insights & Leadership Secrets of the Legendary CEO*. New York: McGraw-Hill, 1998.

Slater, Robert. *Martha: On Trial, in Jail, and on a Comeback*. Upper Saddle River, NJ: Financial Times/Prentice-Hall, 2005.

Slater, Robert. *Soros: The Unauthorized Biography, the Life, Times and Trading Secrets of the World's Greatest Investor*. New York: McGraw-Hill, 1997.

Slater, Robert. *The Wal-Mart Triumph: Inside the World's #1 Company*. New York: Portfolio, 2004 (paperback reprint).

Sloan, Alfred P., Jr. *My Years with General Motors*. New York: Currency, 1990 reissue (originally published, 1964).

Soros, George. *George Soros on Globalization*. New York: PublicAffairs, 2002.

Soros, George. *Soros on Soros: Staying Ahead of the Curve*. New York: Wiley, 1995 (paperback reprint).

Spector, Robert. *Amazon.com: Get Big Fast*. New York: Collins, 2002 (paperback reprint).

Stewart, James B. *Disney War*. New York: Simon & Schuster, 2005.

Stewart, Martha. *The Martha Rules: 10 Essentials for Achieving Success as You Start, Grow, or Manage a Business*. Emmaus, PA: Rodale, 2005.

Strasser, J.D. and Laurie Becklund. *Swoosh: The Unauthorized Story of Nike and the Men Who Played There*. New York: Collins, 1993 (paperback reprint).

Swisher, Kara. *AOL.com: How Steve Case Beat Bill Gates, Nailed the Netheads, and Made Millions in the War for the Web*. New York: Random House, 1998.

Swisher, Kara. *There Must Be a Pony in Here Somewhere: The AOL Time Warner Debacle and the Quest for the Digital Future*. New York: Three Rivers, 2004 (paperback reprint).

Tedlow, Richard S. *Giants of Enterprise: Seven Business Innovators and the Empires They Built*. New York: Collins, 2003 (paperback reprint).

Trump, Donald and Tony Schwartz. *Trump: The Art of the Deal*. New York: Random House, 1987.

Trump, Donald and Meredith McIver. *Trump: How to Get Rich*. New York: Ballantine, 2004 (paperback reprint).

Vise, David A. and Mark Malseed. *The Google Story*. New York: Delacorte, 2005.

Wallace, James and Jim Erickson. *Hard Drive: Bill Gates and the Making of the Microsoft Empire*. New York: Collins, 1993 (paperback reprint).

Walton, Sam, with John Huey. *Sam Walton: Made In America*. New York: Bantam, 1993 (paperback reprint).

Watson, Thomas J., Jr. *A Business and Its Beliefs: The Ideas That Helped Build IBM*. New York: McGraw-Hill, 2003 reissue (originally published, 1963).

Watts, Steven. *The People's Tycoon: Henry Ford and the American Century*. New York: Knopf, 2005.

Welch, Jack, with John A. Byrne. *Jack, Straight from the Gut*. New York: Warner, 2001.

Welch, Jack and Suzy Welch. *Winning*. New York: Collins, 2005.

Wilson, Lucinda. *How They Achieved: Stories of Personal Achievement and Business Success*. Hoboken, NJ: Wiley, 2001.

Winkler, John Kennedy. *Five and Ten: The Fabulous Life of F.W. Woolworth*. Freeport, NY: Books for Libraries Press, 1970.

Young, Jeffrey S. and William L Simon. *iCon Steve Jobs: The Greatest Second Act in the History of Business*. Hoboken, NJ: Wiley, 2005.

Yunus, Muhammad. *Banker to the Poor: Micro-Lending and the Battle Against World Poverty*. New York: PublicAffairs, 2003 (paperback reprint).

BUSINESS DATA AND INFORMATION

These databases and web sites offer a great deal of data and information about companies and their leaders. Some of these resources are subscription-based services; check with your library to see if they offer access to these services at no charge.

www.hoovers.com
Research companies and industries; research corporate executives and decision makers.

www.standardandpoors.com
Provider of independent credit ratings, indices, risk evaluation, investment research, data, and valuations.

www.moodys.com
Investing and finance data; economic analysis.

www.bloomberg.com
Breaking financial, business and economic news worldwide.

www.nyse.com
Official site of the New York Stock Exchange.

www.cnnmoney.com
Internet home of *Fortune*, *Money*, *Business 2.0*, and *Fortune Small Business*, including the Fortune 500.

Index

About the Author

KATERI DREXLER is a freelance writer and editorial project manager, specializing in books and teaching/research materials for the educational and training markets. She is also President and Founder of WestSlope IT, Inc., a research and consulting firm in technology training, market analysis, and advertising. She has served as a professor of business administration and marketing at the University of San Francisco in Quito, Ecuador, and has taught business courses at the University of Colorado Grade School of Business, and has served in a variety of management, marketing, and consulting positions. She is the author or coauthor of several textbooks, including *Strategies for Active Citizenship* and *Keys to Business Success*.